❧ The Mirror of the Medieval ❧

MAKING SENSE OF HISTORY

Studies in Historical Cultures

General Editor: Stefan Berger

Founding Editor: Jörn Rüsen

Bridging the gap between historical theory and the study of historical memory, this series crosses the boundaries between both academic disciplines and cultural, social, political and historical contexts. In an age of rapid globalization, which tends to manifest itself on an economic and political level, locating the cultural practices involved in generating its underlying historical sense is an increasingly urgent task.

For a full volume listing please see back matter.

THE MIRROR OF THE MEDIEVAL

An Anthropology of the Western Historical Imagination

K. Patrick Fazioli

berghahn
NEW YORK · OXFORD
www.berghahnbooks.com

Published in 2017 by
Berghahn Books
www.berghahnbooks.com

© 2017 K. Patrick Fazioli

Library of Congress Cataloging-in-Publication Data
A C.I.P. cataloging record is available from the Library of Congress

British Library Cataloguing in Publication Data
A catalogue record for this book is available from the British Library

ISBN 978-1-78533-544-0 hardback
ISBN 978-1-78533-545-7 ebook

To my mom

Contents

Tables, Figures, and Maps

Tables

Figures

Maps

Acknowledgments

This book would not have been possible without the assistance, support, and encouragement of colleagues, family, and friends. As many of the ideas contained herein had their genesis in the formative years of graduate school, I will always be indebted to my doctoral adviser, T.J. Chevral, and the rest of the faculty members at UB Anthropology from whom I learned so much, especially Sherm Milisauskas, Ezra Zubrow, and Peter Biehl. The chapters in this book also greatly benefitted from conversations with Matthew Bowker, Tim McCorry, Jerry Erion, Ray Whitlow, Josh Kwoka, as well as the comments of four anonymous reviewers. I also greatly appreciate the hard work and patience of my editor at Berghahn, Chris Chappell.

My sincere thanks are also extended to colleagues in Central Europe, who were so generous in sharing not only their data, but also their perspectives on the past. The field and laboratory work that informed the arguments in this book would not have been possible without the help of Christoph Gutjahr, Manfred Lehner, Bernhard Hebert, Stephan Karl, Zvezdana Modrijan, Tina Milavec, Benjamin Štular, Andrej Pleterski, Ivan M. Hrovatin, Hajnalka Herold, the entire Leitinger family, and the numerous American and Austrian students who aided in my fieldwork. Financial support for my research was provided by a National Science Foundation Dissertation Improvement Grant and a Mark Diamond Research Grant from the Graduate Student Association at the University at Buffalo.

Finally, none of this would have been possible without the support, sacrifices, and love of my entire extended family, but particularly my wife Rachel and our three amazing children.

Introduction

Interdisciplinary projects are perilous endeavors. Despite all the lip service paid to inter- and trans-disciplinarity as the future of academic research, the traditional nineteenth-century intellectual division of labor in the human sciences remains largely intact today, and continues to be reinforced by archaic institutional barriers, the hyper-specialized nature of postgraduate training, discipline-specific jargon, and, perhaps above all, the incentive structure of the academic job market. Furthermore, since research questions and lines of inquiry deemed interesting by one disciplinary community often fail to translate to even closely related fields, such projects run a perpetual risk of falling between the cracks, condemning them to a fate far worse than skepticism or criticism: deafening silence.[1]

Consider the relationship between cultural anthropology and medieval history, two fields with broadly convergent agendas that remain institutionally and intellectually isolated from one another.[2] Although, at first glance, medievalists and anthropologists may not seem to have much in common—the former traditionally focused on long-dead (mostly) Christian Europeans, while the latter on (mostly) living, non-Western, non-Christian peoples—what they do share is an interest in human lifeways and social worlds peripheral to Western modernity. In other words, both disciplines are broadly engaged in what Micheal Uebel has termed *heterology*: "the differences, projections, doubleness, and ambivalence attending past and present constructions of otherness."[3] So notwithstanding the occasional moments of fruitful cross-disciplinary borrowing over the past half-century (mostly flowing from anthropology to medieval history), the fact is that very few members in either field see much purpose in staying abreast of the theoretical and methodological developments in the other.[4]

Notes for this section begin on page 7.

This book hopes to address this unfortunate state of affairs by demonstrating the tremendous potential of more robust engagement between medieval history, anthropological theory, and archaeological practice. The essays in this volume seek to bridge geographical, temporal, and disciplinary gaps that have expunged the Middle Ages from the history of anthropology, discouraged many medieval archaeologists from embracing social theory, and kept the study of medieval material culture subservient to the "tyranny" of the historical record.[5] While keeping the aforementioned pitfalls of interdisciplinarity in mind, there is great promise in creating a new framework for the study of Europe's Middle Ages that builds upon and integrates current trends in anthropological, historical, and archaeological approaches to the past. Even if this book fails to fully deliver on such an ambitious goal, at the very least it should demonstrate why investigating the complex relationship between the (medieval) past and present necessitates such a relentlessly transdisciplinary perspective.

The following investigation will unfold in a decidedly nonlinear fashion, as navigating tricky terrain across multiple disciplines, places, and times requires frequent shifts between the medieval, early modern, and contemporary worlds, as well as trekking from the heart of Europe to distant lands in colonial Africa, Asia, and the Americas. Folding space-time in this unorthodox manner not only allows us to tackle an eclectic array of problems and themes, but—more importantly—reveals the subtle and profound connections among them. The seven chapters of this book take us on a whirlwind tour from daily life on fortified settlements in the post-Roman world to the Nazi occupation of East-Central Europe, from the late medieval travels of William of Rubruck to the writings of nineteenth-century colonial administrators in Africa and Asia, and from the Christianization of the early medieval Eastern Alps to recent debates over what it means to be authentically Slovenian. All the while we will consider the broader theoretical implications for sociocultural constructions of history, temporality, and technology.

This topical diversity requires from the outset a clear articulation of the underlying thematic unity. First and foremost, this is a book about the power of the past; specifically, how historical and archaeological narratives shape, and are shaped by, present-day political, cultural, intellectual, and economic agendas. Moreover, since processes of identity formation furnish the past with its ideological potency, we will also trace the sociopolitical dynamics of inclusion and exclusion in both the medieval and modern eras. Therefore, a second overarching theme is the intrinsic human desire to belong to community (real or "imagined"), as well as the resultant urges to exoticize and primitivize the other. Such psychosocial drives are at the heart of the colonialist, imperialist, and nationalist ideologies traced throughout these chapters. Finally, since all investigations of the relationship between past and present are premised upon certain assumptions about temporality and technology, interrogating these two concepts will allow us to better appreciate how group identities are reinforced through historical narrative, as well as how material objects allow the past to persist into the present.

Outline of the Book

Part 1. Anthropology, History, and the Middle Ages

This anthropology of the Western historical imagination is divided in two parts. The first comprises an extended argument for what I will call an *anthropology of historicity*: a project that explores the relationship between past and present by integrating recent insights in anthropology, history, and archaeology. The potential of this new interdisciplinary approach will be illustrated by an analysis of Europe's Middle Ages as history, myth, and mirror to modernity. The first three chapters collectively demonstrate what an anthropological perspective—in the fullest sense—can contribute to the study of the Middle Ages, as well as why anthropologists can no longer afford to ignore the medieval past.

Chapter 1 offers a manifesto for this anthropology of historicity, laying out its main goals, key elements, and guiding questions, as well as situating it in the broader ongoing dialogue between anthropologists and historians. It begins by outlining what distinguishes this project from previous efforts to bridge "history" and "culture": first, it embraces a "principle of symmetry," a concept borrowed from the history of science in which successes and failures in scientific work are examined through the same analytical lens.[6] For an anthropology of historicity, this means making no a priori distinctions when investigating different representations of the past. Whether a particular narrative is deemed scholarly, popular, pseudo-historical, nationalist, mythical, and so on, each can be critically analyzed for the deeper cultural logics that they reflect and reinforce. Secondly, an anthropology of historicity seeks not only to situate individual histories, historians, or historical schools within their cultural context, but also to interrogate the epistemological tenets underlying Western historical thinking writ large. Third, this approach is not content to merely study how the past is narrativized, but also grapples with the more challenging task of developing new methods for studying the past itself.

Chapter 2 shows why Europe's Middle Ages provide an ideal case study for an anthropology of historicity. Although the medieval past is often regarded as irrelevant for (or even antithetical to) the modern world, it constitutes nothing less than the foundational myth of modernity. This chapter outlines how the medieval has been imagined and reimagined over the past five centuries, tracing its ever-shifting place in the Western historical imagination. From the Renaissance to the nineteenth century to the present day, the medieval has continually provided a mirror for modernity, allowing various political and intellectual projects to amplify their cultural and historical achievements. The chapter goes on to expose the manifold ideological interconnections between medievalism and colonialism by detailing how concepts like barbarism, feudalism, and crusading were simultaneously consigned to Western pasts and/or non-Western presents. It concludes by arguing that postcolonial attempts to dispel the myth that "primitive" peoples reside at an anterior stage of human history have only reinforced the temporal logic of modernity, thereby widening—not closing—the epistemological chasm between modern and premodern worlds.

Chapter 3 further develops this analysis of the medieval in the Western historical imagination, but shifts focus from explicitly political contexts (e.g. colonialism and nationalism) to more intellectual and academic ones. Specifically, it considers why the Middle Ages are not only missing from contemporary anthropology's disciplinary agenda, but have been systematically expunged from its intellectual genealogy. A close reading of histories of early anthropological thought highlights the widespread scholarly consensus that Europe's medieval past represented the antithesis of modern anthropological values of tolerance, curiosity, and objectivity. However, this widespread assumption has been challenged by a growing body of literature within medieval studies that reveals how this era produced ethnographic works of a quality comparable (or even superior) to antiquity and early modernity. Finally, it is argued that reintegrating the medieval into the discipline's intellectual history not only provides a more complete account of early ethnological thought, but dovetails with ongoing efforts to transform the epistemic space of a single, dominant Western anthropology into the multiple, contested, and fluid spaces of "world" anthropologies.

Part 2. Identity, Power, and the Medieval Past in the Eastern Alpine Region
Having considered what an anthropology of historicity might contribute to cross-disciplinary dialogues, the second part of the book presents a detailed regional case study to demonstrate this project's potential for exploring the complex relationship between the (medieval) past and present. Chapters 4 through 7 examine how the Middle Ages have been appropriated by various political agendas in the Eastern Alpine region (what is today Slovenia, southern Austria, and northeast Italy), and also seek to develop new approaches to the past that might prove more resistant to sinister manipulation. Each chapter begins with a brief historical synopsis that is then thoroughly analyzed and deconstructed. The narratives outlined in these opening sections are not meant to provide comprehensive accounts of the current scholarship

or even reflect the author's own viewpoint. Rather, their purpose is to encapsulate the various "traditional" interpretations of the enigmatic transition between late antiquity and the early Middle Ages in this region, thereby revealing how scholars working with nearly identical datasets are able to fashion divergent, even contradictory narratives—producing something like a *Rashomon* effect on the early medieval past.[7] It is important to point out that these chapters (particularly 4 and 5) will be less concerned with evaluating the *validity* of individual narratives than understanding how sociopolitical contexts shape the perception and interpretation of textual and material data.

Chapter 4 details how German and Austrian historians used the medieval past to justify their imperial fascination with, and expansion into, East Central Europe during the nineteenth and twentieth centuries. The Middle Ages played a surprisingly important role in advancing the themes of *Volk* and *Raum* that dominated Germanophone social science during this era. From the triumphalist overtones of the *Drang nach Osten* to *Völkisch* fantasies surrounding the medieval peasant, the politically-useful conceit that the Eastern Alps had always been an authentically Germanic region required a very specific reading of the early medieval past. We will see how Slovene-speaking communities in this region were subject to a "colonial gaze" that portrayed them as lacking any meaningful historical or cultural achievements. Finally, a close reading of historical, archaeological, and toponymical scholarship during the National Socialist era reveals striking parallels with colonial ideologies employed by European powers in overseas contexts.

Chapter 5 begins by sketching the traditional Slovenian ethno-nationalist interpretation of the early Middle Ages, which played a critical role in fashioning a shared past for their nascent imagined community. Using John Coakley's tripartite division of ethno-nationalist mythologies as a guiding framework, this chapter traces how the Middle Ages have been indispensable to the formulation and maintenance of Slovenian identity, from their assumed ethnogenesis in the Migration Period to the "golden age" of early medieval Carantania, followed by their prolonged collective suffering under a Germanic yoke. The chapter concludes by considering how the rise of the "Venetic Theory"—which locates the origins of the Slovenian people not in Slavic migrations of the post-Roman period, but rather in a more ancient Iron Age culture—reflects rapidly shifting sociopolitical conditions over the past two decades that have reshaped what it means to be "authentically" Slovenian. Although mainstream scholars regard the Venetic Theory as blatantly pseudo-archaeological, its surprising popularity among the Slovenian public (and diasporic communities in North America and Australia) suggests that it powerfully resonates with deep, primordial aspects of their historical imaginations, as a simultaneous rejection and internalization of longstanding German colonial stereotypes against Slavic peoples.

Having detailed how easily modern political agendas can appropriate the medieval past for their own purposes, Chapters 6 and 7 confront the more challenging task of developing an alternative approach to the Middle Ages that might prove more resistant to such manipulation. Chapter 6 examines the concept of ethnicity, which has proven particularly susceptible to political abuse. Ironically, while the ethnicity paradigm has been dominant in medieval history and archaeology for decades, current subjectivist understandings of this concept in the social science literature make it exceedingly difficult to recover (either historically or archaeologically) from the premodern past. Therefore, this chapter calls for investigating other manifestations of group identity that were equally (or even more) important during this period, such as the "community of practice," in which groups of craftspeople shared a body of knowledge, skilled practices, resources, and a sense of "Us-ness." Although this expression of identity generally lies outside the purview of ancient written sources, it is potentially recoverable through archaeological methods because such technological choices often leave behind discernable traces in the material record. An examination of shifts in coarse-ware pottery production from late antiquity to the early Middle Ages in the Eastern Alps demonstrates the potential of this approach for studying identities beyond ethnicity.

Chapter 7 adds another component of this new approach to the study of the medieval past by revisiting two (unexpectedly) interrelated concepts: time and Christianization. The rise of Christianity across Europe and the Mediterranean in the first millennium CE has been traditionally explained in two ways: either through the intrinsic appeal of the Christian message or as a byproduct of *realpolitik* decisions having very little to do with religious belief. While both of these explanatory frameworks have some merit, neither provides a satisfactory mechanism for the rapid dissemination of Christianity throughout Roman, Celtic, Germanic, and Slavic "pagan" societies. This chapter builds upon recent innovative scholarship that attributes early Christianity's success to its willingness to borrow and assimilate existing religious beliefs and practices into its own theological framework. Convincing people that the new faith would allow them to retain much of their existing cosmological *doxa* and ritual *habitus* was essential to the conversion of whole communities, but this meant that Christianity did not replace paganism as much as merge with it, creating an entirely new and distinct religion. Interestingly, recent archaeological research has provided a glimpse into how this process unfolded across the Eastern Alps, where Christian appropriation of pagan objects, sacred places, and entire landscapes has left important traces in the material record. The chapter concludes by considering what this new syncretic approach to Christianization reveals about the limitations of traditional conceptions of temporality and history, and proposes a non-spatialized time that offers a more sophisticated understanding of the complex relationship between the past and present.

Notes

1. Immanuel Wallerstein, *Unthinking Social Science: The Limits of Nineteenth-Century Paradigms* (Philadelphia, 2001); Jerry A. Jacobs and Scott Frickel, "Interdisciplinarity: A Critical Assessment," *Annual Review of Sociology* 35 (2009); Frédéric Darbellay, "Rethinking Inter- and Transdisciplinarity: Undisciplined Knowledge and the Emergence of a New Thought Style," *Futures* 65 (2015).

2. Here I refer specifically to sociocultural anthropology and medieval European history, as opposed to the broader field of medieval studies.

3. Michael Uebel, *Ecstatic Transformation: On the Uses of Alterity in the Middle Ages* (New York, 2005), 252. The term "heterology" was coined by Michel de Certeau, *Heterologies: Discourse on the Other* (Minneapolis, 1986).

4. Tellingly, most examples of anthropologists interested specifically in medieval Europe are now decades old: A.L. Kroeber, "On the Principle of Order in Civilization as Exemplified by Changes of Fashion," *American Anthropologist* 21 (1919); A.L. Kroeber, *An Anthropologist Looks at History* (Berkeley, 1963); Alan Macfarlane, "The Origins of English Individualism: Some Surprises," *Theory and Society* 6 (1978); Talal Asad, "Notes on Body Pain and Truth in Medieval Christian Ritual," *Economy and Society* 12 (1983); Talal Asad, "Medieval Heresy: An Anthropological View," *Social History* 11 (1986); Jack Goody, *The Development of the Family and Marriage in Europe* (Cambridge, UK, 1983); Kirsten Hastrup, *Culture and History in Medieval Iceland: An Anthropological Analysis of Structure and Change* (Oxford, 1985). More recent exceptions include David Graeber, "The Anthropology of Globalization (with Notes on Neomedievalism, and the End of the Chinese Model of the Nation-State)," *American Anthropologist* 104 (2002); Leigh Symonds, "Death as a Window to Life: Anthropological Approaches to Early Medieval Mortuary Ritual," *Reviews in Anthropology* 38 (2009); Michael W. Scott, "The Matter of Makira: Colonialism, Competition, and the Production of Gendered Peoples in Contemporary Solomon Islands and Medieval Britain," *History and Anthropology* 23 (2012). Medieval historians who have incorporated anthropological perspectives into their work include Mayke de Jong, "The Foreign Past. Medieval Historians and Cultural Anthropology," *Tijdschrift voor Geschiedenis* 109 (1996); Philippe Buc, *The Dangers of Ritual: Between Early Medieval Texts and Social Scientific Theory* (Princeton, NJ, 2001); Aron I. Akovlevich Gurevich and Jana Howlett, *Historical Anthropology of the Middle Ages* (Chicago, 1992); William Ian Miller, *Bloodtaking and Peacemaking: Feud, Law, and Society in Saga Iceland* (Chicago, 1990); Florin Curta, *The Making of the Slavs: History and Archaeology of the Lower Danube Region, ca. 500–700* (Cambridge; New York, 2001); Patrick J. Geary, *Living with the Dead in the Middle Ages* (Ithaca, NY, 1994); and Julia M. H. Smith, *Europe after Rome: A New Cultural History 500–1000* (Oxford; New York, 2005).

5. See John Moreland, "Archaeology and Texts: Subservience or Enlightenment," *Annual Review of Anthropology* 35 (2006); Timothy Champion, "Medieval Archaeology and the Tyranny of the Historical Record," in *From the Baltic to the Black Sea: Studies in Medieval Archaeology*, ed. D. Austin and L. Alcock (London, 1990); and David Austin, "The 'Proper Study' of Medieval Archaeology," in Austin and Alcock, *From the Baltic to the Black Sea*.

6. For the origins of this "symmetrical" approach in the history of science, see David Bloor, *Knowledge and Social Imagery* (London, 1976); this concept was also used, with a slightly different meaning, by Bruno Latour, *We Have Never Been Modern* (Cambridge, MA, 1993).

7. This term is borrowed from Akira Kurosawa's classic 1950 film *Rashomon*, which tells the story of a murder from four distinct, frequently contradictory perspectives. It should also be noted that this term has been applied to ethnographic fieldwork by Karl G. Heider, "The Rashomon Effect: When Ethnographers Disagree," *American Anthropologist* 90 (1988).

Part I

ANTHROPOLOGY, HISTORY, AND THE MIDDLE AGES

CHAPTER 1

Manifesto for an Anthropology of Historicity

A truth that reigns without checks and balances is a tyrant who must be overthrown.

—Paul Feyerabend, "How to Defend Society against Science"

Anthropology, Historical Thinking, and the "Office to Unsettle"

In his 1984 distinguished lecture to the American Anthropological Association, Clifford Geertz proudly reminded anthropologists that they "have, with no little success, sought to keep the world off balance; pulling out rugs, upsetting tea tables, setting off firecrackers. It has been the office of others to reassure; ours to unsettle."[1] More than three decades later, anthropologists still love to invoke Geertz's line (especially to our students) as it perfectly encapsulates our self-image as the intellectual gadflies of the contemporary academy, willing to challenge the most cherished cultural beliefs, values, and norms of Western society. And without question, over the past century the discipline has been remarkably successful in exposing many commonsense ideas (about race, gender, marriage, economics, ethics, and so forth) to be social constructions that are neither universally espoused nor epistemologically incontestable.[2]

However, not all modern ideologies have been equally subject to the intellectual buzz saw of the anthropological critique. Some have managed to escape critical investigation because they are part of the very intellectual foundation upon which anthropological inquiry rests. This chapter argues that *history* is one of these unassailable categories. Although it is true that anthropologists have long been interested in studying both Western and non-Western representations of the past, there has been surprisingly little scrutiny of the underlying cultural assumptions and epistemological implications of *historical thinking* itself. Even as "History" is recognized to be a distinctively modern and Western mode of thought, many anthropologists' theoretical approaches to studying social change have become, paradoxically, increasingly reliant on the assumptions of historicism. Perhaps this explains why so much has been written about "history and anthropology," "the history of anthropology," and "historical anthropology," yet the "anthropology *of* history" (something altogether quite different) remains little discussed, as Stephan Palmié and Charles Stewart have recently observed.[3] The lack of anthropological scrutiny of historical thinking is even more curious given that historicism is arguably the dominant cognitive framework of the contemporary world.[4] One need not be a professional historian to notice that nearly every dimension of Western modernity is steeped in history: it shapes our personal identities; it frames our political discourse; it underwrites our collective memories; it informs our national traditions and public rituals. As the sociologist Karl Mannheim observed some sixty years ago, history forms "the very basis on which we construct observations of the socio-cultural reality."[5]

Surprisingly, while an erosion of trust in traditional religious, political, philosophical, and scientific authorities has been a dominant theme of the last fifty years in the Western academy (and, to a lesser degree, the general public), historical thinking has only strengthened its hold over our collective *Weltanschauung*. Indeed, when faith is lost in all other epistemologies, history emerges as the last reliable guide and teacher. How often do we hear: *those who do not learn from history are doomed to repeat it; knowing where we are going requires knowing where we came from; history will be my judge,* and other such clichés from teachers, politicians, pundits, and scholars? They are the mantra of our always/already historicized world. It is revealing that at a time when common ground on social, economic, or moral issues continues to shrink, reverence for history offers a rare point of unanimity across the political spectrum. Although there is much debate between Left and Right about the meaning and significance of past events, individuals, or movements (from the intentions of America's "Founding Fathers" to the commemoration of the bombing of Hiroshima and Nagasaki, as well as the US government's past treatment of American Indians), what has often gone unrecognized in these so-called "History Wars" is that the *instructive value* of history is an unspoken point of consensus.[6] In contemporary society, the only sin greater than ignorance of history is actively questioning the relevance of the past for the present, a position regarded less as intellectually scandalous than simply unserious.

But is the lack of robust critique of historical thinking really such a bad thing? Is it necessary, or even wise, to turn a critical lens on what Cicero once called *Magistra vitae* ("the teacher of life")?[7] If anthropologists have rightly congratulated themselves for challenging the ideological bases of colonialism, patriarchy, and capitalism, does history deserve to be next in the line of fire? One could reasonably argue that undermining history's credibility is tantamount to aiding and abetting dictators, fundamentalists, bigots, and other scoundrels who seek to distort the past in the service of their own agendas. While such concerns cannot be casually dismissed (indeed, they form a central theme of this book), it is essential to recognize that a critical interrogation of historical thinking need not entail a categorical rejection of the value of this knowledge regime, nor must it lead down some relativistic slippery slope wherein all versions of the past are deemed equally plausible.

The point is that we can accept history's cultural and political importance without lapsing into an undue deference to this mode of thinking. For as Max Horkheimer and Theodor Adorno famously demonstrated, even valuable and benevolent concepts like "enlightenment" or "Reason" can be transformed into totalitarian ideologies if they lose sight of their own epistemological limitations.[8] A similar critique of science was subsequently made by thinkers like Bruno Latour, Steve Fuller, and Paul Feyerabend, the latter of whom provocatively argued that modern science had morphed from a beacon of intellectual freedom to a narrow dogmatism that actually inhibited freedom of thought.[9] While the Sociology of Scientific Knowledge, as this movement is often known, has been accused of giving aid and comfort to fundamentalist and corporate anti-science forces, their work does not deny the value of science, but seeks to reveal a more sophisticated and three-dimensional picture of the production of scientific knowledge.[10] Likewise, a critical anthropological investigation of what it means to think and act historically could potentially provide a richer understanding of how historical knowledge is created and utilized, what it means to live in a historicized world, and even sharpen our ability to identify and refute the abuse of history. In sum, an anthropology of historicity must carefully investigate the strengths and limitations of history, unpack its hidden assumptions and implications, and prudently determine when it is appropriate to think and act historically, and when we may need to think and act (as Nietzsche might say) "un-historically."

A Short History of Historical Thinking in Anthropology

Before we can fully appreciate what anthropology can contribute to this important intellectual endeavor, it is necessary to consider why historical thinking has thus far largely escaped critical analysis, in spite of the longstanding interdisciplinary dialogue between anthropologists and historians. This requires a brief sketch of the ways that cultural anthropologists have incorporated historical concepts and approaches into their research (bracketing off, for the moment, the myriad anthropological concepts that historians have borrowed). From the very beginnings of the discipline, anthropologists engaged with historical thinking in two distinct, albeit interconnected ways; while some scholars studied how non-Western societies represented and performed their past, others sought to incorporate Western ("scientific") historical concepts into the study of culture change. In the early twentieth century, non-Western representations of the past were rarely referred to as "history," since the oral traditions of supposedly "primitive" indigenous peoples around the world were viewed as too suffused with mythical elements to offer any meaningful glimpse into actual past events. Robert Lowie famously dismissed indigenous accounts of the past as "not history in our sense any more than the fact, even if true, of my neighbor's cat having kittens is history," further insisting that "from the traditions themselves nothing can be deduced."[11] Some decades later, the prefix *ethno-* was added to these histories as an unsubtle reminder that while such narratives may have revealed interesting things about the people telling them, they were not to be taken seriously as "true" descriptions of past events.[12]

It is important to point out at this juncture that this two-pronged approach to studying the past in early anthropology (not coincidentally) reflects a semantic ambiguity contained in the term "history," which can refer both to *narratives* of the past as well as to the past *itself.* Using the same word to describe what actually happened and what we say happened allows history to substitute "its own historical sign of the past for the past itself,"[13] and thereby subtly reinforces the popular assumption that the past can be reconstructed, to use Leopold von Ranke's famous expression, *wie es eigentlich gewesen* ("how it really was"). Since it will be essential in the following discussion to distinguish between these two meanings of "history," I will heretofore employ the anthropologist Michel-Rolph Trouillot's categories of *historicity 1* (i.e. the actual past socio-material events and processes) and *historicity 2* (i.e. the various ways in which past events and processes are collectively remembered and/or emplotted in historical narratives).[14] When put in these terms, it is clear that early anthropologists studying indigenous "ethnohistories" were focused primarily on historicity

2, while those calling for the greater incorporation of (Western) historical perspectives into ethnological research were really specifically interested in historicity 1.

Anthropologists in the latter camp, like Franz Boas and Alfred Kroeber, believed that history (historicity 1) could serve as an antidote to what they saw as an overly static account of the development of human societies, arguing that cultural change should be approached from the perspective of historical contingency rather than universal generalizing laws.[15] Even as the theoretical pendulum swung back toward evolutionism with the rise of structural-functionalism and systems approaches in the mid twentieth century, many ethnographers continued to draw on historical data as a means of peeling back the "layers" of history that accreted after European colonial contact, with the goal of reconstructing the "authentic" lifeways of indigenous non-Western groups.[16] History in this sense was equivalent to Western influence because the West was seen to progress at a rapid "historical" pace, while small-scale "primitive" cultures were thought to exist in a state of equilibrium that unfolded in a more gradual, evolutionary manner.[17] Therefore, one might say that non-Western peoples were doubly constructed as "without history": not only did they lack the technological, social, or cognitive ability to develop historically (historicity 1), but they also did not possess written narratives about the past that measured up to Western historical standards (historicity 2).

The colonialist conceits that underwrote what James Faubion later called the "Great Divide" between the West and the Rest were increasingly attacked in the early 1980s, a period that also marked the beginning of the so-called "historic turn" in anthropological research.[18] Structural-functionalist and neo-evolutionary approaches were roundly criticized for taking non-Western peoples "out of time," and a concerted effort was made to demonstrate how indigenous communities were the product of long-term global processes as well as their own internal historical dynamics.[19] The longstanding assumption that non-Western groups were "without history" before colonial contact was rightly abandoned. This period also witnessed the first sustained challenges to the epistemological superiority of Western historicity. While some anthropologists had previously expressed skepticism about the universal validity of Western history,[20] in the 1980s this critique gained widespread traction within the discipline, particularly in response to Marshall Sahlins' provocative call to "explode the concept of history" through a cross-cultural examination of historicity.[21] Within a decade, it had become commonplace in anthropological scholarship to characterize Western history as a "social construction," "cultural phenomenon," and even "a myth—worse, a conceit."[22]

This "historic turn" was a key development in anthropological theory because it simultaneously sought to historicize (non-Western) cultures and culturize (Western) history. Yet despite the importance of these two intellectual innovations, a fundamental tension between historicity 1 and 2 remained unresolved: how can human societies be the product of historical processes if historical narratives are themselves socially constructed? In a scathing review of Sahlins' *Islands of History*, Jonathan Friedman made precisely this point: "If history is already a cultural mode, then it is necessarily subsumed by culture and cannot, of course, entertain a further, external relation to it."[23] Furthermore, if history is merely a social construction of Western culture, then subsuming all societies within a single stream of global time simply replaces one imperialistic conceit (i.e. non-Western peoples "lack history") for another (i.e. all history is *Western* history).[24] By trying to have it both ways—using culture to decenter Western history, but then putting a distinctly Western historicity right back at the center of their analyses of culture change—historical anthropologists trapped themselves in a paradox between these two concepts.

Toward an Anthropology of Historicity

The last two decades have witnessed renewed efforts among anthropologists to navigate the tricky epistemological terrain between the concepts of culture and history, with the publication of seminal studies on localized conceptions and performances of historicities from the Balkans, Greece, and rural France to Cuba, Papua New Guinea, and Madagascar.[25] Over a decade ago, Kevin Yelvington called on anthropologists "to elevate 'the cross-cultural study of the past' to a status alongside such anthropological staples as the comparison of kinship and marriage, religion and rituals, economics and legal systems,"[26] while more recently Stephan Palmié has implored ethnographers "to recognize that the way we have brought a historical dimension to our work remains beholden, not just methodologically but epistemologically, to the terms of a set of North Atlantic particulars that have been paraded as human universals since the second half of the eighteenth century."[27] Yet the most fully developed anthropological critique of history comes from Eric Hirsch and Charles Stewart's call for an "ethnography of historicity" that "draws attention to the connections between past, present and future without the assumption that events/time are a line between happenings 'adding up' to history. Whereas 'history' isolates the past, historicity focuses on the complex temporal nexus of past-present-future. Historicity, in our formulation, concerns the ongoing social production of accounts of pasts and futures."[28]

This book seeks to build upon this exciting and innovative interdisciplinary body of scholarship by proposing a broader *anthropology of historicity* that draws upon all subfields of the discipline, not just ethnography. This requires adopting a holistic and comparative perspective that considers the place of historical narratives, practices, and representations within their broader sociocultural context. In other words, like all dimensions of human culture, history must be understood to be deeply entangled in the "webs of significance" (to borrow Geertz's useful metaphor) through which humans organize and make sense of their world. Therefore, historical thinking, writing, and performing will always reflect and reproduce deeper social, political, and economic logics. An anthropology of historicity seeks to reveal the kinds of cultural values that our historical narratives embody, the political agendas they serve, the social identities they underwrite, the emotional anxieties they alleviate, and the power relationships they reinforce. The overarching goal of this project is not merely to evaluate the validity of individual historical narratives, but to ask broader questions like "What is history for?" and "What purpose does it serve?"

Remaining faithful to the traditional disciplinary division of labor between anthropology and history, much of the aforementioned ethnographic work on historicity has focused upon either non-Western societies or marginal, rural, and local representations of the past within Europe. This book, in contrast, seeks to bring an anthropological perspective directly to the heart of Western historical thinking by examining the place of "the Middle Ages" in the historical imagination. While no single case study can claim to provide a definitive or exhaustive account of the complex and often contradictory implications of Western historical thinking, there is no period of the European past that provides more fertile ground for exploring this phenomenon than the Middle Ages. Therefore, investigating how the idea of "the Middle Ages" has been, and continues to be, entangled with colonial, national, ethnic, and intellectual dynamics should serve as a reminder that scholarly, "scientific" history is no less a culturally specific means of representing and experiencing the past than oral traditions, spirit possession, ritual activities, or dreaming.[29]

Of course, this project also draws upon the venerable historiographical tradition that has sought to place the writing of history within broader sociocultural, political, national, and economic contexts. In particular, there is an extensive body of literature dedicated to understanding the central role of historical scholarship in the creation and maintenance of national identities since the eighteenth century.[30] An anthropology of historicity shares much with these approaches, but its perspective is unique in several ways. For example, it strives to adopt a rigorously "symmetrical" perspective that examines all representations of the past (whether scholarly, popular, nationalist, pseudo-historical, indigenous, etc.) through the same analytical lens. That is to say, it begins with the assumption that "objective" scholarly histories will reflect and reinforce broader cultural ideologies no less than "pseudo," mythical, or distorted representations of the past. While some historians might instinctively recoil from a blurring of epistemological boundaries between "true" histories and "false" mythology, anthropologists have long recognized that all representations of the past (including Western historiography) contain a kernel of myth.[31] Moreover, calling history "mythical" is not the same as calling it false, nor does it force us to treat all representations of the past as equally valid. Rather, myth is what animates our narratives about the past—what gives "historicity 2" its meaning, purpose, and appeal. As Frank Ankersmit has pointed out, "myth is the condition of the possibility of all history and of all historical narrative."[32] Therefore, an anthropology of historicity strives to identify the mythical patterns of thought in all the diverse ways that we represent and imagine the past, and to illuminate the place of such narratives within broader cultural logics.

Another key difference between our anthropology of historicity and traditional historiographical research is that while the latter tends to focus on how particular historians, historical narratives or schools of thought have been shaped by their sociopolitical conditions, the former also interrogates the fundamental tenets underlying all Western historical thinking. It seeks to demonstrate how the hidden and rarely questioned epistemological assumptions upon which historical interpretations are constructed can provide equally important insights into history's place in the modern imagination. To be sure, a number of historians have become interested in critically analyzing Western historical thinking from this broader cross-cultural and theoretical perspective. Ankersmit, one of the foremost theorists of history, has posed critical questions like: "What will or must it mean to us to have an awareness of the past?" and "What must happen to a nation or collectivity to become fascinated by the problem of the past?"[33] while fellow German historian Jörn Rüsen has similarly emphasized the need to question "the unity of historical thinking and its claims for validity" and to recognize how Western, academic histories are only one part of a much wider array of cultural variety, difference, and change in historical thinking.[34] Recent collaborations between anthropologists and historians at the University of Chicago and University College London further suggest that tackling these issues will require a dissolution of traditional disciplinary boundaries that have too often generated antagonism and the strict policing of intellectual territories when it comes to history and culture.[35]

Hidden Assumptions and Consequences of Western Historical Thinking

Having sketched the basic tenets of an anthropology of historicity, we now attempt to unpack some of the underlying assumptions and consequences of Western conceptions of history and temporality. In the modern West, time has been widely assumed to be singular, linear, and homogeneous in nature, flowing like a river along a single course and at a uniform speed. In other words, it is understood to be a fourth dimension of Euclidian space-time, where more recent past events are imagined as nearer to the present than older ones. In this ontological model, space and time are dimensions of the same homogeneous and unbounded medium in which the universe exists, so just as we are aware of the "side-by-sideness" of things in space, we also think about temporal succession as the "side-by-sideness" of things in time.[36] Common expressions referring to "the passing of time" and "looking ahead to the future" reveal how deep-seated the spatialization of time is in our cultural consciousness.[37] This view of temporality is not unique to Western modernity, but is, by all accounts, the most common conception of time cross-culturally.[38] In the Western tradition, the spatialization of time can be traced back at least to the pre-Socratic philosopher Zeno of Elea (fifth century BCE), who illustrated a temporal paradox in the flight of an arrow across the sky: at any particular "moment" of time, the arrow occupies a fixed geometrical space where it appears at rest (as it might in a photograph). But if the arrow is not moving at any of these (potentially infinite) specific instances, asks Zeno, how does it move at all?

We will return to some of the inherent problems and limitations of the spatialization of time in Chapter 7, but here it is important to recognize how it underlies the most fundamental assumption about temporality in Western historical thinking: the absolute separation of the past from the present. This divide imbues the past with its very *pastness*: as completed, inaccessible, and never to return ("perfect," in a grammatical sense). As the historian Constantin Fasolt has noted, this division is essential to the practice of history, which needs to understand the past as a separate, unchanging entity that can only be known through systematic historical investigation. While the separation of the past from present may appear obvious and uncontroversial, in his brilliant book *The Limits of History*, Fasolt has shown how it is the product of a "historical revolt" by a group of seventeenth-century humanist scholars who invented our modern understanding of history in part as a political strategy to undermine the authority of the Holy Roman Emperor and papacy.[39]

These fundamental assumptions about the nature of time inform the principles of historicism: "the epistemological orientation that identifies change over time as fundamental or essential rather than superficial or contingent."[40] While not often explicitly articulated, modern historical scholarship presupposes most, if not all, of the following assertions: (1) nothing has an eternal form, permanent essence, or constant identity that transcends historical change; (2) all human experience and knowledge is contextual and relational, rather than transcendent or universal; (3) no political institution, social movement, artistic creation, or intellectual system can be properly understood or explained outside of its unique "historical context" (cf. the "principle of anachronism"); (4) human agency is the central driving force of historical change; (5) human history has a particular arc, often conceptualized as a series of stages, and commonly understood to be generally moving in a particular (upward, "progressive") direction; (6) the past has instructive value: that it constitutes an important guide for representing the right way of acting and helping us to make decisions for the future.[41]

While historiographical studies have explored the sociopolitical context and consequences of particular historical narratives, less attention has been given to historical thinking *itself*. While its consequences can be complex and even contradictory, here I highlight several that have great relevance to our investigation of the Middle Ages. First, historical thinking can serve the current social and economic order by furnishing it with an authority and authenticity often described as the "weight of history." The potentially insidious effects of historical thinking were recognized by Karl Marx, who famously observed that "the tradition of all dead generations weighs like a nightmare on the brains of the living", as well as Friedrich Nietzsche, who warned that the widespread assumption of history having a particular direction was too often used to intimate the sweeping claim that things were "as they had to be, as men now are they were bound to become, none may resist this inevitability."[42] In other words, if one assumes a singular, linear historical trajectory, the social, political, economic, and/or cultural status quo is subtly imbued with an aura of inevitability that discourages the imagining of alternative presents and futures.[43]

In other words, the assertion that something has "always been this way" can provide a convenient excuse to avoid addressing longstanding economic inequalities, rectifying social injustices, or solving inter-ethnic or sectarian conflicts. Indeed, this *argumentum ad antiquitatem* fallacy has often been invoked to rationalize deeply unjust practices and institutions—including black chattel slavery in the antebellum South, denying women's suffrage, and the recent debate over marriage equality—as well as to deflect Western colonialism's role in fomenting contemporary unrest in the Middle East by claiming that Sunni–Shia conflict "dates back millennia."[44] Of course, Americans are not alone in committing this fallacy; the mayor of a small town in France recently dismissed growing calls to change the name of a nearby hamlet *La-mort-aux-Juifs* ("Death to Jews") for the simple reason that since this place name "goes back to the Middle Ages or even further," it is important to "respect these old names."[45]

Furthermore, the assumption that history has a singular, inescapable trajectory also served as a key ideological justification for European colonial rule. For example, Dipesh Chakrabarty has persuasively shown how historicism "enabled European domination of the world in the nineteenth century" by positing a single scheme of historical development where Europe's past was seen as equivalent to non-Western presents, thereby giving the future of the colonial world (if it had one at all) a distinctly Western face.[46] Jack Goody has similarly demonstrated how this understanding of historical development allowed the West to claim sole credit for ideas and institutions like democracy, science, individualism, capitalism, humanism, and even romantic love.[47]

Second, while historical thinking can encourage an undue reverence or nostalgia for the past, it can also paradoxically foster a self-satisfied presentism where the past is put on trial and judged to be "a kind of moral and intellectual failure."[48] As explored in Chapters 2 and 3, no period of the past has been so frequently "put on trial" as the Middle Ages, a periodization invented to be an absolute Other against which modernity could celebrate its own cultural, political, and economic achievements.[49] Rather than grapple with the complex reality of the past, this "progressive" conception of history looks back upon certain parts of history with the same combination of paternalism and contempt that many colonial peoples experienced, who were themselves imagined to literally "belong to the past." The idea that history progresses in a certain direction is further evident in many progressive activists' insistence that "history is on our side," while their opponents' views will soon be relegated to the "dustbin" of history (interestingly, this powerful trope is also frequently invoked in current debates over marriage equality, but from the opposite side to those described above).

Third, one of the most important political functions of the modern historical imagination has been to fashion a shared past for members of nation-states. The creation of collective memories is essential for the maintenance of "imagined communities" (not only national, but also religious, ethnic, professional, etc.) because it strengthens the identity and unity of a group, binding its members together and distinguishing them from the Other. From childhood, citizens are habitually exposed into what Theodor Adorno called "identitarian thinking"[50] from the fairytale history lessons of primary schools to the public rituals, historical monuments, and national holidays that reinforce the dominant state narrative. This is why becoming an educated citizen means being familiar with past national heroes, enemies, and traitors, improbable military victories and tragic defeats, hallowed traditions, key documents, and each of those seminal moments where the nation came to a fuller realization of its collective destiny.

Historical thinking has also proven useful to nationalist ideologies because it reinforces the idea that every nation has a unique set of qualities or attitudes (a "national character"), which are exemplified in its past. For example, American public history encourages citizens to read their national story through the lens of their most cherished collective values (i.e. freedom, independence, self-reliance, etc.). This fosters the dubious notion that some transhistorical "American spirit" can explain everything from the decision to revolt from the British crown to the Manifest Destiny of nineteenth-century westward expansion, or even more recent imperialistic policies across the globe.[51] While contemporary academics are deeply suspicious of reading the past through such jingoistic glasses, the writing of history (and practice of archaeology) has been undeniably intertwined with the concept of the nation-state and national identity since the origin of the discipline.[52] This theme can also be seen in the growth of the heritage and genealogy industries, which encourage people to find their identity in distant ancestors or even their genetic coding.[53] These themes will be further explored in Chapters 4 and 5 of this book, specifically in the context of competing narratives of the early medieval Eastern Alpine region between German imperialists and Slovenian nationalists.

One key purpose of highlighting the assumptions and consequences of historical thinking is to appreciate that epistemological propositions concerning the nature of temporality and historicism are ultimately unverifiable "articles of faith" rather than logical proofs. All approaches to historicity—Western and non-Western, modern, medieval, and ancient—are premised upon epistemologically untestable "first principles," which shape how a society conceptualizes the relationship among past, present, and future. To take one example, the medieval conception of human history, which saw an omnipotent and benevolent God as its driving force, would surely have considered the "commonsense" modernist idea that history has normative value (i.e. *we must learn the lessons of the past*) unpersuasive, if not completely bizarre. Similarly, the idea that history "progresses" in a particular (upward) direction that so powerfully informs the way that Westerners understand past, present, and future would be nonsensical to societies espousing a cyclical view of time. Even if one decides, in the end, that contemporary "scientific" history is more plausible than ancient (cyclical), medieval (eschatological), or contemporary non-Western conceptions of the past, it is nevertheless absolutely critical to realize that this is a choice, not an inevitability. Moreover, those adhering to other historicities are not wrong or ignorant or misinformed, but simply adopt a different set of first principles.

The Role of Archaeology

Another important contribution of the anthropology of historicity proposed here is its integration of the theoretical and methodological insights of contemporary archaeology. While the discipline of archaeology has always sat at the intersection of anthropological and historical research, it has too often been regarded as a "handmaiden" to these disciplines; archaeological data has been effectively used to answer questions generated by historians and anthropologists, but rarely is seen as meaningfully contributing its own theoretical perspective.[54] However, archaeology's focus on materiality provides an important means of negotiating the paradox between historicities 1 and 2 outlined above. Thinking critically about how particular historical narratives fulfill social, political, and psychological needs is an essential component of an anthropology of historicity, but such questions focus only on a single meaning of history (as a culturally constructed mode of representation), and therefore have little to say about those socio-material processes that actually occurred in the past, and which continue to have inescapable consequences for the present. In other words, an anthropology of historicity seeks to bridge the gap between the need to examine how the past is *narrativized* and the (necessary, if unachievable) goal of understanding the past *wie es eigentlich gewesen*. Just because narratives of the past are shaped to suit the needs of the present does not mean that the past is "infinitely susceptible to the whims of contemporary interest and the distortions of contemporary ideology," as Arjun Appadurai has noted.[55] Reducing history to pure ideology ignores the continuing power of the past on the present. As Trouillot has eloquently observed:

> Constructivism's dilemma is that while it can point to hundreds of stories that illustrate its general claim that narratives are produced, it cannot give a full account of the production of any single narrative. For either we would all share the same stories of legitimation, or the reasons why a specific story matters to a specific population are themselves historical.[56]

Put plainly, history may always serve the needs of the present, but it is not invented out of whole cloth. Even if we can never fully know the past (at least not with a Cartesian certainty), the fact remains that events and processes have occurred whose effects persist into the present in the following ways: (1) through individual memories; (2) through collective memories (including, but not limited to, historical narratives), and (3) through the material consequences of past events. Therefore, we have at least three avenues for investigating the past; although none of these lines of evidence is infallible (memories fade, histories are always partial by their very nature, and archaeological remains do not "speak for themselves"), effectively integrating all three is essential for any effort to reconstruct what actually happened (i.e. historicity 1).

Consider the events in New York City on 11 September 2001. Let's ask a deceptively simple question: how can we know what happened on that fateful day? Anyone old enough can probably recall through their memories what it was like to live in that particular moment (whether by witnessing the events in person or on television). Every individual had a unique experience and interpretation of those events, and psychologists have shown that these memories inevitably change over time, and are always filtered through the lens of the present.[57] Living witnesses may then pass on these memories to their children or grandchildren, establishing an informal oral tradition within their families.

Additionally, there are now many written histories that detail the events of 11 September, based on individual eyewitnesses, video footage, government documents, and numerous other potential lines of evidence. Such historical narratives not only describe the events, but also attempt to explain their causes, consequences, and meaning. As is well known, such histories include not only mainstream, scholarly accounts that attribute these attacks to the transnational terrorist organization Al-Qaeda, but also "conspiratorial" histories that propose radically different interpretations of these events, such as claiming that the American government had knowledge of, or even orchestrated, these attacks. The wildly diverging historical narratives surrounding the causes of the events on 11 September bring into full view the ideological context of the writing of history, and the continuing appeal of such alternative pseudo-historical narratives among a certain segment of the populace offers fertile ground for historiographical and sociological analyses to which an anthropology of historicity could certainly contribute.[58]

However, while it is clear that such historical events can inspire multiple contradictory historical narratives, it must also be recognized that these narratives are not infinitely malleable, for the simple reason that the material consequences of these events can continue to be experienced in the present: the built landscape of New York is forever altered, the people in those airplanes are no longer alive, and the remnants of the destruction are housed in museums across the country. No sane person can honestly claim that the attacks *didn't* happen, or that the Twin Towers remain standing in Lower Manhattan. It is in navigating between the Scylla of social constructivism and the Charybdis of naïve positivism where archaeology can make an essential contribution to the anthropology of historicity, not because its data are somehow more objective or reliable than textual sources, but rather because archaeology's focus on materiality offers two key insights. First, recognizing that material processes from the past continue to exert agency in the present helps us to avoid the temptation of understanding history simply as an empty container that is filled by the needs of the present. Secondly, the nature of material things offers a direct challenge to some of the basic assumptions of historical thinking outlined above. Chapters 6 and 7 will consider how adopting a new approach to studying the past—one based on relationality and materiality—will allow us to better navigate the tensions between historicities 1 and 2. Furthermore, by exploring the past in a way that defies traditional historicist conventions, historians and archaeologists can potentially develop new ways of representing the past that are less susceptible to the political consequences of historical thinking outlined above, specifically in terms of their appropriation by nationalist and colonialist agendas. This is perhaps what Laurent Olivier had in mind when he called on archaeologists in a recent monograph to think beyond a traditional linear, singular, and spatialized conception of historical time and to embrace the polysemous temporality of their material datasets:

> In the conventional approach, historical time is a series of events. Events are linked to each other and are explained in terms of their relation to each other. But for that other form of history that is comprised of an accumulation of physical objects, archaeological time is one of repetition … It is a world where, as opposed to that of conventional history, past and present are entwined, where events can occur in place of, or in replacement for each other, and above all where events do not act upon those closest to them but rather on others far removed, more or less by intermingling with them. The operative logic is not that of a chain of events, but rather one of matter, of filiation of form, and the creation of memory.[59]

It is through such a lens that the following chapters will investigate Europe's medieval past.

Notes

1. Clifford Geertz, "Anti Anti-Relativism," *American Anthropologist* 86 (1984): 275.

2. See Agustin Fuentes, *Race, Monogamy, and Other Lies They Told You: Busting Myths about Human Nature* (Berkeley, 2012); Marilyn Strathern, *The Gender of the Gift: Problems with Women and Problems with Society in Melanesia* (Berkeley, 1988); and David Graeber, *Debt: The First 5,000 Years* (Brooklyn, NY, 2011).

3. See the recent panel session organized by Palmié and Stewart entitled "Beyond the Historic Turn: Toward an Anthropology of History" at the 2013 Annual Meeting of the American Anthropological Association, panel abstract found at: http://neubauercollegium. uchicago.edu/faculty/anthropology_of_history/Toward_an_Anthropology_of_History/.

4. Martin L. Davies, *Imprisoned by History: Aspects of Historicized Life* (New York, 2010); Constantin Fasolt, *The Limits of History* (Chicago, 2004).

5. Karl Mannheim, *Essays on the Sociology of Knowledge* (New York, 1952), 85.

6. See Jill Lepore, *The Whites of Their Eyes: The Tea Party's Revolution and the Battle over American History* (Princeton, NJ, 2010); Richard H. Kohn, "History and the Culture Wars: The Case of the Smithsonian Institution's Enola Gay Exhibition," *The Journal of American*

History (1995); and Vine Deloria, *Custer Died for Your Sins; an Indian Manifesto* (New York, 1969).

7. Marcus Tullius Cicero, *De Oratore* (Cambridge, 1942), II, 36.

8. Max Horkheimer, Theodor W. Adorno, and Gunzelin Schmid Noerr, *Dialectic of Enlightenment: Philosophical Fragments* (Stanford, CA, 2002); Max Horkheimer, *Eclipse of Reason* (New York, 1947).

9. Paul Feyerabend, "How to Defend Society against Science," *Radical Philosophy* 11 (1975).

10. Bruno Latour, *Pandora's Hope: Essays on the Reality of Science Studies* (Cambridge, MA, 1999); Bruno Latour, "Why Has Critique Run Out of Steam? From Matters of Fact to Matters of Concern," *Critical Inquiry* 30 (2004).

11. Robert H. Lowie, "Oral Tradition and History," *American Anthropologist* 17 (1915): 599.

12. For a more detailed overview of the rise of ethnohistory, see Shepard Krech III, "The State of Ethnohistory," *Annual Review of Anthropology* (1991); and Michael E. Harkin, "Ethnohistory's Ethnohistory Creating a Discipline from the Ground Up," *Social Science History* 34 (2010).

13. Davies, *Imprisoned by History*, 67. This would be equivalent to having the same word for "nature" and "physics," as pointed out by Michel de Certeau, *The Writing of History* (New York, 1988), 21.

14. Michel-Rolph Trouillot, *Silencing the Past: Power and the Production of History* (Boston, MA, 1995); the concept of "emplotment" of historical narratives is also explored in Paul Ricœur, *Time and Narrative* (Chicago, 1984) and Hayden V. White, *Metahistory: The Historical Imagination in Nineteenth-Century Europe* (Baltimore, 1973).

15. Franz Boas, "The Aims of Anthropological Research," *Science* 76 (1932); A.L. Kroeber, "History and Science in Anthropology," *American Anthropologist* 37 (1935).

16. Brian Keith Axel, "Introduction: Historical Anthropology and Its Vicissitudes," in *From the Margins: Historical Anthropology and Its Futures*, ed. B.K. Axel (Durham, NC, 2002), 4.

17. Bernard S. Cohn, "History and Anthropology: The State of Play," *Comparative Studies in Society and History* 22 (1980): 199.

18. James D. Faubion, "History in Anthropology," *Annual Review of Anthropology* 22 (1993).

19. See Johannes Fabian, *Time and the Other: How Anthropology Makes Its Object* (New York, 1983); Nicholas Thomas, *Out of Time: History and Evolution in Anthropological Discourse* (Cambridge; New York, 1989); Marshall Sahlins, *Historical Metaphors and Mythical Realities: Structure in the Early History of the Sandwich Islands Kingdom* (Ann Arbor, 1981); and Eric R. Wolf, *Europe and the People without History* (Berkeley, 1982).

20. See, for example, Claude Levi-Strauss's debate with Jean-Paul Sartre, whom he accused of holding "an almost mystical conception" of history by making it "the last refuge of transcendental humanism." Interestingly, Levi-Strauss asserted that the anthropologist "respects history, but does not accord it a special value"; see Claude Levi-Strauss, *The Savage Mind* (Chicago, 1966), 256. Around the same time, E.E. Evans-Pritchard, *Anthropology and History* (Manchester, 1961), 12 called for "sociology of historiography, in which the historians themselves and their books are the phenomena under investigation."

21. Marshall Sahlins, "Other Times, Other Customs: The Anthropology of History," *American Anthropologist* 85 (1983).

22. Quotations are from, respectively, Jonathan Friedman, "The Past in the Future: History and the Politics of Identity," *American Anthropologist* 94 (1992): 854; Faubion, "History in Anthropology," 44; John L. Comaroff and Jean Comaroff, *Ethnography and the Historical Imagination* (Boulder, CO, 1992), 19.

23. Jonathan Friedman, "Review of Islands of History by Marshall Sahlins," *History and Theory* 26 (1987): 76.

24. Kevin Birth, "The Creation of Coevalness and the Danger of Homochronism," *Journal of the Royal Anthropological Institute* 14 (2008).

25. See David E. Sutton, *Memories Cast in Stone: The Relevance of the Past in Everyday Life* (New York, 1998); Michael Lambek, "The Sakalava Poiesis of History: Realizing the Past through Spirit Possession in Madagascar," *American Ethnologist* 25 (1998); Christian Giordano, "Actualizing History in Eastern and Western Europe. The History of the Historian and that of the Anthropologist," *Ethnologia Balkanica* (1998); Eric Hirsch, "Valleys of Historicity and Ways of Power among the Fuyuge," *Oceania* (2007); Kenneth Routon, "Conjuring the Past: Slavery and the Historical Imagination in Cuba," *American Ethnologist* 35 (2008); Matt Hodges, "The Time of the Interval: Historicity, Modernity, and Epoch in Rural France," *American Ethnologist* 37 (2010); Charles Stewart, *Dreaming and Historical Consciousness in Island Greece* (Cambridge, MA, 2012).

26. Kevin A. Yelvington, "History, Memory and Identity: A Programmatic Prolegomenon," *Critique of Anthropology* 22 (2002): 230.

27. Stephan Palmié, "Historicist Knowledge and the Conditions of Its Impossibility," in *The Social Life of Spirits*, ed. R. Blanes and D. E. Santo (Chicago, 2013), 219.

28. Eric Hirsch and Charles Stewart, "Introduction: Ethnographies of Historicity," *History and Anthropology* 16 (2005): 262; for more recent articulations of this approach, see Charles Stewart, "Historicity and Anthropology," *Annual Review of Anthropology* 45 (2016) and Stephan Palmié and Charles Stewart, "Introduction: For an Anthropology of History," *HAU: Journal of Ethnographic Theory* 6 (2016).

29. Jörn Rüsen, ed., *Time and History: The Variety of Cultures* (New York, 2007).

30. See, for example, Stefan Berger, *Writing the Nation: A Global Perspective* (New York, 2007); E.J. Hobsbawm and T.O. Ranger, eds, *The Invention of Tradition* (Cambridge; New York, 1983); Stefan Berger, Mark Donovan, and Kevin Passmore, eds, *Writing National Histories: Western Europe since 1800* (London; New York, 1999); Mario Carretero, *Constructing Patriotism: Teaching History and Memories in Global Worlds* (Charlotte, NC, 2011); Georg G. Iggers, *Historiography in the Twentieth Century: From Scientific Objectivity to the Postmodern Challenge* (Hanover, NH, 1997); John Coakley, *Nationalism, Ethnicity and the State: Making and Breaking Nations* (London, 2012); Anthony D. Smith, *The Antiquity of Nations* (Cambridge; Malden, MA, 2004); Susana Carvalho and François Gemenne, *Nations and Their Histories: Constructions and Representations* (Houndmills; New York, 2009).

31. Levi-Strauss, *The Savage Mind*, 254; Friedman "The Past in the Future," 837; see also William H. McNeill, "Mythistory, or Truth, Myth, History, and Historians," *The American Historical Review* 91 (1986); and Joseph Mali, *Mythistory: The Making of a Modern Historiography* (Chicago, 2003).

32. Frank R. Ankersmit, *Sublime Historical Experience* (Stanford, CA, 2005), 364.

33. Ibid., xv.

34. Rüsen, *Time and History*, 2.

35. The webpage for the "Historical Consciousness" research cluster in the Anthropology program at University College London can be found at http://www.ucl.ac.uk/anthropology/isci/historical-consciousness; the webpage for the (now completed) project in "The Anthropology of History" at the Neubauer Collegium for Culture and Society (University of Chicago) can be found at http://neubauercollegium.uchicago.edu/faculty/anthropology_of_history/.

36. John Alexander Gunn, *Bergson and His Philosophy* (London, 1920).

37. Common examples of this linguistic metaphor include "time passes," and "looking ahead to the future." For the time=space metaphor, see Dedre Gentner, Mutsumi Imai, and Lera Boroditsky, "As Time Goes By: Evidence for Two Systems in Processing Space → Time Metaphors," *Language and Cognitive Processes* 17 (2002); for the notion of "historical distance," see Jaap Den Hollander, Herman Paul, and Rik Peters, "Introduction: The Metaphor of Historical Distance," *History and Theory* 50 (2011).

38. There is an ongoing debate as to whether lexical space-time mapping is universal among human groups, outlined in Chris Sinha, Vera Da Silva Sinha, Jörg Zinken, and Wany Sampaio, "When Time Is Not Space: The Social and Linguistic Construction of Time Intervals and Temporal Event Relations in an Amazonian Culture," *Language and Cognition* 3 (2011).

39. Fasolt, *The Limits of History*.

40. Johannes C. Wolfart, "The Rise of the Historical Consciousness," *Religion Compass* 3 (2009): 88.

41. Frederick C. Beiser, *The German Historicist Tradition* (Oxford, 2011); Mannheim, *Essays on the Sociology of Knowledge*.

42. Karl Marx, *The Eighteenth Brumaire of Louis Bonaparte* (London, 1926); Friedrich Wilhelm Nietzsche and R.J. Hollingdale, *Untimely Meditations* (New York, 1997), 107; Martin L. Davies, "The Redundancy of History in a Historicized World," *Rethinking History* 15 (2011): 336–37.

43. Davies, "The Redundancy of History."

44. On marriage equality, see Peter Baker, "'Millennia' of Marriage Being between Man and Woman Weigh on Court," *The New York Times*, 29 April 2015. A recent example of the supposed "ancient" conflict between Sunni and Shia Muslims can be found in President Obama's 2016 State of the Union Address, transcript found at https://www.whitehouse.gov/the-press-office/2016/01/12/remarks-president-barack-obama-%E2%80%93-prepared-delivery-state-union-address.

45. "Le hameau 'La-mort-aux-Juifs' va-t-il devoir changer de nom?" *Le Huffington Post*, 12 August 2014, http://www.huffingtonpost.fr/2014/08/12/la-mort-aux-juifs-hameau-va-devoir-changer-nom_n_5671231.html. Original French : "C'est ridicule, tempête l'élu. Ce nom a toujours existé. Personne n'en veut aux Juifs, bien sûr. Cela ne m'étonne pas que cela revienne encore une fois sur le tapis. 'Il faudrait pour changer de nom une décision du conseil municipal, mais cela m'étonnerait bien' a-t-elle encore dit. Pourquoi changer un nom qui remonte au Moyen-Age, ou à plus loin encore? Il faut respecter ces vieux noms."

46. Dipesh Chakrabarty, *Provincializing Europe: Postcolonial Thought and Historical Difference* (Princeton, NJ, 2000), 7; see also Immanuel Wallerstein, "Eurocentrism and Its Avatars: The Dilemmas of Social Science," *New Left Review* 226 (1997).

47. Jack Goody, *The Theft of History* (Cambridge, 2006).

48. Barry Hindess, "The Past Is Another Culture★," *International Political Sociology* 1 (2007): 328; Nietzsche and Hollingdale, *Untimely Meditations*, 76.

49. Catherine Brown, "In the Middle," *Journal of Medieval and Early Modern Studies* 30 (2000): 549; Carol Symes, "When We Talk about Modernity," *The American Historical Review* 116 (2011): 721; John Dagenais, "The Postcolonial Laura," *MLQ: Modern Language Quarterly* 65 (2004): 374.

50. Theodor W. Adorno, *Negative Dialectics* (New York, 1973).

51. Daniel Little, "Philosophy of History," *Stanford Encyclopedia of Philosophy*. Winter 2012 Edition (Stanford, CA, 2012).

52. For history, see note 30 above; for archaeology, see Bruce G. Trigger, *A History of Archaeological Thought* (Cambridge; New York, 1989); and Margarita Díaz-Andreu García, *A World History of Nineteenth-Century Archaeology: Nationalism, Colonialism, and the Past* (Oxford, 2007).

53. Two prime examples of this are Ancestry.com, a for-profit corporation that allows people to trace their family genealogies, and even have their DNA tested to "get personalized details about your ethnic origins," as well as the PBS television show *Finding Your Roots*, where host Henry Louis Gates does this same thing for celebrities.

54. Austin, "The 'Proper Study' of Medieval Archaeology"; Moreland, "Archaeology and Texts."

55. Arjun Appadurai, "The Past as a Scarce Resource," *Man* 16 (1981): 201.

56. Trouillot, *Silencing the Past*, 13.

57. Daniel L. Schacter, "The Seven Sins of Memory: Insights from Psychology and Cognitive Neuroscience," *American Psychologist* 54 (1999).

58. Michael Barkun, *A Culture of Conspiracy: Apocalyptic Visions in Contemporary America* (Berkeley, 2013).

59. Laurent Olivier, *The Dark Abyss of Time: Archaeology and Memory* (Lanham, MD, 2012), 10–11.

CHAPTER 2

Mirror of the Medieval

[T]he specter of the medieval is a prior presence and an ongoing
horror in the mirror of modernity.
—Saurabh Dube, "Introduction: Enchantments of
Modernity"

Beginning in the Middle

Like a negative space looming at the center of Western history, the
medieval past has always been defined as what it is not. It is not the classical world, the embryo of Western civilization when the ancient Greeks
laid the bases for Western philosophy, literature, art, and politics, and
the Romans built a vast empire through military precision, engineering
ingenuity, and cold bureaucratic efficiency. No, the beginning of the
medieval world constituted the tragic end of this millennium of growth
and prosperity, as marauding barbarians plunged the European continent into a Dark Age marked by a rapidly shrinking population, political
chaos, endemic warfare, and the near complete extinction of classical
learning.

 Standing also in stark contrast to the medieval past is the modern
world, the most recent five centuries of human history that brought
unprecedented technological, economic, and intellectual progress,
first to Europe, and then (slowly but inevitably) to the rest of the world.
In fact, modernity only became possible when a series of revolutionary events woke Europe from its deep medieval slumbers: Renaissance

---

humanists rediscovered classical ideas and ideals; Protestant reformers finally broke a thousand years of Roman Catholic political and theological hegemony; mercantilists opened new markets and reinvigorated economic growth; early scientists developed a powerful new method for studying the natural world; intrepid explorers discovered "New Worlds" and shattered the insular medieval worldview. Even if this road to the modern world was not always smooth, it marked the gradual triumph of reason over superstition, tolerance over prejudice, liberty over servitude, and provided humanity with a previously unimaginable control over nature, our bodies, and our collective destiny.

Lying between these two eras of historical progress, technological innovation, and cultural flourishing lies the Middle Ages, an unfortunate detour in the otherwise ascending arc of Western civilization. During this dark and dismal thousand-year epoch, economic growth was stymied by a sclerotic feudal-manorial system, intellectual curiosity was actively repressed by an authoritarian Catholic hierarchy, and an effete aristocracy was largely indifferent to the nasty, brutish, and short lives of the impoverished and illiterate peasantry. Medieval justice was capricious and brutal, women and children valued as little more than property, and the entire society lived under constant fear of violence, famine, and disease. Although some intellectual achievements—like the Magna Carta, Gothic architecture, and the establishment of the university—did occur during this era, these were only really significant in presaging the modern world.

While guaranteed to make medievalists cringe, there is no denying that the above picture of the Middle Ages remains deeply entrenched in the public's historical consciousness. This "Dark Ages" image of the medieval past—backwards, violent, insular, incurious—continues to powerfully inform cultural, political, and even scholarly discourse, and can be found in contemporary film, television, video games, marketing, journalism, amateur history websites, and even schoolbooks. Even the word *medieval* itself (the *Oxford English Dictionary* lists one definition as "exhibiting the severity of illiberality ascribed to a former age; cruel, barbarous") reveals how deeply seated this motif rests in the modern historical imagination. Even the more nostalgic and romanticized versions of the Middle Ages (chivalrous knights, fair maidens, and beautiful castles) are premised upon a stark difference between the medieval and modern worlds.

Many readers of this book will surely be aware that decades of historical scholarship have shown nearly every one of the aforementioned depictions of medieval society to be grossly exaggerated, if not completely fabricated.[1]

Moreover, many of the "illiberal" practices and beliefs frequently derided as "medieval" were equally prevalent during antiquity and/or early modernity. So how then do we account for the pervasiveness of the Dark Ages motif in our collective historical consciousness, despite the ceaseless efforts of medievalists to debunk these crass stereotypes? Explanations that fault a historically myopic public due to the poor state of history education contain some truth, but are not fully satisfactory. Widespread misconceptions about particular episodes of the past are neither random nor innocent, but often serve specific sociopolitical purposes, as we are reminded every year on Columbus Day and Thanksgiving.[2] Just as our sanitized histories of European exploration of the New World provide Americans with a positive national identity and sense of collective pride and purpose, so does the historical mythology surrounding the Middle Ages perform important ideological functions. Indeed, the fact that the medieval past is arguably the least well understood part of Western history suggests a deep and powerful role in the ideology of modernity.

This chapter traces how and why the Middle Ages have become "one of the most pervasive cultural myths of the modern world."[3] It investigates the place of the medieval as mythistory[4] through its complex conceptual connection to two of the most powerful political forces of the modern era: colonialism and nationalism. Admittedly, this does not exhaust the various ideological purposes that the medieval has served in the modern world, but since the use of the medieval past for political purposes forms a central theme of this book, this chapter offers a broad overview of the origin and evolution of this historical myth. How did the millennium between the fifth and fifteenth centuries come to be defined as a single historical era? Why does it continue to symbolize all that is cruel, ignorant, and backward in the modern world? How have the ideologies of colonialism and nationalism shaped our understanding of the medieval past? What will become clear in the course of this chapter is that the Middle Ages are not an innocent periodization of European history, but serve a key purpose in the temporal logic of modernity. Moreover, this purpose is not monolithic or static, but has significantly shifted over the past several centuries, and continues to do so today.

Inventing the Middle Ages

The very term *Middle* Ages powerfully reinforces the master narrative of Western history outlined above: an entire era that was nothing more than a long interruption in the ascendancy of Western civilization, birthed in antiquity and coming to fruition in modernity. It is therefore necessary to begin our investigation by tracing the origins of this curious term. It may come as no surprise that people living in Europe between the fifth and fifteenth centuries did not generally consider themselves to be in a "middle" age (except in the sense of being between Creation and the Final Judgment). Since medieval Europe was a predominantly Christian society, its histories typically adopted the scripturally derived "Seven Age" system, which identified their own era as the penultimate stage, directly preceding the Parousia.[5]

The ideological origins of our current periodization of the Middle Ages can be traced to Renaissance Italy during the fourteenth century, a time when early humanists were attempting to revive certain philosophical ideals, literary forms, and cultural values of classical antiquity. In order to underscore the historical significance of their intellectual project, these scholars sought to distinguish themselves from their predecessors, whose work they widely considered to lack literary or cultural merit. This was likely what the renowned poet Francesco Petrarch had in mind when, in a 1359 letter, he was the first to describe the period preceding his own as *tenebrae* ("dark" or "shadowy"). While this metaphor was normally invoked to describe the time of "darkness" before the light of Christianity (i.e. pagan antiquity), Petrarch cleverly shifted the meaning of this term from a religious to a cultural connotation, which meant that the *post*-classical era was now the real Dark Ages.[6]

Whether or not he intended to inaugurate a new periodization of the Western past, Petrarch's "dark ages" was subsequently adopted by influential Renaissance scholars like Leonardo Bruni and Giovanni Andrea Bussi—both of whom also began to employ the term *medias tempestas* ("middle ages")— as well as English philosopher Francis Bacon, who was eager to contrast his modern method with the preceding era. In his *Novum Organum* (1620), Bacon explicitly identified three periods where he believed that learning flourished: ancient Greece, classical Rome, and his own "modern" Europe. In contrast, Bacon argues, the intervening centuries "were not flourishing or fertile for the growth of knowledge," since during this time neither the "Arabs" nor "schoolmen" (i.e. medieval scholastic philosophers) added anything significant to philosophy or science, but crushed the search for new knowledge "with the weight of their books."[7] By the end of the seventeenth century, the now-familiar ancient/medieval/modern schema had become a widely accepted organization of European history, particularly after the publication of Christoph Cellarius's *Universal History Divided into an Ancient, Medieval, and New Period* (1688). The key point here is that the invention of the "Middle Ages" was not an innocent, value-free attempt at periodizing the European past, but ultimately derived from humanists' self-serving efforts to underscore the historical import of their own intellectual efforts.

Once firmly entrenched in the modern historical imagination, the notion of a singular, homogeneous "middle ages" stretching from the end of antiquity to the Renaissance could be easily appropriated by any political or ideological agenda seeking to profit from this crass historical caricature. For example, Protestant theologians equated this era with the political and religious power of the Roman Church and papacy, which they were eager to characterize as corrupt, authoritarian, and debauched. Similarly, eighteenth-century philosophers like Voltaire, Montesquieu, and Kant found in the medieval mind a convenient straw man that could be portrayed as superstitious, incurious, and overly deferential to tradition and authority (in other words, the very antithesis of their modern, "enlightened" thinker). On the other hand, artists and philosophers of the Romantic Movement during the nineteenth century found in the Middle Ages an era of lost simplicity, authenticity, and rootedness that provided the ideal counterpoint to the modern forces of industrialization, urbanization, and secularization that they viewed with suspicion and contempt.

Despite the markedly different goals of these various ideological projects, and their idiosyncratic images of the medieval past, it is clear that the Middle Ages offered modern historical imaginations a temporal Other upon which any social needs, ideological desires, or strategic political goals could be readily foisted. Whether used to celebrate or critique the modern condition, the Middle Ages provided a mirror for modernity, ultimately revealing less about the (medieval) past than it did about the (modern) present. In fact, when one considers how fundamental the notion of *rupture* (i.e. breaking from ancient texts, traditions, and authorities) has been to modernity, the invention of a primitive medieval begins to look almost like an inevitable consequence of this ideology.[8]

The Middle Ages as Colonial Other

As the careful reader may already have noticed, the invention of the Middle Ages as a temporal Other against which modernity could define itself bears a striking resemblance to the way in which Europe secured its own identity by imagining a cultural/racial/geographical Other in the colonized world. That is to say, the Middle Ages became, like the colonized world, "a sort of surrogate and even underground Self" for the West, as Edward Saïd famously argued in *Orientalism*.[9] This strongly suggests that the near simultaneous emergence of the non-Western and premodern in the historical-colonial imagination was no coincidence; rather, both were the product of the same colonizing move. In Caroline Brown's pithy observation: "The Middle Ages were invented to be a foreign country."[10]

Therefore, it should not be surprising that the ideologies of colonialism and medievalism have been deeply entangled since the very beginning of the modern project. Indeed, John Dagenais and Margaret Greer have pointed out that "the history of 'The Middle Ages' begins at the precise moment when European imperial and colonial expansion begins," and have demonstrated how Renaissance figures like Petrarch and Dante were inventing a premodern "dark ages" while also fantasizing about European colonial expansion into Africa and the Canary Islands.[11] In other words, over a century before Columbus's transatlantic voyages, the myth of the medieval was already taking shape because it was essential for making Western colonialism "not just doable but thinkable."[12] As an aside, this conflation of the medieval and colonial may also explain why medieval architecture and literature were often described in the sixteenth and seventeenth centuries as vaguely "eastern" or "Saracen," in contrast to the more "authentically European" forms of classical antiquity.[13]

The ideological connection of colonialism and medievalism is further revealed through a close examination of the origins and function of historical categories like "barbarian," "feudalism," and "crusading." While the term "barbarian" etymologically derives from ancient Greece, in the early modern era it was often used to describe both non-Western *and* premodern peoples, with the medieval period sometimes even referred to as the "Barbarous Ages."[14] For this reason, colonial administrators brought deeply ingrained historical images of early medieval barbarians to their dealings with colonial peoples both within and beyond Europe. For example, sixteenth-century English writers like Edmund Spenser and John Davies were eager to compare the customs and traditions of their colonial Irish subjects to ancient barbarian peoples (e.g. Germans, Gauls, and Britons) as well as their own medieval ancestors, finding no contradiction in drawing "indifferently from the first, eighth, twelfth, and fifteenth centuries," as Debora Shuger has shown.[15] Several centuries later, British officials in colonial Southern Africa similarly assumed that local tribal groups were organized by "kinship, communal ownership of land, language, and ethnicity" like their early medieval counterparts. This led to a number of cultural miscommunications; for example, when asked for their "tribal name" by colonial officials, Africans usually responded with the name of their chief, which was then erroneously taken as an ethnonym.[16]

Like barbarism, feudalism—one of the most important concepts in medieval historiography—was shaped within a distinctly colonial context. The term "feudalism" has traditionally been used to describe a set of reciprocal socio-legal obligations whereby a lord granted part of his land holdings (the fief) to another, lesser member of the aristocracy (the vassal), usually in exchange for military or other kinds of service.[17] However, this term was never used in the Middle Ages, but was actually coined by French and English legal scholars in the early modern era. Moreover, as Kathleen Davis has brilliantly shown, the shift from the narrow concept of "feudal" law to the broader idea of "feudalism" occurred during the seventeenth and eighteenth centuries as part of a deliberate effort to turn the latter into a narrative of servitude tied directly to the Middle Ages. Making servility, absolutism, and feudalism a thing of Europe's past, rather than its present, permitted Western intellectuals to imagine slavery as a fundamentally premodern institution, even as millions of Africans were forcibly moved across the Atlantic into the New World.[18] Davis has argued that such a periodizing break was necessary to establish state sovereignty and secular politics as distinctively modern, allowing scholars to avoid the obvious contradiction between modern liberty and chattel slavery.[19]

A third key intersection between medievalism and colonialism can be found in modern political uses of the Crusades, those (in)famous medieval military campaigns in which the pope called upon European armies to retake the Holy Land from Islamic forces. According to Jonathan Riley-Smith, crusading imagery and rhetoric was invoked in two distinct ways during the nineteenth and twentieth centuries: *paracrusading* "had within it some elements drawn from the old movement, although chosen selectively and distorted," while *pseudocrusading* "had no correspondence to the old reality, but borrowed rhetoric and imagery to describe ventures—particularly imperialist ones—that had nothing at all to do with the Crusades."[20] Examples of the former include the Institut des Frères Armés (a modern "crusading order" established by French Archbishop Charles Lavigerie to protect Catholic missionaries in East-Central Africa) and the nineteenth-century restoration of the French Knights of Malta. The latter notion was commonly employed by European powers who drew heavily on medieval imagery to legitimate their colonial goals across the Islamic world, such as the French conquest of Algeria in the 1830s, the Spanish invasion of Morocco in the 1850s, and the British occupation of Palestine after World War I.[21]

The Middle Ages as Nationalist Self

The historical trope of "medieval as Other" was central to the creation of the myth of the Middle Ages and played a variety of roles in the justification of Western colonial domination. However, this was not the only way in which the medieval served modern political agendas. In fact, since the late eighteenth century, the historical potency of the medieval past has often been drawn upon in precisely the opposite manner by nationalist movements in Europe. Rather than constructing the medieval past as radically Other in order to emphasize the significance of the present era, many nationalists emphasized the sameness of the Middle Ages with contemporary European peoples.

A full understanding of why the medieval was ripe for such appropriation requires an appreciation of the importance of historical narratives in the development and justification of nationalist ideologies. As numerous scholars have detailed, one of nationalism's central goals has been to create "imagined communities" that encourage a particular group of people to think of themselves as part of a single nation, even when they do not necessarily share familial, geographical, religious, ethnic, class, or other social bonds.[22] One of the most effective ways to foster this sense of belonging is to invent a past that provides its members with a set of collective memories and a shared sense of historical purpose or destiny. Although the particular content and emphasis of these nationalist historical narratives depends on the sociopolitical context, there are nevertheless many common underlying themes. For example, nationalist histories provide an "origin story" by identify a past "golden age" when the nation expressed itself in its finest form; they explain how this golden age disintegrated into an era of suffering or servitude (typically under a foreign yoke), and, often implicitly, offer some prescriptions for returning the nation to its former glory and prosperity.[23]

Nationalist histories thereby widen the circle of the imagined community to include long-dead ancestors who can inspire and instill a sense of purpose among its living members. The key goal for nationalist scholars of the past—not only historians, but also archaeologists, folklorists, philologists, and so forth—is to invent a long and venerable past for a national community that is, in most cases, a very recent creation. This not only lends an aura of credibility and authority to the efforts at nation-building, but also addresses the very practical need to identify and justify a particular historical territory (i.e. homeland) for that national group. Patrick Geary has referred to this kind of historically justified land claim as "primary acquisition": that mystical moment when a nation established their "right" to a particular territory, thereby invalidating the land claims of any previous or subsequent groups.[24]

While nationalist historians have drawn upon various parts of the distant and recent past to create their narrative or justify their political goals, many European nation-states locate their origins in the early medieval past, perhaps because this was the period when so many ethno-linguistic groups first appeared on the "historical stage," so to speak. Groups like the Franks, Angles, Saxons, Lombards, Magyars, and Bavarians all give their names to modern nation-states or regions in Central Europe. Many English historians have looked back to their Anglo-Saxon past—particularly the reign of Alfred the Great (849–99 CE)—as the first true expression of an English state and sense of national identity. Irish scholars have similarly romanticized their early medieval past as a golden age of "saints and scholars" before falling under the yoke of English imperialism.[25] One also finds great interest in the early Middle Ages among modern Slavic countries, since it was during this period that Slavic-speaking groups are believed to have spread through-out much of Eastern and Central Europe (see Chapter 5). Even Austria, an ethnically heterogeneous state that did not exist until 1919, has sought the origins of their nation in the Middle Ages, specifically the signing of the *Ostarrîchi* document in 996 CE, which created an eastern march out of the Duchy of Bavaria.[26]

Yet not all European nations have a decidedly positive view of their early medieval past. Most German-speaking historians showed little inter-est in ancient Germanic peoples before the mid-nineteenth century, but by the time of the National Socialist regime, these "ancestors" were frequently invoked to emphasize the racial superiority of early Germanic groups as the predecessors of all Nordic and Aryan peoples (see Chapter 4).[27] In France, the search for ancestors was often sharply divided along class lines, with the aristocracy claiming a direct line from the early medieval Merovingian dynasty, while the peasantry was imagined to be descended from the Gallo-Roman population that was conquered by the Franks. This is why during the French Revolution the Celtic past, and the figure of Vercingetorix in particular, provided a powerful historical role model of courage and resis-tance.[28] A similarly ambiguous relationship has existed between modern Italians and the early medieval Lombards, who—depending on the socio-political circumstances—were alternately portrayed as virtuous ancestors and malevolent foreign conquerors.[29]

In sum, while the place of medieval past in European nationalism is complicated, there is no doubt that it serves a very different purpose than in the ideology of modernity-colonialism: rather than being irrelevant, archaic, and easily forgotten, the Middle Ages offer nationalist ideologues an essential site of origins, identity, and collective memory. Instead of the epistemologi-cal gap that exists between medieval and modern in the colonial imagina-tion, nationalists seek to collapse the temporal distance between past and present, rendering medieval figures and events quite germane to contem-porary political issues, land claims, and border disputes. Patrick Geary has warned that this entanglement of the medieval past in contemporary political disputes threatens to turn our understanding of the Middle Ages into "a toxic waste dump."[30] Yet despite such concerns from scholars, politicians continue to invoke historical narratives in this dangerous way, and not just those of nationalist historians, but also the work of scholars ideologically opposed to such nationalist ends.[31] This theme of the relationship between nationalism and the medieval past will be further developed in Chapters 4 and 5, where we will see how the early medieval past has been used in the service of both German imperial expansion and Slovenian ethnic nationalism. Chapter 6 offers an attempt to study the medieval past without relying on the concept of ethnicity that has so often lent itself to political manipulation.

Neither Self nor Other: Medieval Natives in the Spatiotemporal Hierarchy

Above, it has been argued that the myth of "the Middle Ages" was largely a product of the temporal logic of modernity and has been, since the Renaissance, deeply entangled with the ideological development of Western colonialism. Yet at the zenith of Western imperial domination during the nineteenth century, this dual colonization of space and time became even more explicit, as Europeans fundamentally reconceptualized their justifications for dominating the rest of the world. While Western domination of the colonial Other had been justified by perceived religious, cultural, and/or racial superiority since the beginning of European expansion, by the nineteenth century Europeans began to imagine themselves as the most *historically* advanced civilization. Although some aspects of this conceit appear in seventeenth- and eighteenth-century writings,[32] the rise of evolutionary and geological models of time (e.g. Charles Lyell, Charles Darwin, and Herbert Spencer) as well as the new anthropological concept of "primitive society" (e.g. John Lubbock, Lewis Henry Morgan, and Edward Tylor) bestowed an aura of scientific credibility on the concept of a single trajectory of historical development for all human societies.[33] Predictably, Europeans placed themselves at the pinnacle of this progressive geo-temporal schema, relegating non-Western societies to the various lower stages of historical development. The creation of this *spatiotemporal hierarchy* (as it will be hereafter described) encouraged Europeans to imagine contemporary non-Western peoples as analogous to their own long-dead ancestors (Figure 2.1).[34]

This new temporal/historical way of conceptualizing human sociocultural diversity—what Peter Osborne later described as "the projection of

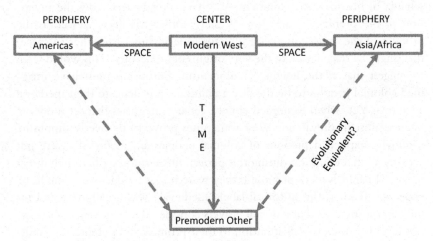

Figure 2.1. The spatiotemporal hierarchy.

certain people's presents as other people's futures"[35]—provided one of the most potent intellectual legitimations of colonial rule during the height of the Age of Empire. Since Europeans had already passed through whatever historical stage colonized peoples were presently situated in, they could claim to be in an ideal position for "guiding" the colonial world toward their destiny of assimilation into Western-style modernity and civilization (the only alternative being extinction). In this way, history itself became, as Dipesh Chakrabarty has noted, "somebody's way of saying 'not yet' to somebody else," effectively relegating Indians, Africans, and other colonial peoples to "an imaginary waiting room of history."[36] European imperial domination and colonial rule could therefore be rebranded as benevolent tutelage—essentially, a temporal justification of the white man's burden.

While a significant body of postcolonial scholarship has investigated this pernicious process of allochronism,[37] what much of the literature on the nineteenth-century spatiotemporal hierarchy tends to overlook is that this process entailed a double colonization, not only of contemporary colonial peoples, but also of Europe's own premodern past. If the spatiotemporal hierarchy insinuated that the future of the colonial world (if it had one) would have a distinctly European face,[38] then it logically follows that Europe's premodern past must have looked very much like the contemporary colonial Other. Perhaps then it is not surprising that while Western colonial ethnologists were imagining a linear developmental schema for global indigenous cultures, archaeologists and historians were developing similar linear evolutionary trajectories for the European past, such as the prehistoric Stone-Bronze-Iron Age system as well as the aforementioned ancient-medieval-modern periodization.[39]

The present concern lies with the place of "the Middle Ages" in this schema of historical development. We have already seen how the invention of the premodern and non-Western Other has been viewed as the product of the same colonizing impetus (one in time, the other in space) that might be traced back to the very origins of modernity. This would seem to suggest that at the height of colonialism, Europeans must have imagined colonial peoples to be the direct cultural equivalents to their medieval ancestors. Yet, when examined closely, binary categories that set modern/West against medieval/not-West sometimes prove to be overly simplistic. Tellingly, explicit depictions of colonial peoples as "medieval" were not actually all that common during this period; furthermore, when such direct historical parallels were proposed, they were not as derogatory as might be expected. Rather, the historical label "medieval" was usually reserved for indigenous societies that colonial powers considered *more* advanced because this term was used to call attention to their promise and potential as candidates for modernization.

British-occupied Malaysia offers an excellent case study of how "native medievals" were imagined in the nineteenth-century spatiotemporal hierarchy. Sociologist Daniel P. S. Goh has combed through the correspondences of British colonial administrators and intellectuals during this period in order to highlight the widespread assumption that native Malays were, in essence, a medieval people "sharing the same psychological, cultural, and sociological make-up as Western society of the feudal past."[40] These letters draw frequent parallels between the European Middle Ages and Malaysian society, such as the supposedly feudal nature of their social relations, the corruption and despotism of their governmental elite, their religious superstitions and widespread belief in "witchcraft," and even their "chivalric" warrior culture. Although colonial administrators looked upon Malay society with a combination of contempt and paternalistic admiration, there was general agreement that these "medieval" people did in fact possess the cultural capacity to become politically and socially modernized. The debate among colonial officials primarily concerned how rapidly this goal of modernization could be realistically accomplished. While the naturalist Alfred Russel Wallace argued that the Malays would soon be ready for modernization and advancement within the British Empire, other politicians like Resident Minister Hugh Clifford expressed skepticism that the natives could evolve so quickly out of their medieval "stage," warning that "to crush into twenty years the revolutions in facts and in ideas, which, even in energetic Europe, six long centuries have been needed to accomplish" was an ill-advised idea that would only lead to further cultural degradation.[41] It is clear that, for Clifford, some additional time in Chakrabarty's aforementioned "imaginary waiting room of history" would be necessary before Malays would be ready for the next stage in historical development.

The indigenous people of South Asia were another "advanced" colonial society that the British analogized to their medieval past. This is why, as A. J. Kabir has argued, colonial administrators found the Roman historian Tacitus's famous description of ancient Germanic tribes (*De Origine et situ Germanorum*) a useful guide for understanding the nature of traditional Indian village life.[42] The twenty-sixth chapter of the *Germania* was deemed particularly salient because it described how to effectively tax Germanic agrarian communities. In addition, the notion that Indian society resided at a medieval stage of development encouraged British colonial authorities to transform the local *zamindars* (elites) into a version of the medieval "landed gentry" with the power to extract (on behalf of the colonial government) as much revenue as possible from the *ryots* (poor tenant farmers).[43] It is important to note that the perceived parallels between nineteenth-century Indian society and medieval Europe operated in both directions. In other words, as Kathleen Biddick has shown, British scholars in the employ of the Imperial

Civil Service drew upon their ethnographic experiences with traditional South Asian lifeways as a basis for imagining everyday life in the Middle Ages, leading her to the remarkable conclusion that "the medieval English village was invented by the India Service"![44] Similarly, during the 1886 Colonial and Indian Exhibition at South Kensington, it was no accident that displays of South Asian flora, fauna, and material culture were placed directly adjacent to a historic reconstruction of a medieval London street.[45]

Taken together, these examples suggest a fundamental shift in the relationship between the colonial and medieval in the nineteenth century. While the Middle Ages had constituted a site of radical Otherness since the Renaissance, the medieval occupied a very specific place in the logic of the nineteenth-century spatiotemporal hierarchy: the penultimate historical stage through which societies must pass before they achieve full modernization. So while "medieval" was decidedly inferior to "modern," it represented a higher stage of historical development than other non-literate "barbarians" living in simple farming communities, not to mention the "savage" groups that subsisted only by hunting and gathering.[46]

A Return to Otherness? Political Medievalisms in the Postcolonial World

It is tempting for the contemporary reader to look back at these blatantly ethnocentric nineteenth-century scholarly depictions of "medieval" colonized peoples with a certain dismissive and condescending smugness. Yet, in reality, not only is the medievalizing of non-Western societies arguably a more prominent feature of twenty-first-century political discourse than a century and a half earlier, but the progressive optimism (however paternalistic) that accompanied this mythistorical label during the nineteenth century has been replaced by categorically negative connotations of backwardness, cruelty, and fanaticism. Rather than being the penultimate stage of historical progress, the medieval now inhabits the Western historical imagination as stagnant, moribund historical space—not unlike that first proposed by Petrarch some six centuries earlier.[47]

Ironically, a term that was once used to mark a society as on the cusp of modernization is now deployed against non-Western groups expressing an overt antipathy toward Western cultural and political hegemony. To wit, those most frequently derided in contemporary discourse as "medieval" are Islamic (and, to a lesser extent, Christian) fundamentalist groups whose ideology explicitly opposes Western values of modernization, secularization, and capitalism. In recent decades, such historical comparisons have been frequently drawn with the Taliban ("they're barbarians" with a "1200 AD mentality" according to former Blackwater CEO Erik Prince[48]), al-Qaeda (who offered "a trip back to the Dark Ages" according to US Army Col. Michael Walker[49]), and most recently the so-called Islamic State in Iraq and Syria (ISIS or ISIL).[50] The Western press has been eager to medievalize this most recent manifestation of Islamic extremism, with recent newspaper headlines like "The New Dark Ages: The Chilling Medieval Society Isis Extremists Seek to Impose on Iraq" (*The Daily Express*, June 2014) and "With Videos of Killings, ISIS Sends Medieval Message by Modern Method" (*The New York Times*, September 2014).[51] Many Western politicians have also been eager to employ this kind of rhetoric, from former US Secretary of State John Kerry (who once called the beheading of an American journalist "an act of medieval savagery") to former British Prime Minister David Cameron (who characterized ISIS fighters' behavior as "literally medieval in character"). However, this notion of a temporal struggle between the West and Islam has been most thoroughly developed by Israeli Prime Minister Benyamin Netanyahu who in a 2012 speech to the United Nations contrasted "the forces of modernity" (defined by their protection of individual rights, respect for human life, and high regard for education) and "the forces of medievalism" (characterized by the subjugation of women and minorities, suppression of knowledge, and glorification of death).[52] Even more discouragingly, some scholars have given this misleading historical parallel an air of intellectual credibility. In a much-discussed 2015 article in *The Atlantic*, the Princeton political scientist Bernard Haykel insisted that ISIS militants were not just "cherry-picking from the medieval tradition" but "are smack in the middle of the medieval tradition and are bringing it wholesale into the present day."[53]

The problem with carelessly invoking such dubious analogies is not only that is distorts and mischaracterizes the medieval past, but also that it fails to recognize these radical ideologies as fundamentally modern—not medieval—in nature. When the Taliban infamously dynamited the Bamiyan Buddhas in 2001, this act was widely decried by the international community as exhibiting "medieval" religious intolerance, but many journalists failed to notice that the Afghani government justified their actions based on the distinctly modern notion of state sovereignty, since the Buddhist statues were located within the recognized national borders of Afghanistan.[54] Furthermore, supposedly medieval organizations like al-Qaeda and ISIS have proven to be highly proficient users of new communication technologies and social media, and understand all too well the power of media images for spreading fear and propaganda in the twenty-first century. However, it is not just the technology, but the very ideology of extremist Islamic groups that is as indebted to modern as medieval thought. As the philosopher John Gray has shown, Sayyid Qubt (1906–66)—often described as the grandfather of radical Islamic thought—was deeply influenced by the revolutionary politics of nineteenth-century Europe, particularly its rejection of traditional authorities, utopian social vision, and rationalization of using violence to overthrow the current geopolitical order.[55]

Paradoxically, when Western politicians and journalists identify Islamic fundamentalist groups as "medieval," or invoke the "clash of civilizations" rhetoric of Samuel Huntington and Bernard Lewis, they are unwittingly reinforcing the very historical narratives that such groups hope to propagate, in order to lend their political agendas a historical legitimacy. This is why Osama bin Laden deliberately and frequently referred to the United States and its Western allies as "global crusaders," and characterized the American invasion of Afghanistan as "a recurring war" that was reviving the original crusades "brought Richard [the Lionheart] from Britain, Louis from France, and Barbarus [Frederick Barbarossa] from Germany." By drawing such specific historical analogies, bin Laden clearly hoped to portray al-Qaeda as the contemporary torchbearer of a long and noble tradition of Muslim resistance to Western imperial intrusions stretching back not decades but centuries.[56] Similarly, one of ISIS's explicit goals is to reestablish a glorious medieval caliphate, in a move that bears a striking resemblance to the "golden ages" trope of the medieval past invoked by European ethno-nationalists. On the other hand, one might just as easily describe ISIS's millenarian theology as *anti*-medieval, in that it explicitly rejects the traditions of religious tolerance, scientific inquiry, and artistic, literary, and philosophical movements in the Islamic world that can be traced to the Abbasid (c. 750–1250 CE) and Fatamid (c. 900–1150 CE) dynasties.[57]

How to explain this recent "return to Otherness" of the Middle Ages in the Western historical-colonial imagination? One underappreciated factor has been the impact of postcolonial theory on anthropology, history, and related disciplines, which rejected the universalizing narratives of progress that underwrote the assumption that the medieval was, essentially, almost modern. The recognition that non-Western peoples had their own unique histories and were not simply following the single course of Western civilization (as assumed in the spatiotemporal hierarchy) was, of course, a welcome development in the humanities and social sciences. But the problem with this critique of the "politics of time" was that it often failed to recognize the double colonization at work, which primitivized the premodern as well as non-Western Other. So while longstanding ethnocentric stereotypes about non-Western peoples were rightly challenged, those *chrono*-centric biases and periodizations first articulated by Renaissance humanists have not only been left intact, but have actually gained strength. Once again, the medieval provides a mirror, functioning as the antithesis of what we *want* modernity to be. When journalists and politicians (and even some scholars) describe unusually cruel or horrific behaviors as "medieval," they are not just invoking a lazy historical comparison, but helping to cleanse modernity of its own undesirable elements. In light of Kathleen Davis's argument that equating feudalism with servitude resolved the cognitive dissonance between "modern" values of freedom and liberty with the expansion of chattel slavery in the eighteenth century, so too does labeling ISIS as "medieval" comfort us that its brutal methods and ideology come from some other place and time for which we cannot be held responsible.

Notes

1. For a historical debunking of numerous common myths about Europe's Middle Ages, see Régine Pernoud, *Pour en finir avec le Moyen Age* (Paris, 1977) and Stephen J. Harris and Bryon Lee Grigsby, eds, *Misconceptions about the Middle Ages* (New York, 2008).

2. James W. Loewen, *Lies My Teacher Told Me: Everything Your American History Textbook Got Wrong* (New York, 1995).

3. Brian Stock, "The Middle Ages as Subject and Object: Romantic Attitudes and Academic Medievalism," *New Literary History* 5 (1974): 543.

4. *Sensu* Mali, *Mythistory*.

5. F.C. Robinson, "Medieval, the Middle Ages," *Speculum* 59 (1984).

6. T.E. Mommsen, "Petrarch's Conception of the 'Dark Ages'," *Speculum* 17 (1942): 234.

7. Francis Bacon, *Novum Organum* (Oxford, 1878) [orig. 1620].

8. Couze Venn and Mike Featherstone, "Modernity," *Theory, Culture & Society* 23 (2006); Gurminder K. Bhambra, *Rethinking Modernity: Postcolonialism and the Sociological Imagination* (New York, 2007).

9. Edward W. Said, *Orientalism* (New York, 1978), 3. Tzvetan Todorov, *The Conquest of America: The Question of the Other* (New York, 1984), has similarly explored how European encounters with American Indians were shaped by the question of the Other. Victor Li, *The Neo-primitivist Turn: Critical Reflections on Alterity, Culture, and Modernity* (Toronto, 2006), has also recently argued that the category of the "primitive" continues to serve as an Other against which the West can define itself.

10. Brown, "In the Middle," 547.

11. John Dagenais and Margaret Greer, "Decolonizing the Middle Ages: Introduction," *Journal of Medieval and Early Modern Studies* 30 (2000): 431.

12. Dagenais, "The Postcolonial Laura," 366.

13. John M. Ganim, *Medievalism and Orientalism: Three Essays on Literature, Architecture, and Cultural Identity* (New York, 2005), 5.

14. Robinson, "Medieval, the Middle Ages," 749.

15. Debora Shuger, "Irishmen, Aristocrats, and Other White Barbarians," *Renaissance Quarterly* (1997): 504.

16. Norman Etherington, "Barbarians Ancient and Modern," *The American Historical Review* 116 (2011): 47.

17. François Louis Ganshof, *Feudalism* (Toronto, 1964).

18. See also Susan Buck-Morss, *Hegel, Haiti and Universal History* (Pittsburgh, 2009).

19. Kathleen Davis, *Periodization and Sovereignty: How Ideas of Feudalism and Secularization Govern the Politics of Time* (Philadelphia, 2008), 24.

20. Jonathan Riley-Smith, *The Crusades, Christianity, and Islam* (New York, 2008), 54.

21. Ibid., 61.

22. See especially Benedict Anderson, *Imagined Communities: Reflections on the Origin and Spread of Nationalism* (London, 1983); and Anthony D. Smith, "Authenticity, Antiquity and Archaeology," *Nations and Nationalism* 7 (2001).

23. Anthony D. Smith, "The 'Golden Age' and National Renewal," in *Myths and Nationhood*, ed. G. Hosking and G. Schopflin (New York, 1997).

24. Patrick J. Geary, *The Myth of Nations: The Medieval Origins of Europe* (Princeton, NJ, 2002), 12.

25. For England, see Chris Wickham, "The Early Middle Ages and National Identity," *Storica* 27 (2006); for Ireland, see Jerry O'Sullivan, "Nationalists, Archaeologists and the Myth of the Golden Age," in *Early Medieval Munster: Archaeology, History and Society*, ed. M. Monk and J. Sheehan (Cork, 1998).

26. Walter Pohl, "Ostarrîchi Revisited: The 1946 Anniversary, the Millennium, and the Medieval Roots of Austrian Identity," *Austrian History Yearbook* 27 (1996).

27. Ian Wood, "Barbarians, Historians, and the Construction of National Identities," *Journal of Late Antiquity* 1 (2008): 72. It should be noted that feelings about ancient Germans diverged within the Nazi movement: while Himmler was obsessed with the ancient Germans, Hitler expressed embarrassment at their lack of cultural achievement in comparison to Romans; Bettina Arnold, "The Past as Propaganda: Totalitarian Archaeology in Nazi Germany," *Antiquity* 64 (1990).

28. Michael Dietler, "'Our Ancestors the Gauls': Archaeology, Ethnic Nationalism, and the Manipulation of Celtic Identity in Modern Europe," *American Anthropologist* 96 (1994).

29. Wood, "Barbarians, Historians, and the Construction of National Identities."

30. Geary, *The Myth of Nations*, 15.

31. In his introduction to *The Myth of Nations*, Geary himself recounts his surprise and revulsion upon reading an article in *Le Monde* that used his earlier monograph *Before France and Germany* as historical evidence of the need to further restrict French immigration policies.

32. As early as the seventeenth century, John Locke famously quipped that, "In the beginning, all the World was America" (cited in T. Carlos Jacques, "From Savages and Barbarians to Primitives: Africa, Social Typologies, and History in Eighteenth-Century French Philosophy," *History and Theory* 36 [1997]: 203). In the eighteenth century, a range of influential European thinkers, including Friedrich Schiller, Edmund Burke, G. W. F. Hegel, and Immanuel Kant, also proposed the idea that non-Western peoples belonged to the past; see Barry Hindess, "'Been There, Done That…'," *Postcolonial Studies* 11 (2008).

33. See especially Adam Kuper, *The Invention of Primitive Society: Transformations of an Illusion* (New York, 1988); Bernard McGrane, *Beyond Anthropology: Society and the Other* (New York, 1989); and Fabian, *Time and the Other*.

34. Perhaps the best example of this is John Lubbock's early "ethno-archaeological" attempt to use what he described as "the manners and customs of modern savages" to explain the behavior of prehistoric peoples in Europe. John Lubbock, *Pre-historic Times, as Illustrated by Ancient Remains, and the Manners and Customs of Modern Savages* (New York, 1872).

35. Peter Osborne, "Modernity Is a Qualitative, Not a Chronological, Category," *New Left Review* 192 (1992): 75.

36. Chakrabarty, *Provincializing Europe*, 8.

37. Fabian, *Time and the Other*.

38. Wallerstein "Eurocentrism and Its Avatars," 97.

39. The stages of European prehistory were developed by Thomsen and Worsaae; see Robert F. Heizer, "The Background of Thomsen's Three-Age System," *Technology and Culture* 3 (1962); for an early example of the ancient-medieval-modern periodization, see Henry Marcus Cottinger, *Elements of Universal History for Higher Institutes in Republics and for Self-Instruction* (Boston, 1884).

40. Daniel P.S. Goh, "Imperialism and 'Medieval' Natives," *International Journal of Cultural Studies* 10 (2007): 333.

41. Cited in ibid., 330.

42. While Tacitus was obviously an ancient rather than medieval figure, his work on the ancient Germans was widely believed to also apply to the various Germanic societies (such as the Goths or Alamanni) of the early Middle Ages.

43. Ananya Jahanara Kabir, "An Enchanted Mirror for the Capitalist Self: The Germania in British India," in *Medievalisms in the Postcolonial World: The Idea of "the Middle Ages" outside Europe*, ed. K. Davis and N. Altschul (Baltimore, MD, 2009).

44. Kathleen Biddick, *The Shock of Medievalism* (Durham, NC, 1998), 67.

45. Ganim, *Medievalism and Orientalism*, 9.

46. This is the way that Lewis Henry Morgan understood the different levels of human societies: savages (no farming), barbarians (farming, no writing), and civilization (writing); see Lewis Henry Morgan, *Ancient Society; or, Researches in the Lines of Human Progress from Savagery through Barbarism to Civilization* (London, 1877).

47. Bruce W. Holsinger, *Neomedievalism, Neoconservatism, and the War on Terror* (Chicago, 2007), 9.

48. Quoted in Jeremy Scahill, "Secret Erik Prince Tape Exposed", *The Nation*, published online 4 May 2010, https://www.thenation.com/article/secret-erik-prince-tape-exposed/.

49. Quoted in Peter R. Mansoor, *Surge: My Journey with General David Petraeus and the Remaking of the Iraq War* (New Haven, 2013), 125.

50. Kathleen Davis, "Time behind the Veil: The Media, the Middle Ages, and Orientalism," in *The Postcolonial Middle Ages*, ed. J. Cohen (New York, 2000); Thomas Barfield, "Is Afghanistan 'Medieval'?," *Foreign Policy*, published online, 2 June 2010, http://foreignpolicy.com/2010/06/02/is-afghanistan-medieval-2/.

51. Adrian Lee, "The New Dark Ages: The Chilling Medieval Society Isis Extremists Seek to Impose in Iraq," *The Daily Express*, published online, 21 June 2014, http://www.express.co.uk/news/world/483920/Iraq-Isis-Extremists-Dark-Ages-Muslim-Baghdad-Jihadist; David Carr, "With Videos of Killings, ISIS Sends Medieval Message by Modern Method," *The New York Times*, published online 7 September 2014, http://www.nytimes.com/2014/09/08/business/media/with-videos-of-killings-isis-hones-social-media-as-a-weapon.html.

52. A full transcript of Netanyahu's speech can be found at http://www.algemeiner.com/2012/09/27/full-transcript-prime-minister-netanyahu-speech-to-united-nations-general-assembly-2012-video/.

53. Graeme Wood, "What ISIS Really Wants," *The Atlantic*, March 2015.

54. Saurabh Dube, "Introduction: Enchantments of Modernity," *South Atlantic Quarterly* 101 (2002).

55. For the connections between Islamic fundamentalism and modernity, see John Gray, *Al Qaeda and What It Means to Be Modern* (London, 2015).

56. The full quote from his 2001 interview with Tayseer Alouni: "What do Japan or Australia or Germany have to do with this war? They just support the infidels and the crusaders. This is a recurring war. The original crusade brought Richard [the Lionheart] from Britain, Louis from France, and Barbarus from Germany. Today the crusading countries rushed as soon as Bush raised the cross. They accepted the rule of the cross." The full interview can be found online at http://www.justresponse.net/Bin_Laden2.html.

57. Robert G. Hoyland, *In God's Path: The Arab Conquests and the Creation of an Islamic Empire* (New York, 2014).

CHAPTER 3

Anthropology's Lost Medieval Heritage

Every image of the past that is not recognized by the present as one of its own concerns threatens to disappear irretrievably.
—Walter Benjamin, *Illuminations*

Introduction

In the previous chapter, we explored the place of "the Middle Ages" in the modern historical imagination and, in particular, its entanglement with colonialist and nationalist ideologies. This chapter further argues that the consequences of the medieval/modern periodization have not been limited to such explicitly political projects.[1] On the contrary, the assumption of a primitive Middle Ages can be traced to the very foundations of modern social theory, and continues to underwrite a wide range of intellectual and disciplinary agendas in the contemporary academy. Karl Marx famously understood the shift from the medieval to modern world in terms of changing modes of production (feudalism to capitalism),[2] while Max Weber posited a fundamental distinction between a premodern and modern *mentalité* (the former being irrational, enchanted, and bound to tradition, and the latter rational, secular, and bureaucratic).[3] The notion of an epistemic break between the medieval and modern world similarly informs the work of intellectual figures from G. W. F. Hegel, Jacob Bruckhardt, and Oswald Spengler to Anthony Giddens, Jürgen Habermas, Benedict Anderson, Reinhart Koselleck, and Edward Saïd.[4]

Notes for this section begin on page 63.

Since social theory has long been premised on investigating the "modern condition" as a unique historical phenomenon, there would seem to be little reason to seriously engage with ideas or events before its emergence.[5] This is likely why the medieval continues to be ghettoized (if not entirely omitted) from the scholarly discourse, graduate programs, and college curricula of so many academic disciplines (history, literature, science, philosophy, political science, art, and so forth). As Margreta de Grazia has observed: "Whether you work on one side or the other of the medieval/modern divide determines nothing less than relevance. Everything after that divide has relevance to the present; everything before it is irrelevant … it works less as a historical marker than a massive value judgment, determining what matters and what does not."[6]

Building on a number of recent studies seeking to recover the missing medieval element from political science, sociology, geography, literary, and postcolonial studies, this chapter examines how the medieval/modern periodization has shaped the discipline of sociocultural anthropology.[7] While Chapter 1 offered a case for bringing a more robust anthropological perspective to the investigation of historical thinking, a truly reflexive anthropology of historicity must turn the analytical lens back on itself, which requires recognizing the subtle but profound ways in which the anthropological project has been shaped by the temporal logic of modernity. Therefore, this chapter begins by considering the reasons behind the curious lack of anthropological interest in the medieval period, as well as the overwhelmingly negative manner in which the Middle Ages have been characterized in histories of early anthropological thought. After debunking some of the most prevalent misconceptions, the chapter ends by imploring anthropologists to come to terms with how their discipline continues to be shaped by the temporal logic of modernity.

Whither the Historical Anthropology of the Middle Ages?

Historical anthropology has been one of the most innovative and exciting areas of anthropological research in recent decades. Bringing a unique perspective to the study of past and present societies by combining ethnographic and archival methods, historical anthropologists have examined a range of case studies from the origins of the modern world-system and the dynamics of nineteenth-century European colonialism to cultural histories of sugar, money, and the family.[8] However, with a few notable exceptions, they have limited the scope of their inquiry to the modern (i.e. post-1500) world, showing comparatively little sustained interest in the ancient and medieval societies of Europe and the Mediterranean basin. This lack of scholarly attention is all the more perplexing given anthropology's longstanding interest in investigating "exotic" cultural practices and worldviews. Paradoxically, as medieval historians have increasingly embraced anthropological theories and approaches in their research, anthropological studies of Europe's Middle Ages have become *less* common in recent decades.

How do we account for the apparent lack of interest in the medieval world among historical anthropologists? One cannot ignore the practical barriers of such interdisciplinary work. For example, doing archival research on medieval documents requires a specialized set of skills (i.e. reading fluency in Latin) that few anthropologists acquire during their graduate training. Longstanding institutional and disciplinary boundaries between anthropology and medieval history in particular have also surely discouraged work on this period. Furthermore, since anthropology as a discipline has traditionally concerned itself with the study of non-Western peoples, historical anthropologists have usually been drawn to the modern world, when interactions between Europeans and non-Europeans became far more sustained and impactful.

While these factors may help to explain why historical anthropologists prefer to remain on one side of the medieval/modern periodization, there is something deeper and more ideological at work. As noted at the end of Chapter 2, the postcolonial turn in anthropological theory over the past several decades has unwittingly helped reinforce a narrative premised upon a medieval/modern periodization. When, beginning in the 1970s and 1980s, anthropologists rejected the ethnocentric logic that underwrote the notion of a single trajectory for all human societies, they understandably focused their criticism on the idea that non-Western peoples were somehow "from the past," but rarely extended this critique to analogous stereotypes about premodern peoples. Furthermore, universalizing theories of human behavior upon which the anthropological project had long been based were increasingly assumed to reflect a racist and colonialist worldview, so transhistorical comparisons were deemed not only unfashionable, but downright irresponsible.

For these reasons and others, most sociocultural anthropologists lost any appreciation of the relevance of the premodern past for the study of contemporary peoples.[9] Medieval historian Daniel Smail has recently pointed out the irony of this situation, noting, "It is a curious feature of historical practice in the last two or three decades that, even as historicity has been rightly restored to East Asia, Africa, and to all the people supposedly without history, it is being denied to the European Middle Ages."[10] This situation, in my view, has subtly encouraged anthropologists to accept the traditional narrative that posits a culturally isolated, intolerant, and intellectually stagnant medieval mentality. But since a simple lack of anthropological interest in the

Middle Ages provides little direct evidence of this hypothesis, we must turn to another place where anthropologists have expressed many of the familiar stereotypes of the medieval: histories of early anthropological thought.

The Medieval in Histories of Early Anthropology

Many histories of anthropology begin their story in the late nineteenth century, since it was during this period that the first ethnological societies were established in Europe and North America. While this is a perfectly logical starting point, other historians have adopted a broader perspective that explores the origins of the "ethnographic imagination" in the centuries (even millennia) before the professionalization of the discipline. Of course, such early "para-ethnographic" writings do not meet the rigorous standards of modern scholarship (and, indeed, it would be unfair to expect this), but their desire to broach distinctively anthropological questions nevertheless merits a place in what has been described as the discipline's "prehistory."[11] Since anthropology lacks a neatly defined proto-discipline, there has been great debate about precisely when and where to locate the *naissance* of the anthropological impulse,[12] with most scholars falling into three broad camps: (1) those who see its origins in the Enlightenment and/or Romantic ideals of the eighteenth and nineteenth centuries; (2) those who trace it to the rise of humanism, modern science, and Western exploration during the fifteenth and sixteenth centuries; and (3) those who go back even further to Greek and Roman thought in the classical Mediterranean world.[13] In stark contrast, almost all histories of pre-professional anthropology either overlook—or explicitly reject—the existence of authentic anthropological inquiry during Europe's Middle Ages (c. 500–1400 CE).[14]

A close examination of several influential histories of early anthropology published over the past half-century will serve to illustrate this point. In a seminal 1965 essay on the Renaissance foundations of anthropological thought, John H. Rowe unambiguously asserted: "It is a fact that there was no continuous anthropological tradition of comparative studies in Classical antiquity and the Middle Ages," and went on to insist that "the intellectual climate of Europe was not favorable to a native development of anthropology" during the medieval era.[15] James Slotkin expressed a similar sentiment in his *Readings in Early Anthropology*, which also located the origins of the discipline in the early modern world. Although, to his credit, Slotkin included several medieval thinkers (like Aquinas and Dante) in his compilation of anthropological readings, he nevertheless clearly asserted in the book's Introduction his belief that the intellectual bases of anthropology "were established in the sixteenth and seventeenth centuries."[16] A decade later, John J. Honigmann reaffirmed this position in *The Development of Anthropological Ideas*, casually remarking to his readers that the medieval world "contains little to hold us" since during this era "anthropological thought came almost to a halt before it was resuscitated and stimulated by the impact of classical learning, in which interest revived, and by discoveries made in the New World and other parts of the globe."[17]

Finally—lest one mistakenly assume that this image of the medieval has improved in recent decades—consider Paul Erickson and Liam Murphy's *A History of Anthropological Theory* (fourth edition published in 2013), which claimed that "the door was opened for anthropology to develop" only after an "intellectually precarious" medieval worldview was discredited by Renaissance humanism, European voyages of discovery, and the Scientific Revolution.[18] The few paragraphs that Erickson and Murphy dedicate to the Middle Ages reduce the entirety of the scholastic tradition to a familiar (but historically dubious) caricature of "seeing how many angels can fit on the head of a pin."[19]

It is perhaps unsurprising that these histories, which link the possibility for authentic anthropological inquiry to the rise of a distinctly modern worldview, show little interest in the Middle Ages. On the other hand, one might expect to find more sympathetic treatment of medieval thought in those histories that trace the origins of anthropological thought to ancient Greece and Rome, since classical ethnographies (like their medieval counterparts) had a tendency to intersperse realistic cultural descriptions with literary, mythical, or otherwise fantastical elements. As ancient historian Wilfried Nippel reminds us: "Ancient approaches to alterity are characterized by a varying mixture of empiricism and speculation, visual evidence and literary tradition, honest attempts to understand foreign cultures as cherishing values of their own and crude ethnocentrism, admiration for cultural achievements and legitimation for conquering allegedly less developed peoples."[20]

Unfortunately, characterizations of medieval thought are little improved in these histories of anthropological thought. The best example is Margaret Hodgen's landmark *Early Anthropology in the Sixteenth and Seventeenth Centuries*, which generally espoused a nuanced and historically contextualized view of ancient ethnographies. Herodotus, for example, is described as "a cheerful, inquisitive, and rationalistic extrovert who traveled over his world to discover the facts, who took delight in telling a good story but usually avoided the temptation to wander very far from sober common sense."[21] While admitting that his ethnographies were not always reliable (such as his accounts of the one-eyed Arimaspi culture of China and the goat-footed peoples of the eastern steppe), Hodgen wisely cautions against overly harsh judgment, noting that for premodern thinkers "remoteness lends a kind of plausibility."[22]

Yet, inexplicably, Hodgen does not see fit to extend a similar generosity in her analyses of medieval ethnographic writing. Despite the obvious parallels between constructions of alterity in the ancient and early medieval worlds, and their similar penchant for blending of realism and fantasy, Hodgen describes medieval ethnographies as a product of "twisted imaginations," "mental apathy," and "careless repetition and invention,"[23] further insisting that:

> ... the general body of medieval anthropo-geographical notions is the end product of an impairment of a far superior system of ideas which has been current in Greek antiquity ... medieval scholarship purveyed a preposterous and fabulous sediment of what had once been a comparatively realistic antique ethnography ... Medieval man was indifferent to the ideas and behavior of the near-by European barbarian or savage—probably because medieval man was so often the very savage the ancients had seen fit either to eulogize or belittle.[24]

This flagrant double standard in assessing the value of classical and medieval ethnographies which were, in so many ways, actually quite similar, demands some explanation. Revealingly, Hodgen employs the term medieval not only in a chronological, but also in an evaluative sense, characterizing it as a particular "state of mind"[25] that could transcend temporal boundaries. For example, she castigates Renaissance figures like Peter Martyr d'Anghiera (1457–1526) and Francois Rabelais (1494–1553) for being "too medieval," while Christopher Columbus (1451–1506) is admiringly described as a "modern" man. While a few late medieval travelogues do garner some begrudging respect from Hodgen, she is quick to point out that they were exceptions in an era that was otherwise a "twilight of the mind."[26]

Medieval Anthropologies: Myths and Reality

What this brief survey of histories of early anthropology reveals is that (when not completely ignored) Europe's Middle Ages have been widely imagined to be a retreat into an intolerant, insulated, and rigid intellectual orthodoxy that was antithetical to the spirit of anthropological inquiry. To be fair, not every historian of anthropology has equally indulged in such crass stereotypes, but there is no question that the Middle Ages have been effectively written out of the discipline's intellectual genealogy.[27] Yet the dismal portrait of medieval Europe painted by many anthropologists has been challenged by a significant body of scholarship that highlights the rich and diverse anthropological and ethnographic traditions of this era.[28] Over thirty years ago, the historian Felipe Fernandez-Armesto described the Middle Ages as "the most remarkable and least remarked" period in the history of anthropological thought.[29] Literary scholar Shirin Khanmohamadi has more recently echoed this sentiment, arguing that the medieval period "produced ethnographic data and consciousness deserving of study in and of itself, and not as a mere 'prelude' or 'prehistory' to the inception of real, that is scientifically-minded, anthropology in the west."[30] The historian Joan Pau Rubiés has similarly insisted that the quality of ethnographic writing during the late Middle Ages was equal, if not superior, to its classical and early modern counterparts, describing the ethnographic genre as "one of the original creations of the late medieval period" that not only developed before the rise of humanism, but also "articulated European views of other cultures no less decisively than would be the case after the Renaissance."[31]

What lies behind this striking disparity in portrayals of medieval ethnography? Have anthropologists ignored a key part of their intellectual heritage, or are medieval scholars exaggerating the anthropological value of medieval thought? Ultimately, the answer to this question depends on how one chooses to draw the boundaries around the anthropological project; in other words, what attitudes, practices, or approaches are required for authentic anthropological inquiry? How do we demarcate conceptions of the human, or constructions of the Other, that are legitimately anthropological from those that are not? Of course, such questions open up an array of epistemological issues that continue to be highly contested within the discipline.[32] Fortunately, determining whether the Middle Ages deserve greater inclusion in the history of anthropology does not require us to untie the Gordian knot of "what is anthropology?" but only to address a more circumscribed question: is it possible to identify anthropological inquiry and/or ethnographic writing during the Middle Ages that is of comparable quality to classical or early modern thought that has long merited inclusion in the discipline's autobiography? While most histories outlined above clearly answer this question in the negative, their stated objections are underwritten by several prevalent historical myths that demand clarification.

Myth #1: Medieval Thinkers Did Not Meaningfully Engage with Anthropological Questions

The Western European Middle Ages are often closely associated with the theological and philosophical dominance of the Roman Church, and it is true that most major intellectual figures of this era were devout (if not necessarily orthodox) Catholic Christians whose worldviews were deeply informed by the basic tenets of this religious faith. However, this historical reality has given rise to a widespread misconception that medieval thinkers' concern with the supernatural realm precluded any sustained interest in the natural or social world around them. Before the rise of humanism in the Renaissance—so this argument usually goes—intellectual curiosity was primarily directed toward theological rather than anthropological questions.[33]

Yet, in reality, many medieval thinkers were deeply concerned with questions that are undeniably anthropological in nature: what are the essential qualities and characteristics of being human? What sets humans apart from the rest of the natural world? How do we explain the physical and cultural diversity evident among human groups?

Contrary to the common notion that classical thought was "lost" during the Middle Ages,[34] medieval philosophers drew heavily from the ideas of Plato, Aristotle, Herodotus, Cicero, Pliny, and other ancient thinkers to address these profound anthropological questions. Indeed, Greek and Roman ideas exerted a major influence on the way that medieval philosophers thought about everything from the importance of climate and geography in explaining human physical and cultural variation, to the division of the world into "civilized" and "barbarian" societies, and the fundamental tension in human nature between reason and the passions.[35] The innovation of medieval thinkers was to integrate these ancient "pagan" concepts into a Christian framework premised upon the authority of scripture and the writings of the Church fathers. For example, any credible explanation of human diversity had to account for the uncontestable fact that all people, no matter how different, were descended from a single ancestor (Adam) and therefore shared a common human nature and capacity for reason. By synthesizing these two distinct intellectual traditions, medieval thinkers (especially after the twelfth century) developed sophisticated intellectual models for addressing questions that continue to be debated by contemporary anthropologists.[36] In the thirteenth century alone, Albertus Magnus explored the ontological boundaries between human and animal, Thomas Aquinas developed a comprehensive account of human nature that synthesized Aristotelian and Christian metaphysical frameworks, and Roger Bacon speculated about a comparative approach to understanding human societies.[37]

Myth #2: The Middle Ages Lacked a Coherent Tradition of Realistic Ethnographic Writing

Even if medieval thinkers did broach explicitly anthropological questions, these intellectual debates remained largely confined to the insularity and comforts of European universities, so one might protest that they lacked a truly *intercultural* dimension necessary for authentic anthropological inquiry. In order to address this challenge, we should consider how Europeans during this period imagined and encountered the cultural and racial Other. Here we encounter a second misconception of medieval ethnographic writings: that they were more fantasy than reality, filled with outlandish accounts of quasi-human monsters (e.g. Cyclopses, giants, people with dog heads or eyes on their shoulders) who inhabited the margins of the known world.[38] While such bizarre descriptions can indeed be found in a variety of medieval writings—from Isidore of Seville's seventh century *Etymologies* to the popular fourteenth-century pseudo-travelogue *Travels of Sir John Mandeville*—we should not forget that such monstrous accounts are also prevalent in classical and early modern travelogues. Moreover, this objection overlooks a parallel tradition of more sober and realistic ethnographic writing that emerged during the later Middle Ages, particularly in the context of Christian missionary journeys to the East.[39]

While there are quite a few examples of empirical ethnography during the latter half of the Middle Ages, this section focuses on Gerald of Wales' *Descriptio Kambriae*[40] ("Description of Wales," composed in 1194) and Friar William of Rubruck's *De Moribus Tartarorum*[41] ("On the Mores of the Tartars," composed in 1255), as these two works illustrate both the diversity and common underlying themes of the medieval ethnographic genre.[42] The former was written by an aristocratic bishop who spent years traveling and reporting on Celtic societies in service of the English monarchy, while the latter was the account of a Flemish Franciscan monk sent on a missionary journey by King Louis IX to the court of Mongol khan Möngke. Drawing on ethnographic experiences with exotic cultures at the geographical periphery of the medieval European world, these works provide not only realistic and accurate depictions of Welsh and Mongol cultures, but also provide fascinating insights into the medieval *mentalité*.

Contemporary anthropologists may be astonished at how closely these works follow the form and structure of a traditional ethnographic monograph, with descriptions of subsistence practices, economy, law, kinship, marriage, food culture, dress, personal hygiene, religion and ritual, warfare, material culture, language, and so on. Since both of these works were the product of firsthand intercultural experiences, they are conspicuously devoid of the imaginative and fantastical elements that can be found in the aforementioned *Etymologies* and *Mandeville*. Rubruck is particularly skeptical of hearsay and rumor, writing: "I enquired about the monsters or human freaks who are described by Isidore and Solinus, but was told that such things had never been sighted, which makes us very much doubt whether [the story] is true."[43] When he does relate strange or exotic practices—like the people of Tebet who were said to drink from the skulls of their ancestors—he always emphasizes that such information was gathered from credible eyewitness sources.[44] For his part, Gerald of Wales' admirable commitment to ethnographic accuracy is evidenced by his accounts of pre-Christian practices (such as a soothsaying) that not only would have been disturbing to his ecclesiastical audience, but undermined the overall goal of his trip, which was to emphasize the Christian piety and orthodoxy of the Welsh.[45] He could have easily omitted such practices in his ethnographic accounts, but for some reason decided that they needed to be included in order to provide a complete account of tribal Welsh society.

More importantly, Rubruck and Gerald not only provide reliable and accurate ethnographic descriptions, but also employ comparative analyses to explain the strange cultural practices they encounter. Gerald frequently situates Welsh customs in broader cross-cultural contexts, noting their similarity to, or difference from, similar practices among contemporary (English, Irish, French, Scandinavian, German) and historical (Roman, Greek, Teutonic, Biblical) peoples. In one interesting example, Gerald deduces that the shaving habits of Welsh men (who leave only a moustache) must be an ancient practice, since a similar description is found in Julius Caesar's accounts of the Britons.[46] Gerald also explains differences in musical traditions between the English and Welsh by offering a plausible diffusionist interpretation; Welsh singing styles, he hypothesizes, must have been influenced by Danes and Norwegians "by whom these parts of the island were more frequently invaded, and held much longer under their dominion."[47]

Rubruck also employs comparative analysis, such as when he describes exotic Mongol rituals in terms of practices that would have been more familiar to his European audience: their practice of sprinkling mare's milk on the ground is "like the custom that obtains among us in some places regarding wine on the feast of St. Bartholomew or St. Sixtus, or with fruit on the feast of Saints James and Christopher."[48] In sum, Gerald's desire to place Welsh practices in broader cultural and historical context and Rubruck's attempts to make the strange seem familiar indicate an anthropological dimension to their thinking that surely deserves greater inclusion in disciplinary histories.

Myth #3: Medieval Society Was Profoundly Intolerant toward the Other

The third common objection to the inclusion of medieval anthropologies in disciplinary histories draws on what is arguably the most pervasive myth about this period: the Middle Ages were characterized by a profound cultural intolerance and intellectual dogmatism that is antithetical to authentic anthropological inquiry. To be sure, medieval Europeans did often hold ethnocentric attitudes toward the Other (including Muslims, Jews, heretics, homosexuals, and women) that offend our contemporary sensibilities, but we should be cautious not to let our conception of the medieval worldview lapse into unhelpful caricature. Medieval Europe was quite obviously not an "open society" by Popperian standards, but neither was it an age of rigid orthodoxy or mindless conformity as often presumed. For example, even though Western Europe was nominally united under a single faith, regional and local variations of Christian worship—often syncretically blended with pre-Christian beliefs and customs—were more common than most people recognize, as Gerald's account of the Welsh makes clear.[49] Furthermore, scholars in the nascent universities of the late Middle Ages were given a surprising degree of intellectual latitude on philosophical and doctrinal matters, and were even permitted to explore the work of ancient pagan and contemporary Islamic thinkers. As political scientist Cary Nederman has argued: "If never quite formally institutionalized, freedom of intellectual inquiry into matters of central concern to orthodoxy seems to have been remarkably well preserved by the medieval Church, both before and after the rise of universities."[50]

While medieval European society has long been portrayed as the epitome of religious, political, and cultural prejudice, a growing body of historical scholarship has provided a more balanced and nuanced approach to medieval conceptions of tolerance.[51] Albrecht Classen's investigations of medieval German literature provide an interesting case study of cultural tolerance during this period. *Herzog Ernst* (composed c. 1180 CE) and *Die Heidin* (composed c. 1280 CE) were popular fictional tales about the travels of German-speaking knights to distant lands populated by monstrous races that would have been familiar to medieval audiences. Despite fanciful descriptions of their physical bodies (crane heads, swan-like feet, a single eye), Classen points out that these cultural Others are portrayed no differently than European Christians in terms of personal character, intelligence, and nobility. In other words, despite their strange appearances, these "monstrous races" are generally depicted as honorable and trustworthy beings deserving of respect. Classen contends that the underlying messages of these tales— "acknowledging the multiplicity of peoples and races in this world and accepting them as part of a universal community" and to "demonstrate that interaction and peaceful cohabitation with people from 'the other world' is possible and can be fruitful for both sides involved"—express a remarkably enlightened attitude toward the Other.[52]

William of Rubruck's aforementioned missionary journey to the heart of the Mongol Empire provides another fascinating encounter with a cultural and religious Other. Although the explicitly proselytizing nature of his trip would seem to indicate a narrow-mindedness, Rubruck is always careful to present himself as a model of tolerance and reasonableness in negotiating the distinctly multiethnic context of Möngke's court. While expressing disgust at certain cultural practices (such as the Mongol penchant for moving "no further away than one could toss a bean" when defecating) and passing moral judgment at times (such as his sharp condemnation of corrupt Nestorian priests), the overall tone of Rubruck's work is one of respect and open-mindedness. When engaging in intense theological debates at the khan's court with Nestorians, Muslims, and Buddhists, he recognizes that his arguments must be grounded in reason rather than the authority of scripture (as he quickly recognizes, "if you tell them one story, they will quote you another"). Moreover, in a revealing sign of mutual respect in spite of religious disagreement, he describes how the participants would all engage in song and drink at the conclusion of the debates.[53]

Khanmohamadi has argued that it is the missionary nature of William's journey that leads him to paint a strikingly even-handed, even intimate picture of the Mongols, at a time when many Europeans saw them as demonic harbingers of the apocalypse. Seeing them as potential converts to Christianity, William continually "goes out of his way to affirm Mongol humanity, eschewing in all but rare instances the varied discourses of dehumanization available to him in favor of an affirmation of Mongolian humanity and reason."[54]

Reintegrating Medieval Anthropologies

It is important to stress once again that advocating for a greater inclusion of medieval thought in the history of anthropological inquiry does not imply that the Middle Ages were a paragon of multicultural openness or unfettered intellectual inquiry. Because medieval approaches to human nature and the Other rested on a metaphysical framework and a set of cultural assumptions that were quite distinct from ancient, early modern, or contemporary anthropologies, we must eschew the whiggish temptation to highlight only those particular elements of medieval thought that foreshadow contemporary ideas, while ignoring those aspects that do not. Rather, adopting a truly anthropological approach means evaluating the strengths and limitations of medieval thought on its own terms. To paraphrase James Boon, just as anthropologists rightly reject invidious ethnocentric comparisons between cultures, historians of anthropology must similarly avoid making chrono-centric judgments regarding premodern *mentalités*.[55] Restricting the boundaries of legitimate anthropological inquiry to a modern and Western worldview serves to exclude any conception of the human that does not comport with this particular conceptual framework.

We must recognize that ancient, medieval, modern, and postmodern ideologies are each premised upon a particular set of metaphysical assumptions and ideals—whether supernatural or materialist, religious or humanist—that provide meaning for individuals, and shape the way society understands the Self and constructs the Other. The anthropological project would be hollow without these epistemological convictions.[56] This chapter concludes by providing two brief examples of how reintegrating medieval anthropologies in the discipline's intellectual genealogy might help to illuminate both the similarities and differences between modern and premodern approaches to important anthropological issues.

Shifting Concepts of the Human from the Medieval to Early Modern Worlds

One of the central tenets of medieval anthropology, as noted above, was the belief in a single moment of creation and shared human nature. This concept was articulated as early as the fourth century by Augustine of Hippo, who wrote in *The City of God*: "But whoever is anywhere born a man, that is, a rational, mortal animal, no matter what unusual appearance he presents in color, movement, sound, nor how peculiar he is in some power, part, or quality of his nature, no Christian can doubt that he springs from that one protoplast."[57] While this idea was echoed by numerous philosophers over the next thousand years, during the Renaissance and European voyages of discovery this commitment to monogenism was gradually replaced by polygenism, which ardently denied a single universal humanity. In the sixteenth century, theories began to circulate that various peoples encountered by European explorers were, in fact, not part of the human family, but rather soulless beings descended from "another Adam" or perhaps spontaneously generated from the earth.[58] Valerie Flint has traced this ideological shift at the onset of modernity through changing popular attitudes toward the Antipodes, a mythical continent thought to be located on the opposite side of the world. While the medieval church rejected the possibility of an inhabited antipodal world, this idea gained greater acceptance during the sixteenth and seventeenth centuries—an ideological shift often used to illustrate the birth of a more open, less rigidly orthodox mentality. However, Flint points out that it equally reflected a shift from medieval conceptions of a shared humanity to a framework of racial hierarchy that justified an emerging colonial/imperial order.[59]

James Boon's analyses of early modern European travelogues in Tierra del Fuego vividly illustrate the consequences of this shifting ideology. While early sixteenth-century explorers described the inhabitants of this region as "Patagonians" (giants reminiscent of medieval monstrous races), Boon points out that the native peoples would continue to be depicted as inhuman in Western travel accounts well into the nineteenth century. Although after the Enlightenment the underlying approach to difference shifted from Christian categories of the "Saved" and "Damned" to more purportedly "scientific" measurements of racial characteristics, Boon argues that the underlying ethnocentric assumptions not only remained, but actually intensified: "Does a secular analysis of harems and human sacrifice as abstract variables mark an epistemological advance over pre-Enlightenment interpretations that, for all their value-ladeness, often contained as much ethnographic information? Is the difference a matter of increased rationality, as Enlightenment philosophers needed, culturally, to think? Or is this difference, too, a kind of simplification?"[60]

While Boon is contrasting Renaissance and Enlightenment-era travelogues, he further argues that such a critique must extend to anthropological treatments of the Middle Ages, noting that to "overlook the diversity admitted even in negative medieval ethnological imagery is to ignore the social, political, and cultural context of church history and theological exegesis—not a very anthropological policy."[61] This shift from medieval universalism to early modern racial difference complicates standard historical narratives in which the supposedly "intellectually precarious" medieval synthesis was replaced by early modern commitments to humanism, rationality, and liberalism.[62] While the Middle Ages are often the era most closely associated with stifling orthodoxy, religious fanaticism, and pervasive social violence, one might recall that the concept of a "Divine Right" of kings, the height of the Spanish and Roman Inquisitions, and the most destructive religious wars in European history all occurred during early modernity. This chronological disconnect has led Carol Symes to speculate that the medieval "functions as a kind of penal colony wherein modernity's own undesirable elements are imprisoned and conveniently redefined as 'medieval'."[63]

The Colonial Imagination of Medieval Anthropologies

A comparison between medieval and modern anthropologies can also highlight parallels just as illuminating as the aforementioned differences. Returning to Gerald of Wales' *Descriptio Kambriae*, we can identify several striking similarities with modern colonial anthropology. A member of the Anglo-Norman aristocracy, Gerald wrote in the service of a colonial power for the expressed purpose of military conquest and imperial domination.[64] After conquering England in 1066, the Norman dukes directed their political interests toward Wales, making significant territorial gains during the reign of Henry I (1100–1135).[65] Strikingly, in the final few chapters of the *Descriptio*, Gerald specifically articulates the best manner in which to conquer and govern the Welsh people, and his arguments uncannily echo nineteenth-century colonial anthropology.[66] Gerald's advice for conquering the Welsh draws upon the time-honored strategy of *divide et impera*: "Let him divide their strength, and by bribes and promises endeavor to stir up one against the other, knowing the spirit of hatred and envy which generally prevails amongst them."[67]

Being part of a hierarchical state-level society, Gerald identifies the decentralized nature of Welsh political authority as the fundamental problem at the root of their primitiveness. He notes that of the main things which "ruin this nation, and prevent its enjoying the satisfaction of a fruitful progeny" is a refusal of a population to "subject themselves to the dominion of one lord and king."[68] In a fascinating echo of the modern colonial trope that "savage" peoples could only benefit from the structure and efficiency of colonial rule, Gerald observes: "Happy and fortunate indeed would this nation be, nay, completely blessed, if it had good prelates and pastors; and but one prince, and that prince a good one."[69]

Throughout much of his work, Gerald develops a discourse of inferiority and backwardness among the Welsh that alternates between images of romanticized "noble savages" (Book 1) and depraved, dangerous barbarians (Book 2). The primitiveness of Welsh society is a recurrent theme throughout Gerald's work, which he links to their limited agriculture and crude material culture. Gerald often imagines the Welsh as an extension of the animal world, noting that they are as wild as "the beasts of the field,"[70] and that "they neither inhabit towns, villages, nor castles, but lead a solitary life in the woods."[71]

A final unexpectedly modern element of Gerald's ethnography is his personal ambivalence about facilitating colonial conquest that becomes increasingly apparent in Book 2. Gerald's reaction to the Welsh vacillates between admiration and revulsion, and their strange practices evoke both his curiosity and condemnation. This schizophrenic attitude may reflect Gerald's own ambiguous identity; although part of the Anglo-Norman elite, he was also a descendant of the Welsh princess Nest, and therefore, in some sense, a "native ethnographer."[72] During an era without stable state borders and national identities, Gerald's hybrid cultural identity and conflicted political loyalties make his ethnography undeniably compelling. He readily acknowledges that he is "equally connected by birth with each nation" and therefore feels compelled to "instruct them in the art of resistance."[73] In fact, the final chapter of his work—entitled "In What Manner This Nation May Resist and Revolt"—includes advice for struggling *against* the English colonizers, and a call to "encourage the daring spirit of rebellion" among the Welsh![74]

Conclusion

By linking their disciplinary origins to early modernity, anthropologists implicitly reinforce one of the central tenets of modernist ideology: its own sense of historical and cultural exceptionalism, and refusal to acknowledge the relevance of anything before the medieval/modern divide. Considering the intimate (if not indistinguishable) relationship between modernity and colonialism, anthropological theory cannot be fully decolonized until it begins to problematize the medieval/modern periodization that lies at the very core of the modernist ideologies of rupture and difference. Opening up the conceptual space for premodern, specifically medieval anthropologies should also be conceptualized as part of a larger, quite urgent project that seeks to transform the single epistemic space of a dominant anthropology into the multiple, contested, and fluid spaces of "other" or "world" anthropologies.[75] Although indigenous and postcolonial anthropologies might find medieval studies an unexpected fellow traveler, calls for a greater alliance between these two disciplines have been made elsewhere.[76] Michael Herzfeld has also recently acknowledged that "the apparent anachronism of calling pre-19th century scholarship anthropology ... finds a spatial and cultural analogue in the dilemmas faced by Indian, Chinese, and other non-Western scholars."[77] After all, if we truly wish to "take seriously the multiple and contradictory historical, social, cultural and political locatedness of the different communities of anthropologists and their anthropologies,"[78] can these not occupy other times as well as other places?

Notes

1. A previous version of this chapter appeared as K. Patrick Fazioli, "The Erasure of the Middle Ages from Anthropology's Intellectual Genealogy," *History and Anthropology* 25 (2014).

2. Karl Marx, *Grundrisse* (New York, 1993).

3. Max Weber, *Economy and Society: An Outline of Interpretive Sociology* (Berkeley, 1978).

4. For a critique of Saïd, see Kathleen Biddick, "Coming Out of Exile: Dante on the Orient(alism) Express," *The American Historical Review* 105 (2000); for a critique of Benedict Anderson, see Michel Bouchard, "A Critical Reappraisal of the Concept of the 'Imagined Community' and the Presumed Sacred Languages of the Medieval Period," *National Identities* 6 (2004); for a critique of Anthony Giddens, see Charles R. Cobb, "Archaeology and the 'Savage Slot': Displacement and Emplacement in the Premodern World," *American Anthropologist* 107 (2005); and for a critique of Reinhart Koselleck, see Davis, *Periodization and Sovereignty*.

5. Although, ironically, the medieval is actually more embedded in social theory than one might expect, as brilliantly demonstrated by Bruce W. Holsinger, *The Premodern Condition: Medievalism and the Making of Theory* (Chicago, 2005).

6. Margreta de Grazia, "The Modern Divide: From Either Side," *Journal of Medieval and Early Modern Studies* 37 (2007): 453.

7. For the missing medieval in contemporary geography, see Keith D. Lilley, "Geography's Medieval History," *Dialogues in Human Geography* 1 (2011); for sociology, see Bhambra, *Rethinking Modernity*; for political science, see Davis, *Periodization and Sovereignty*; for literature, see Carol Symes, "The Middle Ages between Nationalism and Colonialism," *French Historical Studies* 34 (2011); and for postcolonial studies, see Jeffrey Jerome Cohen, *Medieval Identity Machines* (Minneapolis, 2003).

8. The body of scholarship on "historical anthropology" is vast, but some of the more significant contributions include Macfarlane, "The Origins of English Individualism"; Renato Rosaldo, *Ilongot Headhunting, 1883–1974: A Study in Society and History* (Stanford, CA, 1980); Sahlins, *Historical Metaphors and Mythical Realities*; Wolf, *Europe and the People without History*; Sidney Wilfred Mintz, *Sweetness and Power: The Place of Sugar in Modern History* (New York, 1985); Comaroff and Comaroff, *Ethnography and the Historical Imagination*; Trouillot, *Silencing*

the Past; Han F. Vermeulen and Arturo Alvarez Roldán, eds, *Fieldwork and Footnotes: Studies in the History of European Anthropology* (London; New York, 1995); Goody, *The Theft of History*; Ann Laura Stoler, *Along the Archival Grain: Epistemic Anxieties and Colonial Common Sense* (Princeton, NJ, 2009); Graeber, *Debt: The First 5,000 Years*.

9. Shannon Lee Dawdy, "Clockpunk Anthropology and the Ruins of Modernity," *Current Anthropology* 51 (2010); and Cobb, "Archaeology and the 'Savage Slot'."

10. Daniel Lord Smail, "Genealogy, Ontogeny, and the Narrative Arc of Origins," *French Historical Studies* 34 (2011): 34.

11. Here I borrow the phrase "para-ethnographic" from Michel-Rolph Trouillot, "Anthropology and the Savage Slot: The Poetics and Politics of Otherness," in *Recapturing Anthropology: Working in the Present*, ed. R.G. Fox (Sante Fe, 1991); and the term "prehistory" of anthropology from M. Harbsmeier, "Towards a Prehistory of Ethnography: Early Modern German Travel Writing as Traditions of Knowledge," in Vermeulen and Roldan , *Fieldwork and Footnotes*.

12. Harry Liebersohn, "Anthropology before Anthropology," in *A New History of Anthropology*, ed. H. Kulick (Malden, MA, 2008), 18.

13. Scholars who have located the discipline's origins in the "Age of Enlightenment" (because of its emphasis on rationalism and empirical science) include Robert H. Lowie, *The History of Ethnological Theory* (New York, 1937); Michel Foucault, *Les mots et les choses; une archéologie des sciences humaines* (Paris, 1966); Marvin Harris, *The Rise of Anthropological Theory; a History of Theories of Culture* (New York, 1968); Clifford Geertz, *The Interpretation of Cultures: Selected Essays* (New York, 1973); E.E. Evans-Pritchard and André Singer, *A History of Anthropological Thought* (New York, 1981); David Denby, "Herder: Culture, Anthropology and the Enlightenment," *History of the Human Sciences* 18 (2005); Bruce Kapferer, "Anthropology and the Dialectic of Enlightenment: A Discourse on the Definition and Ideals of a Threatened Discipline," *The Australian Journal of Anthropology* 18 (2007); and Larry Wolff and Marco Cipolloni, eds, *The Anthropology of the Enlightenment* (Stanford, CA, 2007). Those who have focused on the Romantic Movement cite this movement's emphasis on cultural relativism and tolerance, such as George W. Stocking, *Race, Culture, and Evolution; Essays in the History of Anthropology* (New York, 1968); R. A. Shweder, "Enlightenment's Romantic Rebellion against the Enlightenment, or There's More to Thinking than Reason and Evidence," in *Culture Theory: Essays on Mind, Self and Emotion*, ed. R.A. Schweder and R. Levine (Cambridge, 1984); Fritz W. Kramer, "Empathy—Reflections on the History of Ethnology in Pre-Fascist Germany: Herder, Creuzer, Bastian, Bachofen, and Frobenius," *Dialectical Anthropology* 9 (1985); John H. Zammito, *Kant, Herder, and the Birth of Anthropology* (Chicago, 2002); and Daniel Purdy, "Immanuel Kant and Anthropological Enlightenment," *Eighteenth-Century Studies* 38 (2005). The idea that anthropological inquiry really began with Renaissance humanism has been one of the most popular positions, with advocates including James Sydney Slotkin, *Readings in Early Anthropology* (Chicago, 1965); John Howland Rowe, "The Renaissance Foundations of Anthropology," *American Anthropologist* 67 (1965); John Joseph Honigmann, *The Development of Anthropological Ideas* (Homewood, IL, 1976); Regna Darnell, "History of Anthropology in Historical Perspective," *Annual Review of Anthropology* 6 (1977); G. Gliozzi, *Adamo et il nuovo mondo. La nascita dell'antropologia come ideologia coloniale: dalle genealogie bibliche alle teorie razziali (1500–1700)* (Florence, 1977); Murray J. Leaf, *Man, Mind, and Science: A History of Anthropology* (New York, 1979); Anthony Pagden, *The Fall of Natural Man: The American Indian and the Origins of Comparative Ethnology* (New York, 1982); Britta Rupp-Eisenreich, *Histoires de l'anthropologie: XVIe–XIXe siècles: Colloque la Pratique de l'anthropologie aujourd'hui, 19–21 novembre 1981, Sèvres* (Paris, 1984); Claude Blanckaert, *Naissance de l'ethnologie? Anthropologie et missions en Amérique XVIe–XVIIIe siècle* (Paris, 1985); Justin Stagl, *A History of Curiosity: The Theory of Travel, 1550–1800* (London, 1995); Harbsmeier, "Towards a Prehistory of Ethnography"; Daniel Carey, "Anthropology's

Inheritance: Renaissance Travel, Romanticism and the Discourse of Identity," *History and Anthropology* 14 (2003); Paul A. Erickson and Liam D. Murphy, *A History of Anthropological Theory* (Peterborough, ON, 2008); and Liebersohn, "Anthropology before Anthropology." Finally, those tracing it back to ancient Greek and Roman authors include R.R. Marett, ed., *Anthropology and the Classics* (Oxford, 1908); E.E. Sikes, *Anthropology of the Greeks* (London, 1912); A.L. Kroeber and Clyde Kluckhohn, *Culture; a Critical Review of Concepts and Definitions* (Cambridge, MA, 1952); Clyde Kluckhohn, *Anthropology and the Classics* (Providence, 1961); Margaret T. Hodgen, *Early Anthropology in the Sixteenth and Seventeenth Centuries* (Philadelphia, 1964); Dell H. Hymes, *Reinventing Anthropology* (New York, 1972); Fred W. Voget, *A History of Ethnology* (New York, 1975); Robert Ackerman, "Anthropology and the Classics," in Kulick, *A New History of Anthropology*; and Joseph Skinner, *The Invention of Greek Ethnography: From Homer to Herodotus* (New York, 2012).

14. It is interesting that while medieval Western Europe has been widely ignored, Islamic and Byzantine thought during this period are occasionally included in histories of early anthropology; see John W. Bennett, "Comments on 'the Renaissance Foundations of Anthropology,'" *American Anthropologist* 68 (1966); Michael A. Hoffman, "The History of Anthropology Revisited—A Byzantine Viewpoint," *American Anthropologist* 75 (1973); and Voget, *A History of Ethnology*.

15. Rowe, "The Renaissance Foundations of Anthropology," 1, 8.

16. Slotkin, *Readings in Early Anthropology*, vii; some of the premodern figures that Slotkin deemed worthy of inclusion are Paul of Tarsus, Thomas Aquinas, and Dante Alighieri.

17. Honigmann, *The Development of Anthropological Ideas*, 41.

18. Erickson and Murphy, *A History of Anthropological Theory*, 28.

19. Ibid. This supposed archetype of medieval philosophical triviality was actually a straw man invented by seventeenth-century Protestant historians as a way to attack Roman Catholic theology.

20. Wilfried Nippel, "Facts and Fiction: Greek Ethnography and Its Legacy," *History and Anthropology* 9 (1996): 131.

21. Hodgen, *Early Anthropology in the Sixteenth and Seventeenth Centuries*, 28.

22. Ibid., 27.

23. Ibid., 21, 33, 34.

24. Ibid., 29, 34, 35.

25. Ibid., 33.

26. Ibid., 71.

27. See especially Hoffman, "The History of Anthropology Revisited"; Annemarie de Waal Malefijt, *Images of Man; a History of Anthropological Thought* (New York, 1974); Michael Herzfeld, *Anthropology through the Looking-Glass: Critical Ethnography in the Margins of Europe* (Cambridge; New York, 1987); and James A. Boon, "Comparative De-enlightenment: Paradox and Limits in the History of Ethnology," *Daedalus* 109 (1980).

28. James Muldoon, *Popes, Lawyers, and Infidels: The Church and the Non-Christian World, 1250–1550* (Philadelphia, PA, 1979); James Muldoon, "The Nature of the Infidel: The Anthropology of the Cannon Lawyers," in *Discovering New Worlds: Essays on Medieval Exploration and Imagination*, ed. S. Westrem (London, 1991); James Muldoon, ed., *Travellers, Intellectuals, and the World beyond Medieval Europe* (Burlington, VT, 2010); Felipe Fernandez-Armesto, "Medieval Ethnography," *Journal of the Anthropological Society of Oxford* 13 (1982); J. K. Hyde, "Ethnographers in Search of an Audience," in *Literacy and Its Uses. Studies on Late Medieval Italy*, ed. D. Waley (Manchester, 1991); Westrem, *Discovering New Worlds*; A. Samarrai, "Beyond Belief and Reverence: Medieval Mythological Ethnography in the Near East and Europe," *Journal of Medieval and Early Modern Studies* 23 (1993); Seymour Phillips, "The Outer World in the European Middle Ages," in *Implicit Understandings: Observing, Reporting and Reflecting on the Encounters between Europeans and Other Peoples in the Early Modern Era*, ed. S.B. Schwartz

(Cambridge, 1994); Peter Jackson, "William of Rubruck in the Mongol Empire: Perception and Prejudices," in *Travel Fact and Travel Fiction. Studies on Fiction, Literary Tradition, Scholarly Discovery and Observation in Travel Writing*, ed. Z. von Martels (Leiden, 1994); Kurt Flasch and Udo Reinhold Jeck, eds, *Das Licht der Vernunft: die Anfänge der Aufklärung im Mittelalter* (Munich, 1997); Joan Pau Rubiés, "The Emergence of a Naturalistic and Ethnographic Paradigm in Late Medieval Travel Writing," in *Voyages and Visions: Towards a Cultural History of Travel*, ed. J. Elsner and J. P. Rubiés (London, 1999); Joan Pau Rubiés, ed., *Medieval Ethnographies: European Perceptions of the World Beyond* (Burlington, VT, 2009); Albrecht Classen, ed. *Meeting the Foreign in the Middle Ages* (New York, 2002); Geraldine Heng, *Empire of Magic: Medieval Romance and the Politics of Cultural Fantasy* (New York, 2003); Richard Gyug, *Medieval Cultures in Contact* (New York, 2003); Shirin Khanmohamadi, *Proximate Others and Distant Selves: Writing Culture in Late Medieval Europe* (New York, 2005); Shirin Khanmohamadi, "The Look of Medieval Ethnography: William of Rubruck's Mission to Mongolia," *New Medieval Literatures* 10 (2008); Shirin Khanmohamadi, *In Light of Another's Word: European Ethnography in the Middle Ages* (Philadelphia, 2014); and Debra Higgs Strickland, "The Exotic in the Later Middle Ages: Recent Critical Approaches," *Literature Compass* 5 (2008).

29. Fernandez-Armesto, "Medieval Ethnography," 275.

30. Khanmohamadi, *Proximate Others and Distant Selves*, 2.

31. Rubiés, "The Emergence of a Naturalistic and Ethnographic Paradigm," xx, xiii.

32. James Clifford, "Rearticulating Anthropology," in *Unwrapping the Sacred Bundle: Reflections on the Disciplining of Anthropology*, ed. D. Segal and S. Yanagisako (Durham, NC, 2005).

33. For example, Hodgen, *Early Anthropology in the Sixteenth and Seventeenth Centuries*, 50.

34. For example, Honigmann, *The Development of Anthropological Ideas*, 41.

35. For the indebtedness of medieval thought to ancient predecessors on the question of human variation, see Robert Bartlett, "Medieval and Modern Concepts of Race and Ethnicity," *Journal of Medieval and Early Modern Studies* 31 (2001); on questions concerning the "barbarian," see W. R. Jones, "The Image of the Barbarian in Medieval Europe," *Comparative Studies in Society and History* 13 (1971); for reason and the passions, see Oscar De-Juan and Fabio Monsalve, "Morally Ruled Behaviour: The Neglected Contribution of Scholasticism," *The European Journal of the History of Economic Thought* 13 (2006).

36. For a general survey of the way that medieval thought shaped the Western intellectual tradition, see Marcia L. Colish, *Medieval Foundations of the Western Intellectual Tradition, 400–1400* (New Haven, CT, 1997).

37. On Albertus Magnus, see H. W. Janson, *Apes and Ape Lore in the Middle Ages and the Renaissance* (London, 1952); for a recent study on Thomas Aquinas's anthropology, see Robert Pasnau, *Thomas Aquinas on Human Nature: A Philosophical Study of Summa Theologiae, 1a 75-89* (Cambridge, 2002).

38. John Block Friedman, *The Monstrous Races in Medieval Art and Thought* (Syracuse, NY, 2000).

39. Rubiés, "The Emergence of a Naturalistic and Ethnographic Paradigm"; Muldoon, *Travellers, Intellectuals*.

40. I use Sir Richard Colt Hoare's English translation from the J.M. Dent edition: Richard Colt Hoare and Geraldus Cambrensis, *The Description of Wales* (London, 1912). Citations are given with book and chapter numbers.

41. I use Peter Jackson and David Morgan, *The Mission of Friar William of Rubruck: His Journey to the Court of the Great Khan Möngke, 1253–1255* (London, 1990). Citations are given with chapter and page numbers from this translation.

42. For an excellent discussion of these two works, see Khanmohamadi, *Proximate Others and Distant Selves*, Ch. 1 and 3.

43. XXIX, 46.

44. XXVI, 3.

45. Book 1: XVI.

46. Book 1: XI.

47. Book 1: XIII.

48. XXXV, 4.

49. The degree to which aspects of non-Christian belief and ritual were incorporated into medieval religion remains a contentious issue, and is also related to the debate over whether a meaningful distinction can be drawn between "high" and "popular" cultures; see Jean-Claude Schmitt, *The Holy Greyhound: Guinefort, Healer of Children since the Thirteenth Century* (Cambridge, 1983); and John Arnold, *Belief and Unbelief in Medieval Europe* (London, 2005). See also Chapter 7 below.

50. Cary J. Nederman, "Introduction: Discourses and Contexts of Tolerance in Medieval Europe," in *Beyond the Persecuting Society: Religious Toleration before the Enlightenment*, ed. J.C. Laursen and C.J. Nederman (Philadelphia, 1998), 18.

51. On the notion of tolerance in medieval Europe, see I. Bejczy, "Tolerantia: A Medieval Concept," *Journal of the History of Ideas* 58 (1997); Laursen and Nederman, *Beyond the Persecuting Society*; and Glenn Olsen, "The Middle Ages in the History of Toleration: A Prolegomena," *Mediterranean Studies* 16 (2007).

52. Albrecht Classen, "Multiculturalism in the German Middle Ages? The Rediscovery of a Modern Concept in the Past: The Case of *Herzog Ernst*," in *Multiculturalism and Representation*, ed. J. Rieder and L. Smith (Honolulu, 1996), 212; see also Albrecht Classen, "Die Heidin: A Late-Medieval Experiment in Cultural Rapprochement between Christians and Saracens," *Medieval Encounters* 11 (2005).

53. XXXIII, 22; cf. Cary J. Nederman, *Worlds of Difference: European Discourses of Toleration, c. 1100–c. 1550* (University Park, PA, 2000), 64.

54. Khanmohamadi, "The Look of Medieval Ethnography," 94.

55. Boon, "Comparative De-enlightenment," 73.

56. Malefijt, *Images of Man*, 33.

57. Chapter 8; Augustine of Hippo and Marcus Dods, *The City of God* (Peabody, MA, 2009), 479.

58. Pagden, *The Fall of Natural Man*, 22.

59. Valerie I. Flint, "Monsters and the Antipodes in the Early Middle Ages and Enlightenment," *Viator* 15 (1984): 78.

60. Boon, "Comparative De-enlightenment," 78.

61. Ibid., 80.

62. See, for example, Erickson and Murphy, *A History of Anthropological Theory*, 28.

63. Symes, "When We Talk about Modernity," 721.

64. Robert Bartlett, *Gerald of Wales, 1146–1223* (Oxford, 1982), 186; Khanmohamadi, *Proximate Others and Distant Selves*, 38–53.

65. R. R. Davies, *The Age of Conquest: Wales, 1063–1415* (Oxford, 2000).

66. Cf. Talal Asad, *Anthropology & the Colonial Encounter* (New York, 1973).

67. Book 2: VIII.

68. Book 2: IX.

69. Book 1: XVIII.

70. Book 1: VIII.

71. Book 1: XVII.

72. Cf. Bartlett, *Gerald of Wales*, 9–26.

73. Book 2: X.

74. Ibid.

75. Gustavo Lins Ribeiro, "World Anthropologies," *Critique of Anthropology* 26 (2006).

    76. Symes, "When We Talk about Modernity," 718; Cohen, *Medieval Identity Machines*, 14.

    77. Michael Herzfeld, "Purity and Power: Anthropology from Colonialism to the Global Hierarchy of Value," *Reviews in Anthropology* 39 (2010): 290.

    78. Eduardo Restrepo and Arturo Escobar, "'Other Anthropologies and Anthropology Otherwise'," *Critique of Anthropology* 25 (2005): 100.

Part II

Part II

IDENTITY, POWER, AND
THE MEDIEVAL PAST IN THE
EASTERN ALPINE REGION

CHAPTER 4

German Imperialism and the Early Medieval Past

*The German Middle Ages are Germany's destiny. The Middle
Ages belong to us, as their destiny can only ever belong to a people.*
—Herman Heimpel, *Deutschlands Mittelalter
Deutschlands Schicksal*

The Early Medieval Eastern Alps: A German Narrative

For Herman Heimpel, and many of his late nineteenth- and early twentieth-century colleagues, Europe's medieval past was, above all, a story of German achievement.[1] In their view, Germanic-speaking peoples during the Middle Ages exerted an unparalleled political, economic, and cultural influence on societies from the Pyrenees to the Urals, leaving an indelible mark on medieval life across the European continent. The Eastern Alpine region—which today includes Slovenia, southern Austria, and northeastern Italy—lay at the center of this Germanic sphere of influence, and in the view of many historians, remained firmly under German control from the end of classical antiquity to the early twentieth century. This is the story that they told:

> Shortly after the collapse of the western Roman Empire in the fifth century CE, the imperial provinces of the Eastern Alpine region were absorbed into Theodoric the Great's Ostrogothic kingdom, which

---

Notes for this section begin on page 88.

came to control most of the Italian peninsula and Balkans by the time of his death in 526 CE. A few years later, Byzantine Emperor Justinian launched a campaign to bring this region back under imperial authority, and during the subsequent Gothic-Byzantine war, the Eastern Alps changed hands between several Germanic groups. It was first controlled by the Franks before being taken over by the Lombards, who had conquered most of northern Italy by 568 CE. Around the same time, the Avars—a nomadic steppe people who established khaganate across the Pannonian plain (Hungary)—also expanded into the Eastern Alps, bringing with them Slavic-speaking peoples who settled along the valleys of the Mura, Drava, and Sava rivers.

After a period of political instability, the Eastern Alps came formally under Bavarian control in the mid-eighth century, when the Alpine Slavs pledged their fealty to the Agilolfing dukes in exchange for military assistance against their Avar overlords. Once the Avar threat was repealed, the Bavarians began a program of colonization and Christianization, bringing an influx of German-speaking farmers to settle the sparsely populated land and missionaries from the Archbishopric of Salzburg to convert the pagan Slavs. However, in 788 CE the Bavarian duke Tassilo III was deposed by Charlemagne (for supposedly conspiring against him with the Avars), and the Frankish Empire absorbed the Eastern Alps, annexing not only the Bavarian realm but also the Lombard duchies to the west and Byzantine Istria to the south. In the ninth and tenth centuries, Carolingian rulers reorganized this region into a series of defensive "marches" (Carinthia, Styria, Carniola, and Istria) that provided a buffer zone between the imperial heartland and hostile groups to the east, such as the Avars, Magyars, and Bulgars.

From this point forward, the Eastern Alps formed a part of the medieval Holy Roman Empire, and the region was gradually Germanized, becoming a true Germanic *Kulturboden*. Although the population remained culturally and linguistically diverse, Germans dominated the political and social spheres in the growing urban centers, while the Slavs constituted much of the poor peasantry in the countryside. It was not until after World War I, when the Treaty of Saint-Germain-en-Laye placed the southern parts of these traditional duchies under the control of the new state of Yugoslavia, that these regions came under the Slavic sphere of influence, unjustly tearing apart what had been a single unified region for a millennium.

The present chapter investigates how this traditional historical narrative of the medieval Eastern Alps was used to explain and justify German dominance of this region from the eighteenth to twentieth centuries. It further develops the ideological connections between medievalism and colonialism introduced in the first part of the book by demonstrating how certain ethnic groups within Europe were subject to a "colonial gaze" not unlike the indigenous peoples of Africa, Asia, and the Americas. Specifically, we will consider how Slavic-speaking communities in East Central Europe were embedded in the same east/west slope of civilization that underwrote Orientalist discourse.[2] Not coincidentally, explicit parallels between Slavic and "Oriental" cultures were frequently drawn in eighteenth- and nineteenth-century scholarship, from historical arguments that placed the origins of the Slavs in the Middle East or Central Asia to anthropological research that described the traditions, customs, and even skull shapes of Slavs to be characteristically Asiatic.[3] In addition to the two axes of the spatiotemporal hierarchy outlined in Chapter 2 (Europe/not-Europe and modern/premodern), we will see how a similar developmental hierarchy was erected between Western and Eastern Europe (Figure 4.1).

This chapter will not only explore the role of medieval history and archaeology in articulating intellectual justifications for colonial authority, but also highlight some striking rhetorical and thematic similarities between German imperialism in East Central Europe and Western overseas colonialism. In order to understand why such parallels exist, we must first appreciate how all empires seek to intellectually justify their domination over subservient groups. That is to say, the structural violence that enforces imperial authority is almost always accompanied by a concerted effort to ideologically legitimize—indeed normalize—the exploitative relationship between conquerors and conquered. Since German imperialism in East Central Europe and Western colonial powers overseas faced a common dilemma of justifying

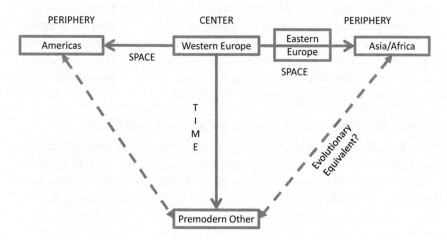

Figure 4.1. The spatiotemporal hierarchy (revised).

the confiscation of land from indigenous peoples whose chronological primacy would otherwise appear to give them inviolable rights of ownership, it makes sense that they would invoke many of the same ideological strategies for legitimating their power and authority.

We begin with an investigation of the various means by which German scholars—operating within the *Volk und Raum* paradigm of nineteenth- and early twentieth-century German social science—invented a medieval past that conveniently supported German colonial ambitions in Central and Eastern Europe. After considering how this narrative was employed in different parts of East Central Europe, the second half of the chapter examines more closely the intersections of medievalism, imperialism, and German social science in the Eastern Alpine region. We will trace how local Slovene-speaking populations morphed from "noble savages" to "dangerous Slavs" in the German colonial imagination, as well as detail how medieval history, archaeology, and toponymy were used to "prove" the historical Germanness of this region in order to legitimate National Socialist expansion and control.

Imperialism and Medievalism in Nineteenth-Century German Social Science

Over the past several decades, an extensive body of scholarship has highlighted the role that various social and historical sciences (ethnology, physical anthropology, history, geography, archaeology, psychology, folklore studies, etc.) played in supporting German colonialism during the nineteenth and early twentieth centuries.[4] However, the place of the Middle Ages in this political agenda has received considerably less scholarly attention, despite the fact that historical narratives of the medieval past were central to justifying German imperial projects throughout Eastern Europe. Therefore, in the following section, we will consider how the two dominant themes of German social science research—*Volk* (race) and *Raum* (space)—shaped, and were shaped by, images of Germany's medieval past.[5]

Space: Lebensraum, Kulturkreislehre, *and the* Drang nach Osten

The prominent role of space in German social science[6] can be largely attributed to the influence of the geographer Friedrich Ratzel (1844–1904), whose interdisciplinary method known as *Anthropo-geographie* asserted that the primary determinant for the success or failure of all living organisms was the sufficient acquisition of *Lebensraum* ("living space"). Ratzel's innovative anti-evolutionary framework influenced a range of disciplines in the late nineteenth century, including geography, zoology, anthropology, archaeology, and political science. For example, Ratzel's student Leo Froebnius brought the concept of *Kulturkreis* (Cultural Circles) to ethnology, where it would constitute a key idea of the *Kulturkreislehre* (Cultural Circles School), which emphasized migration and diffusion (rather than social evolution) as the driving forces of culture change. Fritz Graebner and Wilhelm Schmidt helped to popularize this school of Viennese ethnology during the early twentieth century, at a time when sociopolitical conditions within the multi-ethnic Austro-Hungarian monarchy were ideal for such an approach to flourish.[7] Although this hyper-diffusionist paradigm was abandoned relatively quickly, the *Kulturkreislehre* had an important impact on the direction of cultural anthropology in both Europe and North America.[8] In the early twentieth century, the *Kulturkreis* framework was also adopted by many European archaeologists, since its method of identifying human cultures through an "inventory" of particular traits seemed well suited for connecting patterns in the material record with the movement of prehistoric peoples. Most infamously, the German archaeologist Gustaf Kossinna would marry this "culture-history" approach to a Germanic racial chauvinism in his *Siedlungsarchaologie*, which became the archetype of archaeological research during the National Socialist period, as discussed below.[9]

The most politically consequential application of Ratzel's work was undoubtedly the *Geopolitik* School of political science, which used the concept of *Lebensraum* to argue for the necessity of a new supranational order across Central and Eastern Europe under German leadership that would then be able to "exercise its influence all over the world."[10] This order was to be divided between a German Empire in the north and Austro-Hungarian Empire in the south, and would consist of an inner *Volksboden* populated by ethnic Germans surrounded by an outer *Kulturboden* of non-German peoples, but where German culture (language, art, literature, folklore, architecture, etc.) would nevertheless predominate.[11] It was within this latter zone that much of Eastern Europe was imagined to fit.[12] The effort to develop an intellectual edifice that made German political and cultural hegemony over the whole of Eastern Europe appear legitimate, desirable, and inevitable was taken up enthusiastically by members of the *Ostforschung*, a constellation of scholars and academic institutions dedicated to proving the cultural and historical rights of German imperial rule in the "East."[13] It is not coincidental that many prominent medievalists—including Albert Brackmann, Hermann Heimpel, and Hermann Aubin—played key roles in founding the *Ostforschung* and advancing its central mission.[14]

But why exactly did the Middle Ages represent an important ideological building block of the *Ostforschung* project? One likely reason is that the most compelling historical precedent for German political control of Eastern Europe was the so-called *Drang nach Osten* ("Drive to the East"), an umbrella term used to describe various episodes of German colonization of Eastern Europe throughout the medieval period. Beginning in the second half of the nineteenth century, German historians increasingly viewed the *Drang nach Osten* as proof of the superiority of Germanic over Slavic culture, arguing that Germans were ultimately responsible for bringing agriculture, urban life, and other elements of "civilization" to Eastern Europe.[15] Various episodes of German eastward migration—from the aforementioned eighth-century migration of Bavarian farmers into the Eastern Alps to the ninth-century Varangian conquest of the Kievan Rus, as well as the establishment of the "State of the Teutonic Order" in the thirteenth century—were framed as different manifestations of a single long-term historical process by which industrious German-speaking peoples transformed the feral landscapes of the east into a "land of blessed productivity."[16] Some German historians and archaeologists went even further, asserting that all complex, state-level societies in the east were the product of Germanic (not Slavic) ingenuity, pointing to Carolingian expansion across Europe and the establishment of *Terra Mariana* by German knights during the Livonian Crusade, as well as (more controversially) claiming that the founding members of medieval Slavic dynasties such as the Rurik in Russia, Piast in Poland, and Přemyslid in Bohemia were actually of "Nordic stock."[17]

A careful examination of the concept of *Drang nach Osten* reveals a striking number of colonialist tropes, such as the "Right of Civilization": the notion that political control over a region should be determined by the "relative contribution by a people to [a territory's] economic transformation, expansion, and use"; or, put more bluntly, "the right of civilized nations to take the land from barbaric peoples."[18] This dubious concept had a long tradition in Western political thought, with its origins in the medieval claim that Christians could legitimately take land from "pagans" who violated the laws of God and nature. John Locke would later develop a similar argument that agriculturalists, but not foragers, have an inherent right to the land, since uncultivated land is basically without value.[19] Since Western legal traditions seemed to justify the confiscation of territory that was either under-utilized, sparsely populated, or inhabited by local peoples deemed "uncivilized," the Right of Civilization was regularly invoked in the colonial world, from the Australian government's infamous policy of *terra nullius*—which legally voided all aboriginal land claims on the grounds that they were racially inferior—to the American concept of Manifest Destiny, which justified Indian removal policies based on the idea that native peoples "did not in any true sense own or occupy" their territory, as Theodore Roosevelt once wrote.[20] German imperialists similarly claimed a "Right of Civilization" in East Central Europe, which many considered their own colonial birthright, equivalent to British India or French Indochina. Strikingly, such connections were already being made in the late eighteenth century by German philosopher Christoph Meiners, who wrote: "Inherent privileges are acceptable and natural when based on inherent superiority. By right, the Germans enjoy the liberties they were born with in all the Slavic lands where they have settled. By right Europeans occupy all foreign parts of the world, where they dominate or merely tolerate the black, red, yellow or brown inhabitants of these lands."[21]

A century later, German historian Ludwig Schlesinger similarly opined that medieval Bohemia was for Germany what California is to the United States,[22] a sentiment later echoed by the eminent American historian James Westfall Thompson, who admiringly described the *Drang nach Osten* as "the great deed of the common people of medieval Germany, just as the making of the American West has been the achievement of the common people of America."[23] For Thompson, the parallels between the two colonizing shifts were obvious: "In both instances, the work was the work of the common people and independent of governmental initiative, the work of the pioneer and the settler subjugating the forest with the ax, the fields with the plow, and driving the Slav or the redman, as the case may be, before him by his prowess in arms."[24]

Race: Anthropology, Völkism, and the German Middle Ages

A second overarching theme of nineteenth- and early twentieth-century German social science research was race. Indeed, many of the aforementioned arguments detailing German imperial expansion into, and domination of, Eastern Europe were premised upon German cultural and/or racial superiority over Slavs. While the concepts of "space" and "race" were deeply entangled during this period, there was nevertheless an underlying tension between them, perhaps best exemplified in the 1928 split of the department of "Anthropologie und Ethnologie" at the University of Vienna into separate entities, with the former more closely allied with German racial physical anthropology and the latter with the Viennese *Kulturkreislehre* approach to ethnology mentioned above.[25]

Here we will be concerned less with how German anthropology sought to empirically measure and classify physical differences among human groups (what would eventually become the dubious field of "racial science"), and more on the *völkisch* movement, which held a more humanistic, organic, even mystical view of ethno-cultural variation. Inspired by the Romantic writings of J. G. Herder and J. G. Fichte, Völkism asserted that every "people" (*Volk*) possessed a unique and eternal "spirit" (*Geist*) that could never be fully described by scientific means. This spirit was instead expressed in the traditions, customs, dress, and other aspects of "folk culture" among rural peasant communities, which were seen as vestigial leftovers from a distant (medieval) past. It should not be surprising then that the *völkisch* movement—from the folktales of the Brothers Grimm to Wagner's operas and the pre-Raphaelite Brotherhood—drew heavily upon romanticized, prelapsarian images of the Middle Ages.[26] Similarly, as the geographer Joshua Hagen has written, the medieval walled town in Germany would come to represent "a close-knit classless community of citizens bound together by tradition, civic pride, and the need for common defense."[27] Such historical fantasies of the simple, authentic, and enchanted world of the medieval peasant offered a stark contrast to the modern European urbanite, whose anomie stemmed from the modern ills of industrialization, secularization, and materialism.

Although Völkism was not initially premised on German racial superiority, by the early twentieth century its image of "an idyllic medieval past of cosmic and social harmony and unity" had become increasingly tied to fascist assumptions of a "historically superior but repressed German people."[28] The task of studying this supposedly "repressed German people" was taken up by medieval historians like Otto Brunner, Karl Bosl, Walter Schlesinger, and other pioneers of *Volksgeschichte* ("people's history"), an approach to history that eschewed the traditional historiographical focus on political elites in favor of studying the social, cultural, economic, and political totality of the German nation. While this interdisciplinary approach to history was methodologically innovative and theoretically promising (not unlike the contemporaneous *Annales* School in France), it was poisoned by a racial ideology that underwrote its ulterior political motives, such as a desire to prove the "German-ness" of regions beyond Germany's truncated post-World War I borders.[29]

Of course, racial superiority was also a recurrent theme in Western overseas colonialism. It is important to recognize that both German imperialists in Eastern Europe and Western colonialists abroad conceptualized the world as divided into two kinds of societies: advanced civilizations that were the driving force of history, and "primitive" peoples who lacked true history, politics, or culture. Such a "colonizer's model of the world"—which deeply informs the work of Hegel, Marx, John Stuart Mill, and others—was a key corollary of the "Right of Civilization" described above, since primitive African, American, and Australian peoples could only "progress" under the tutelage of advanced societies (see Chapter 2).

Slavic-speaking peoples in Eastern Europe were frequently included in the category of static, backwards people, incapable of possessing "true" culture. Just as colonial archaeology was used to demonstrate that native peoples were frozen in a primitive state,[30] archaeological work in East Central Europe was premised upon a division between Germans as *Kulturträger* ("carriers of culture") and Slavs without culture. For example, in a 1928 article, German archaeologist Paul Reinecke emphatically rejected the possibility of

Slavic political or cultural autonomy during the early Middle Ages, arguing that they passed from being "under the dominion of the Avars" to "falling under strong political and therefore cultural dependence on the Carolingian Empire."[31] For Reinecke, their lack of culture made the Slavs predisposed to rapid Germanization: "The Slavs adopted many forms of new cultural material from their Germanic neighbors ... the notion of a self-sufficient Slavic culture with exclusively Slavic forms is out of the question, and their dependence on the details of the Germanic circle is absolute."[32]

This emphasis on the difference between "primitive" Slavs and advanced, culture-bearing Germans can be detected in early twentieth-century archaeological writings throughout East Central Europe. At the site of Opole in Upper Silesia (Poland), German archaeologist Bolko von Richthofen underscored the "extremely great" differences between Slavic and Germanic groups, noting how the early medieval Germans had brought "enormous cultural progress" to this region.[33] Similarly, archaeological reports for the nearby site of Zantoch described "Slavic" settlement layers as technologically primitive and dirty, in contrast to the German layers, which were interpreted as much cleaner, better organized, and constructed with greater care and sophistication. Interestingly, the very phrase "Slavic culture" was frequently placed in scare quotes, perhaps in order to highlight the perceived irony of this term.[34]

Slovenians in the German Imperial Imagination

Thus far, we have seen how particular narratives of the medieval past were used to provide an intellectual justification for German imperial expansion into East Central Europe, by offering a historical precedent of "benevolent" German rule over Slavic peoples as well as identifying the medieval peasant as the authentic bearer of a superior German culture and identity. We have also uncovered how German justifications for imperial control over the "Slavic East" mirrored Western colonial domination of indigenous peoples in Africa, Asia, and the Americas. The second half of this chapter turns to investigating how this potent combination of colonial ideology, Völkism, and medievalism was used to establish political and cultural hegemony over Slovene-speaking communities in the Eastern Alpine region.

Primitivizing Slovenians (c. 1750–1900)

Some of the earliest evidence of a German "colonial gaze" toward the indigenous peoples of the Southeastern Alps can be found in eighteenth-century Habsburg travelogues. In these proto-ethnographic accounts written by imperial officials, German-speaking peasants are generally characterized as sincere, honorable, faithful, thrifty, and clean, while their Slavic-speaking counterparts tend to be depicted as pugilistic, lazy, and dirty (if also merry, generous, and hospitable).[35] Such ethnic stereotypes were clearly informed by a broader colonial imaginary that contrasted a rational, masculine, and civilized German culture with an irrational, feminine, exotic, and mythical Slavic culture.[36] However, unlike other Slavic-speaking groups (like the Poles) for whom German imperialists expressed almost nothing but contempt, Slovenians were often portrayed as simple, unassuming peasants, closely connected to the land, traditions, and spirituality. In other words, they were archetypal *Naturmensch* ("noble savages"). As one German traveler to the Eastern Alps wrote in 1812: "The Slavonic peasant is modest in his tastes; he is satisfied with maize, millet, and oats, with the milk from his little cow. He is unconcerned that German *Knecht* [servant] consumes so much during his *Hauptfesten* [feast days], as he is pleased if his whole family have enough."[37]

Thanks to their deep historical and cultural ties with the Germanic world (outlined in the narrative at the beginning of this chapter), Slovenians had achieved a status of "quasi-Germans" whose assimilation into the *Volksboden* was seen as a natural and inevitable historical eventuality.[38] To be sure, since advancement within Habsburg society required becoming culturally German, many Slovene speakers during this period expressed greater affinity with Germanic culture than with other South Slavic peoples (e.g. Croats, Serbs, and Bosnians) whom they derided as "semi-savages."[39] Nevertheless, despite holding a relatively privileged place in the German imperial imagination, it was not uncommon for Slovenians to be riddled with some of the same tropes as colonized peoples abroad. In particular, they were widely seen as lacking any meaningful "cultural" (i.e. literary or artistic) or historical achievements. As remarked by one character in the popular turn of the century novel *Zwölf aus der Steiermark*: "the Slovene nation? It has no past and no monuments. Only a bit of Glagolitic script. No heroism, no divine thoughts; nothing but the idol of Triglav."[40]

Ironically, it was precisely their status as a "non-historical nation" within the Habsburg Empire that made Slovenians ideal candidates for Germanization. Without any authentic culture or history of their own, they offered a kind of *tabula rasa* upon which superior German identity could be inscribed. Following this circular logic, any historical achievements or successes of the Slovenian people were retroactively attributed to their proximity to the German *Kulturkreis*. Such assumptions of cultural dependency were the basis of an 1863 speech given by Count Anton Alexander von Auersperg—an ethnically German politician from Ljubljana—in which he asserted that the Slovene people "live and thrive under the influence of the German spirit, German cultural accomplishments. That is how it always was and how it is and, God willing, how it should also remain. Whatever Carniola [a Slovenian province] has of prosperity, spiritual wealth, legal institutions and other advantages, it owes to the influence of the German spirit."[41]

Count von Auersperg even considered Slovenians "advanced" enough to have raised the possibility of political independence at some indeterminate future date, remarking: "Slovenia should walk a while longer with the aid of its elder sister, Austria, and should not be ashamed of accepting such guidance ... Once it achieves full maturity, the separation will also be natural—and therefore less painful." [42] Not coincidentally, John Stuart Mill offered a nearly identical argument against indigenous sovereignty only two years earlier in *Representative Government*, noting that colonial peoples who were not in a "sufficiently advanced state to be fitted for representative government" should continue under the direction of their imperial masters in order to "facilitate their transition to a high stage of improvement."[43] This serves as an important reminder that non-Western peoples were not the only ones who were asked to wait in the "imaginary waiting room of history."

Rise of Slovenian Nationalism and the Impact of World War I (c. 1900–1939)

As we have seen, throughout the Habsburg era Slovene-speaking communities were encouraged to embrace German language, culture, and identity, with the ultimate goal of facilitating their complete assimilation into the German *Kulturkreis*. However, by the end of the nineteenth century, concerns over rising social mobility in the empire compelled the political elite to severely restrict the availability of German identity from anyone willing to adopt a particular set of cultural values to only those individuals of a particular ethno-linguistic heritage.[44] This new, less inclusive concept of "Germanness" served to foster within the Slovenian-speaking community a greater sense of solidarity with other South Slavic peoples—a shift their German neighbors witnessed with a mixture of incredulity and anxiety. Fears over this increasing "Slavicization" of Slovenians were felt most strongly on the traditional borderlands between the German and Slavic worlds, such as the Eastern Alpine duchies of Styria, Carinthia, and Carniola. Responding to a perceived (but demographically unsubstantiated) threat that looming "Slavic masses" would soon overrun these regions, pan-Germanist organizations in the early twentieth century began to fund efforts to resettle groups of ethnic Germans there.[45] Predictably, as more Slovenians expressed greater kinship with Belgrade than Vienna, their favored status as "quasi-Germans" quickly disappeared, and they would be increasingly saddled with familiar negative Slavic stereotypes.[46]

Yet despite this surge of pan-Slavic nationalism at the turn of the twentieth century, mainstream Slovenian political parties still expected their goal of a unified South Slavic nation to be fulfilled within the Austrian Empire.[47] However, everything changed with the defeat of the Triple Entente in World War I. The Paris Peace Conferences dramatically reshaped the territorial boundaries and political balance of power in the region, with the Treaty of Saint-Germaine-en-Laye dissolving the Austro-Hungarian Empire and giving large portions of the Eastern Alps to the newly formed state of the Slovenes, Croats, and Serbs.[48] While the new border between a "German" Austria and "Slavic" Yugoslavia was justified based on the geographical distribution of ethno-linguistic groups, Germans were furious with what they saw as an unjust separation of the historical *Volksboden*. Similar developments were concurrently unfolding throughout postwar East Central Europe, as new nations like Poland, Czechoslovakia, and the Baltic states were carved out of former German territories.

In response to what was widely perceived as humiliating treatment at the Paris Peace Conferences, Germans increasingly turned to the political, economic, and cultural achievements of their (medieval) ancestors as a source for renewed national pride. German imperialist scholars set about devising a new set of arguments that, in addition to denying the cultural autonomy of Slavic peoples, also sought to demonstrate the historical injustices of the boundaries established by the Allied Powers. This meant redoubling the intellectual efforts to show that the entire political, social, and cultural infrastructure of these areas was the result of German colonization that could be traced back to the Middle Ages. Not surprisingly, scholarly interest in the *Drang nach Osten* grew significantly during the interwar period, to the point where, as Polish historian Jan Piskorski has noted, "nearly every historical work identified medieval colonization of Central and Eastern Europe as the greatest achievement of Germany's medieval period; and cast that colonization in a strongly pragmatic light, namely, as proof of Germany's right to East Central Europe."[49] In other words, if the medieval historian could show that Czechs, Poles, and Slovenians had always been simple peasants, wholly dependent on a German upper class for their culture and prosperity, then political independence would surely be ill advised, even dangerous.[50]

When the Third Reich rose to power, they would draw upon these historical arguments to gin up support among ethnic Germans living in these nascent Slavic states. During a visit to Maribor—a majority German border city in northern Yugoslavia—Adolf Hitler is reported to have stood on the balcony of the City Hall and called upon the gathered crowd to "make this land German again."[51] A year later, the *Drang nach Osten* was the thematic focus of the German history periodical *Jomsburg*, published on the eve of the Third Reich's invasion of Poland.[52]

Justifying Conquest and Domination in the National Socialist Period

After the creation of the Yugoslav state, the medieval past became an increasingly potent site of ideological struggle between Yugoslav/Slovenian nationalists and German/Austrian imperialists in the Eastern Alpine region. Historical precedence was seen as the key to determining whether this region was "authentically" Slavic or Germanic, which in turn legitimated territorial claims and political authority. There was widespread scholarly consensus that early medieval Slavic settlement of this region predated German coloniza-tion (as outlined in the narrative above). As further detailed in Chapter 5, most Slavic historians argued that Slavs were not only the dominant ethnic group until at least the eleventh century, but that they established an early medieval state known as Carantania that enjoyed at least a century of political independence before coming under the control of the Bavarian dukes. Slavic archaeologists linked the political boundaries of Carantania to the distribu-tion of a particular style of medieval jewelry known as the *Köttlach* culture, often employing the hyphenated term *Karantanisch-Köttlach* to emphasize this connection.[53]

Not surprisingly, German and Austrian scholars opposed to Slovenian nationalism crafted a very different historical narrative, one that explicitly denied the existence of an independent Slavic polity and asserted unin-terrupted Germanic political authority in the region, from the Goths and Lombards to Bavarians and Franks. Some even disputed the idea that Slavic-speaking peoples were the primary ethnic group during the early Middle Ages, arguing instead that mass immigration of German settlers started in the eighth century or earlier (including some more outlandish claims of German settlement continuity from prehistory).[54] This counter-narrative—which Austrian medievalist Walter Pohl has termed the "German continuity thesis"—first appeared in the late nineteenth century and grew in popularity over subsequent decades.[55] By the National Socialist period, it had become the dominant narrative for German medievalists.

The work of medieval historian and archaeologist Karl Dinklage, head of the department of "Ur- und Frühgeschichte" (Pre- and Proto-History) at the Institut für Karntner Landesforschung (IKL; Institute for Carinthian Regional Studies), provides an illustrative example of this perspective. In the 1940s, Dinklage published a series of articles based on excavations he conducted throughout this region (partially funded by the *Ahnenerbe*) that applied the German continuity thesis to Lower Styria and Carniola. Not only did Germans exercise political control in these regions, Dinklage argued, but the written sources support mass colonization of German groups in the early Middle Ages, writing: "The archives prove the advancing Germanization in the tenth century. It is not possible that these alone were carried out by the motives of the necessarily only relatively few landowners mentioned [in historical sources], without the participation of the Germans brought along."[56]

Dinklage also vehemently disputed the claims of archaeologists like Walter Schmid, who connected the duchy of Carantania with the archaeologist *Köttlach* culture (see Chapter 5). Scoffing at the notion that early medieval Slavs could produce such finely crafted jewelry, Dinklage asserted that *Köttlach*—due to its similarities with Bavarian and Merovingian styles—actually represented the Germanization of this region, noting: "at the time when the finds from Schmid's 'Carantanian culture' were in the *Ostmark* … it is known that there were already Germanic peoples in Carinthia."[57] Dinklage further attempted to demonstrate the Germanic character of *Köttlach* material by arguing that certain recurring designs and motifs like "strong lines with an inside swirl" and representations of eagles and griffins reveal a distinctly Germanic artistic sensibility, observing: "these Germanic thoughts in abstraction, these carefully crafted symbols of pure sense characters [*Sinnzeichen*]" were "renderings of nature [*Naturwiedergabe*]" and show "the course of Germanic artistic development."[58] Unsurprisingly, Dinklage expressed great skepticism at any suggestion of authentic indigenous Slavic culture in the Eastern Alpine region, calling it a "myth" (*Märchen*), and asserting that the archaeological evidence proves "the uniform picture of early German culture in its full extent" across Western and Central Europe.[59]

Historical linguist Eberhard Kranzmayer, another prominent member of the IKL, also sought to prove early Germanic settlement of the Southeastern Alps using place-name and toponymical evidence. For example, he claimed that the etymology of *Glanfurt*, the name of a river in the southern Austrian province of Carinthia, proves Germanic settlers antedated Slavic colonization of this region. Although he admits that the word derives from the Celtic "Lankvart," Kranzmayer argues that "Lankart," for phonetic reasons, "leaves no doubt that the Slovenian name is borrowed from the German. Therefore, the Germans settled along the Glanfurt before the Slavs. The phonetics of Lankart further suggests that the Winds [Slavs] first discovered our river in the eleventh or twelfth century."[60]

A third example of medieval scholarship being used to prove the "German-ness" of the Eastern Alps comes from Karl Starzacher, historian and head archivist for the Reichskommissariat *für die* Festigung deutschen Volkstums (the bureau that oversaw resettlement projects), who wrote in 1943 that Carniola was a *Deutscher Kulturboden* ("German cultural land") in the fullest sense of the term. Like Dinklage, Starzacher assumed historical continuity of Germanic rule and mass colonization in the early Middle Ages, and that German farmers and craftsmen brought true political and cultural development (*Kulturarbeit*) during the High Middle Ages. As for the contribution of the Slavs, Starzacher laments that "the Slavic and Avar attacks at the end of the sixth century demolished much, but did not destroy everything."[61] Furthermore, he argues that it was only recently that "Slovenization" had wiped out the German bonds of this land, turning them inside out and transforming those peasants with "German blood in their veins" into "fanatical village fighters" for the cause of Slovenian nationalism.[62]

Conclusion: German Identity and Medieval Scholarship after World War II

This case study illustrates how history, archaeology, and toponymy were used to fashion an early medieval past amenable to Germanic imperial interests in the Eastern Alpine region, both during and before the National Socialist period. Besides demonstrating the place of the Middle Ages in the Western historical imagination, there are several important takeaways from this example. First, it suggests that the strategies adopted to justify Germanic political and cultural hegemony in the Eastern Alps were drawn from overseas imperial and colonial ideologies, in addition to fascist racial fantasies and national chauvinism. Moreover, as the case of the American West highlights, not only did justification for German eastward expansion explicitly draw inspiration from European colonial experiences abroad, but the latter also perceived the *Drang nach Osten* as its logical historical antecedent. Secondly, it reminds us that political influence on historical and archaeological scholarship did not appear *ex nihilo* with the National Socialist *Machtergreifung* (seizure of power) in 1933, but was already evident in the middle of the nineteenth century, becoming only more pervasive during the interwar period.[63]

In concluding this examination of the place of "the Middle Ages" and "the East" in the German and Austrian historical imaginations during the nineteenth and early twentieth centuries, it is worth considering how these two conceptual categories have continued to shift over the seven decades since the end of World War II. While a comprehensive investigation is beyond the scope of this chapter, a brief excursus is useful for recognizing how the historical imagination continues to adapt to new sociohistorical conditions.

The Cold War (1945–1990)

Germany's defeat in World War II and the subsequent denazification policies and partition of the country into eastern and western halves effectively ended the longstanding German ambition to create an empire in

East Central and Eastern Europe. However, German conceptual geogra-
phies of "the East" were profoundly impacted by the emergence of the
Iron Curtain and the Eastern Bloc. As Merje Kuus has detailed, during
the Cold War, the Soviet Union and Eastern Europe continued to serve
as an "Other" against which Western Europe could define itself, and East
Central Europe was often caught up in this east/west binary thinking,
where all of these nations were treated as a uniform bloc.[64]

The legacy of Nazi atrocities and genocidal projects also exerted a
profound influence over the paradigmatic direction of archaeology and
medieval history, along with the rest of the social sciences and humanities. Archaeology, which had positioned itself as the "pre-eminent national
discipline" during the National Socialist era, was eager to shed this igno-
minious label in the postwar period. The nationalist and racial chauvinist
paradigm of figures like Kossinna and Dinklage was abandoned in favor
of more descriptivist aims that conspicuously lacked any overt political
implications. Likewise, questions about past social identity were largely
replaced by more ostensibly "objective" questions related to economic,
environmental, and technological developments as German archaeology
became famously "atheoretical" and "scientific" in orientation.[65]

Similar developments occurred in medieval history, where the study of
ancient Germans that had been so popular under the Nazi regime quickly
fell out of favor after the war. Although there were some continuities in
the historiographical traditions before and after 1945, there is no question
that this moment marked a sharp turn in both the scholarly questions that
were asked about the medieval past and the kind of language that was used
to describe it. For example, the aforementioned *Volksgeschichte* ("people's
history"), an innovative interdisciplinary approach to social history tainted
by Nazi ideology, later re-emerged as *Strukturgeschichte* ("structural history")
purged of the overtly racist elements that had infected its first incarna-
tion.[66] It was only in 1961 that questions about barbarian social identity
during the early Middle Ages came back into mainstream historiography,
with the publication of Reinhard Wenskus's influential *Stammesbildung und
Verfassung*.[67] As detailed in Chapter 6, Wenskus and his intellectual heirs
sought to shift the historical approach to barbarian identity from biological
and racial factors to social and political ones. The medieval past also played
an important role in the Austrian historical imagination during the postwar
era. As Walter Pohl has argued, the celebration of the 1,500th anniversary
of the signing of the Ostarrîchi charter in 1946 came at a crucial moment
in Austrian politics, where politicians were eager to forget the previous
several decades by reorienting the origins of Austrian identity in the early
Middle Ages.[68]

The Post-Cold War Era (1990–present)

After defeat in World War II, the second most historically significant moment for Germany over the past seventy-five years was the end of the Cold War, which saw the fall of the Iron Curtain and reunification of West and East Germany. Although tensions and disagreements between the former western and eastern halves of the nation did not disappear overnight, a newly unified Germany sought to position itself as the cultural, political, and economic conduit between Western and Eastern Europe. In the years after the Cold War, Germany engaged in *Kulturpolitik*, opening German culture and language centers throughout the former Eastern Bloc nations. At the same time, the expansion of the European Union and North Atlantic Treaty Organization has been premised upon a "reinscription of Otherness" in East Central Europe, playing on age-old stereotypes of an irrational, backwards, uncivilized, and archaic Slavic culture.[69]

Both medieval history and archaeology have reflected these broader sociopolitical trends over the past several decades. As further explored in Chapter 6, questions of ethnicity and ethnogenesis have become increasingly prevalent in the scholarly literature, as both historians and archaeologists look for ways to think about and recover early medieval social identities without lapsing into the essentialist and racialized conceptions of ethnicity that plagued the studies described above. Nevertheless, the early Middle Ages have continued to serve ethno-nationalist agendas, such as during the Balkan War and in border disputes between contemporary nations.[70]

Interestingly, and perhaps ironically, the early medieval past has also been enrolled in recent efforts to cultivate a transnational European identity, which is clearly tied to the expansion of the EU. A number of recent archaeological exhibits and catalogs have emphasized the early Middle Ages—particularly Charlemagne's Frankish Empire—as a kind of historical precursor to contemporary projects to establish an economically and politically unified (Western) Europe. Michael H. Moore has described this notion that Europe is moving into a post-national era that will look not unlike the Middle Ages as "Euro-medievalism."[71] Given recent events that have thrown the durability and longevity of the European Union into question, it will be interesting to see whether the next few decades will bring a more politically and culturally unified Europe or a revival of aggressive and destabilizing nationalism across the continent.

Notes

1. A previous version of this chapter appeared as K. Patrick Fazioli, "From First Reich to Third Reich: German Imperialism and Early Medieval Scholarship in the Southeastern Alpine Region (c. 1919–1945)," *Archaeologies: A Journal of the World Archaeological Congress* 8 (2012).

2. Maria Nikolaeva Todorova, *Imagining the Balkans* (New York, 1997); Milica Bakić-Hayden, "Nesting Orientalisms: The Case of Former Yugoslavia," *Slavic Review* 54 (1995); Jan M. Piskorski, "After Occidentalism: The Third Europe Writes Its Own History. (Instead of Introduction)," in *Historiographical Approaches to Medieval Colonization of East Central Europe: A Comparative Analysis against the Background of Other European Inter-ethnic Colonization Processes in the Middle Ages*, ed. J.M. Piskorski (Boulder, CO, 2002); Attila Melegh, *On the East-West Slope: Globalization, Nationalism, Racism and Discourses on Eastern Europe* (New York, 2006).

3. Catherine Carmichael, "Ethnic Stereotypes in Early European Ethnographies: A Case Study of the Habsburg Adriatic c. 1770–1815," *Narodna umjetnost—Hrvatski časopis za etnologiju i folkloristiku* 33 (1996): 206; P.M. Barford, *The Early Slavs: Culture and Society in Early Medieval Eastern Europe* (London, 2001), 37.

4. For studies on German anthropology during the colonial period, see H. Glenn Penny and Matti Bunzl, eds, *Worldly Provincialism: German Anthropology in the Age of Empire* (Ann Arbor, 2003); for the politics of the social sciences in Germany more broadly, see Woodruff D. Smith, *Politics and the Sciences of Culture in Germany, 1840–1920* (New York, 1991). Bernard Mees, *The Science of the Swastika* (New York, 2008) also provides an interesting perspective on "antiquarian studies" (archaeology, folklore, historical linguistics, philology, etc.) during the Nazi period.

5. While the German word *Volk* is better translated as "people" rather than "race" (*Rasse*), the racial undertones of the idea of *Volk* during this period make this an acceptable translation; see Mark Bassin, "Race Contra Space: The Conflict between German Geopolitik and National Socialism," *Political Geography Quarterly* 6 (1987).

6. In the following discussion, I use the term "German social science" as shorthand for all Germanophone scholarship, even that of German-speaking scholars living in places like the Austro-Hungarian Empire. It should be noted that intellectual developments in early twentieth-century German social science were not monolithic.

7. Katharina C. Rebay-Salisbury, "Thoughts in Circles: Kulturkreislehre as a Hidden Paradigm in Past and Present Archaeological Interpretations," in *Investigating Archaeological Cultures: Material Culture, Variability, and Transmission*, ed. B.W. Roberts and M. Vander Linden, (New York, 2011), 45.

8. Clyde Kluckhohn, "Some Reflections on the Method and Theory of the Kulturkreislehre," *American Anthropologist* 38 (1936).

9. Ullrich Veit, "Ethnic Concepts in German Prehistory: A Case Study on the Relationship between Cultural Identity and Archaeological Objectivity," in *Archaeological Approaches to Cultural Identity*, ed. S. Shennan (New York, 1989).

10. Patricia Chiantera-Stutte, "Space, Grössraum and Mitteleuropa in Some Debates of the Early Twentieth Century," *European Journal of Social Theory* 11 (2008): 186.

11. Benno Teschke, "Geopolitics," *Historical Materialism* 14 (2006): 330.

12. Karl Haushofer, *Grenzen in ihrer Geographischen und politischen Bedeutung* (Berlin; Grunewald, 1927).

13. Michael Burleigh, *Germany Turns Eastwards: A Study of Ostforschung in the Third Reich* (New York, 1988).

14. Albert Brackmann, "Die Ostpolitik Ottos des Grossen," *Historische Zeitschrift* 134 (1926); Hermann Heimpel, *Deutschlands Mittelalter Deutschlands Schicksal* (Freiburg im Breisgau, 1933); Hermann Aubin, *Von Raum und Grenzen des deutschen Volkes; Studien zur Volksgeschichte* (Breslau, 1938); for a deeper examination of Aubin's role in this movement, see Eduard

Mühle, "The European East on the Mental Map of German Ostforchung," in *Germany and the European East in the Twentieth Century*, ed. E. Mühle (Oxford, 2003).

15. Wilhelm Wattenbach, "Die Germanisierung der östlichen Grenzmarken des deutschen Reichs," *Historicsche Zeitschrift* 9 (1863); Gustav Strakosch-Grassmann, *Geschichte der deutschen in Österreich-Ungarn* (Vienna, 1895); for a historiographical review of this literature, see Gerard Labuda, "The Slavs in Nineteenth Century German Historiography," *Polish Western Affairs* 10 (1969).

16. Wiebke Rohrer, "Politics, Propaganda and Polemics: Prehistoric Archaeology in Upper Silesia 1918 to 1933," *Archaeologia Polona* 42 (2004): 180.

17. Of course, the fact that German imperialist scholars were fond of citing such historical examples to justify Germanic control over the east does not mean that Germanic peoples were *not* influential in many medieval societies in Eastern Europe. For example, support for the "Nomanist Theory" of the rise of the medieval Russian state has certainly not been limited to politically compromised German imperialists, but continues to be a site of legitimate scholarly debate; see N. Riasanovsky, "The Norman Theory of the Origin of the Russian State," *Russian Review* 7 (1947); Leo S. Klejn, "Soviet Archaeology and the Role of the 'Vikings in the Early History of the Slavs," *Norwegian Archaeological Review* 6 (1973); and Hans Christian Sørensen, "The So-Called Varangian-Russian Problem," *Scando-Slavica* 14 (1968).

18. Piskorski, "After Occidentalism," 11.

19. John Locke, *Second Treatise of Government: An Essay Concerning the True Original, Extent and End of Civil Government* (Hoboken, NJ, 2014, [orig. 1689]), Chapter 5.

20. Theodore Roosevelt, *The Winning of the West: An Account of the Exploration and Settlement of Our Country from the Alleghanies to the Pacific* (New York, 1917), 55; see also Jo-Anne Claire Pemberton, "The So-Called Right of Civilization in European Colonial Ideology, 16th to 20th Centuries," *Journal of the History of International Law* 15 (2013).

21. Christoph Meiners, *Geschichte der Ungleichheit der Stände unter den vornehmsten Europäischen Völkern* (Hanover, 1792), 600; original German: "Erbliche Vorrechte sind nur als dann gültig und natürlich, wenn sie auf erbliche höhere Vorzüge gegründet sind. Mit Recht also geniessen die Deutschen sast in allen Slawichen Landern, wo sie sich niedergelassen haben, Freiheiten, die man den Eingeboren versagt hat. Mit Recht besitzen die Europäer in allen fremden Weltteilen, wo sie herrschen, oder auch nur geduldet werden, grosse Vorrechte vor den Schwartzen, rothen, gelben, braunen Einwohnern dieser Lander."

22. Jan M. Piskorski, "The Medieval Colonization of Central Europe as a Problem of World History and Historiography," *German History* 22 (2004): 334.

23. James Westfall Thompson, *Feudal Germany* (Chicago, 1928), 527.

24. As quoted in Patrick Geary, *Medieval Germany in America* (Washington, DC, 1996), 27.

25. Rebay-Salisbury, "Thoughts in Circles," 45.

26. For an examination of the role of folklore in the Third Reich, see James R. Dow and Hannjost Lixfeld, *The Nazification of an Academic Discipline: Folklore in the Third Reich* (Bloomington, 1994). The place of the medieval in the Romantic Movement is also investigated by Veronica Ortenberg, *In Search of the Holy Grail: The Quest for the Middle Ages* (New York, 2006).

27. Joshua Hagen, "The Most German of Towns: Creating an Ideal Nazi Community in Rothenburg ob der Tauber," *Annals of the Association of American Geographers* 94 (2004): 208.

28. Ortenberg, *In Search of the Holy Grail*, 96.

29. Examples of this historical approach include Otto Brunner, *Land und Herrschaft: Grundfragen der territorialen Verfassungsgeschichte Südostdeutschlands im Mittelalter* (Baden bei Wien, 1939); Karl Bosl, *Die Reichsministerialität als Träger staufischer Staatspolitik in Ostfranken und auf dem bayerischen Nordgau* (Ansbach, 1941); and Walter Schlesinger, *Die Entstehung der Landesherrschaft. Untersuchungen vorwiegend nach Mitteldt. Quellen. Mit e. Vorbemerkung z. Neudr.* (Darmstadt, 1941). On *Volksgeschichte* and the discipline of history during the Third

Reich, see Willi Oberkrome, *Volksgeschichte: methodische Innovation und völkische Ideologisierung in der deutschen Geschichtswissenschaft 1918–1945* (Göttingen, 1993); Hans Schleier, "German Historiography under National Socialism: Dreams of a Powerful Nation-State and German Volkism Come True," in *Writing National Histories: Western Europe since 1800*, ed. S. Berger, M. Donovan, and K. Passmore (New York, 1999); Karen Schönwälder, "Histories. The Fascination of Power: Historical Scholarship in Nazi Germany," *History Workshop Journal* 43 (1997); and Karl Ditt, "The Idea of German Cultural Regions in the Third Reich: The Work of Franz Petri," *Journal of Historical Geography* 27 (2001).

30. Ian J. McNiven and Lynette Russell, *Appropriated Pasts: Indigenous Peoples and the Colonial Culture of Archaeology* (Lanham, MD, 2005).

31. Paul Reinecke, "Slavish oder Karolingisch?" *Prähistorische Zeitschrift* 19 (1928): 272, 278; original German: "kommen jetzt in mehr oder minder starke politische und dazu auch kulturelle Abhängigkeit vom Karolingerreich."

32. Ibid., 278–79; original German: "Von ihren germanischen Nachbarn übernahmen diese Slawen reichlich Formen neuen Kulturgutes, so vor allem die Keramik, die sich aus einem der Bestandteile bajuwarisch-alamannischer und wohl auch ostfränkisher Keramik zur Merowingerzeit entwickelt hatte, dazu dann auch Schmucktypen u.a. die Schläfenringe. Aber auch jetzt kann einer selbständigen slavischen Kultur mit eigenen, ausschliesslich slavishen Formen hier noch keine Rede sein, da die Abhängigkeit von den Einzelheiten des germanis-schen Kreises eine volkommene ist."

33. Rohrer, "Politics, Propaganda and Polemics."

34. Hubert Fehr, "Prehistoric Archaeology and German Ostforschung: The Case of the Excavations at Zantoch," *Archaeologia Polona* 42 (2004): 211.

35. On Habsburg ethnography in the Alpine-Adriatic region, see Lidija Nikočević, "State Culture and the Laboratory of Peoples: Istrian Ethnography during the Austro-Hungarian Monarchy," *Narodna umjetnost—Hrvatski časopis za etnologiju i folkloristiku* 43 (2006); Ursula Reber, "Concerns of the Periphery / Peripheral Concerns: Tempting Territories of the Balkans," *spacesofidentity* 2 (2002); Carmichael, "Ethnic Stereotypes in Early European Ethnographies."

36. Timothy Beasley-Murray, "German-Language Culture and the Slav Stranger Within," *Central Europe* 4 (2006): 132.

37. As quoted in Carmichael, "Ethnic Stereotypes in Early European Ethnographies," 205.

38. Pieter Judson, "Inventing Germanness: Class, Ethnicity, and Colonial Fantasy at the Margins of the Habsburg Monarchy," *Social Analysis* 33 (1993).

39. Peter Sugar, "The Nature of Non-Germanic Societies under Habsburg Rule," *Slavic Review* 22 (1963): 19.

40. Rudolf Hans Bartsch, *Zwölf aus der Steiermark* (Leipzig, 1908), 171; original German: "Und das Slowenische Volk? Keine Vergangenheit, kein Denkmal, als das bischen glagolithi-sche Schrift; kein helbentum, kein Gottesgedanke als einen dreitöpfigen Götzen."

41. As quoted in Janez Cvirn, "The Slovenes from the German Perspective (1848–1918)," *Slovene Studies Journal* 15 (1993): 53.

42. Ibid.

43. John Stuart Mill, *Representative Government* (Kitchener, ON, 2001 [orig. 1861]), 202.

44. Pieter Judson, "'Whether Race or Conviction Should Be the Standard': National Identity and Liberal Politics in Nineteenth-Century Austria," *Austrian History Yearbook* 22 (1991).

45. Pieter Judson, *Guardians of the Nation: Activists on the Language Frontiers of Imperial Austria* (Cambridge, MA, 2006).

46. Martin Moll, "The German-Slovene Language Border in Southern Austria: From Nationalist Quarrels to Friendly Co-existence (19th to 21st Centuries)," in *Imagining Frontiers, Contesting Identities*, ed. S. Ellis and L. Klusakova (Pisa, 2007), 211.

47. Carole Rogel, *The Slovenes and Yugoslavism, 1890–1914* (New York, 1977), 418.

48. This state would soon become the Kingdom of Yugoslavia.

49. Piskorski, "After Occidentalism," 16; see also Gerard Labuda, "A Historiographic Analysis of the German Drang Nach Osten," *Polish Western Affairs* 5 (1964): 231.

50. Christian Promitzer, "The South Slavs in the Austrian Imagination: Serbs and Slovenes in the Changing View from German Nationalism to National Socialism," in *Creating the Other: Ethnic Conflict and Nationalism in Habsburg Central Europe*, ed. N. Wingfield (New York, 2003), 195.

51. Predrag Novaković, "Archaeology in Five States—a Peculiarity of Just Another Story at the Crossroads of 'Mitteleuropa' and the Balkans: A Case Study of Slovene Archaeology," in *Archaeologies of Europe: History, Methods, and Theories*, ed. P. Biehl, A. Gramsch, and A. Marciniak (New York, 2002), 335.

52. Piskorski, "The Medieval Colonization of Central Europe," 323.

53. Walter Schmid, "Südsteiermark im Altertum," in *Südsteiermark, ein Gedenkbuch*, ed. F. Hausmann (Graz, 1925); Z. Vinski, "Köttlacher Kultur," in *Enzyklopädisches Handbuch zur Ur- und Frühgeschichte Europas*, ed. J. Filip (Stuttgart, 1966); Paola Korošec, *Zgodnjesrednjeveška arheološka slika karantanskih Slovanov* (Ljubljana, 1979); V. Šribar, "Der Karantanisch-Köttlacher Kulturkreis, Aquileja und Salzburg," *Aquileia nostra* 54 (1983); Walter Modrijan, "Der Forschungstand zum Karantanisch-Köttlacher Kulturkreis," *Archäologisches Korrespondenzblatt* 7 (1977); V. Šribar and V. Stare, "Das Verhältnis der Steiermark zu den übrigen Regionen der Karantanisch-Köttlacher Kultur," *Schild von Steier* 15/16 (1978/79).

54. This latter theory, sometimes described as *Wiederverdeutschung des Ostens* ("re-Germanization of the East"), was first proposed by G. Höfken in 1850; see Labuda, "The Slavs in Nineteenth Century German Historiography," 220.

55. Walter Pohl, "National Origin Narratives in the Austro-Hungarian Monarchy," in *Manufacturing Middle Ages: Entangled History of Medievalism in Nineteenth Century Europe*, ed. P.J. Geary and G. Klaniczay (Leiden, 2013), 28, 29.

56. Karl Dinklage, "Frühdeutsche Volkskultur der Ostmark im Spiegel der Bodenfunde von Untersteiermark und Krain," *Mitteilungen der Anthropologischen Gesellschaft in Wien* 71 (1941): 240; original German: "Eine weitere seit dem 10. Jhdt. fortschreitende Eindeutschung auch der slawischen anhängigen Bevölkerung hat Klebel an Hand von Brixner Archivalien nachgewiesen. Es ist unmöglich, dass diese allein auf Veranlassung der notwendigerweise nur verhältnismassig kleinen Grundbesitzerschicht ohne Mitwirkung mitgebrachter deutscher Hintersassen durchgeführt worden ist."

57. Ibid.; original German: "Zu der Zeit, da die Funde von Schmids 'karantanischem Kreis' in der Ostmark getragen wurden, da gab es schon ein deutsches Karnten, da versteht man unter Karantanern bereits deutsche Menschen."

58. Ibid., 244.

59. Ibid., 256; original German: "Möchten schon diese knappen Zeilen dazu beigetragen haben, das Märchen von einer eigenen frühmittelalter Kultur der Slawen in den Ostalpenländern zu beseitigen. Eine zusammenfassende Darstellung des karolingischen Fundguts von Northumberland big Venedig und von Oxford bis Stuhlweissenburg wird bald das einheitliche Bild der frühdeutschen Volkskultur in vollem Umfang zeigen."

60. Eberhard Kranzmayer, "Reste germanischen Lebens in Kärntner Ortsnamen," *Carinthia I* 132 (1942): 106; original German: "Diese Lautung ist entscheidend. Lankart lässt nämlich aus lautlichen Gründen keinen Zweifel darüber offen, dass der slowenische Name bestimmt aus dem Deutscshen entleht ist. An der Glanfurt haben sonach die Germanen vor den Slawen gesiedelt. Die Lautung Lankart lässt sogar erschliessen, dass die Windischen mit unserm Fluss erst im 11. oder 12. Jahrhundert bekannt wurden."

61. Karl Starzacher, "Oberkrain, deutscher Kulturboden," *Deutsche Volkskunde* 5 (1943): 70; original German: "Der Slawen- und Awarensturm zu ende 6. Jahrhunderts hat vieles zerstört, aber nich alles vernichtet."

62. Ibid.

63. R. Bollmus, *Das Amt Rosenberg und seine Gegner: Studien zum Machtkampf im nationalsozialistischen Herrschaftssystem* (Munich, 1970); Frank Fetten, "Archaeology and Anthropology in Germany before 1945," in *Archaeology, Ideology, and Society: The German Experience*, ed. H. Harke (Frankfurt am Main, 2000); Fehr, "Prehistoric Archaeology and German Ostforschung."

64. Merje Kuus, "Europe's Eastern Expansion and the Reinscription of Otherness in East-Central Europe," *Progress in Human Geography* 28 (2004): 474.

65. Heinrich Härke, ed., *Archaeology, Ideology, and Society: The German Experience* (Frankfurt am Main, 2000).

66. Winfried Schulze, *Deutsche Geschichtswissenschaft nach 1945* (Munich, 1989).

67. Reinhard Wenskus, *Stammesbildung und Verfassung; das Werden der frühmittelalterlichen Gentes.* (Cologne, 1961).

68. Pohl, "Ostarrîchi Revisited."

69. Ingrid Hudabiunigg, "The Otherness of Eastern Europe," *Journal of Multilingual and Multicultural Development* 25 (2004); Michal Buchowski, "The Specter of Orientalism in Europe: From Exotic Other to Stigmatized Brother," *Anthropological Quarterly* 79 (2006); Todorova, *Imagining the Balkans.*

70. Geary, *The Myth of Nations.*

71. Michael E. Hoenicke Moore, "Euro-Medievalism: Modern Europe and the Medieval Past," *Collegium: News from the College of Europe = nouvelles du Collège d'Europe* 24 (2002). It might also be noted that the origins of a unified Europe have also been traced to the Celtic past and even the Bronze Age; see Mark Pluciennik, "Archaeology, Archaeologists and 'Europe'," *Antiquity* 72 (1998); Cris Shore, "Imagining the New Europe: Identity and Heritage in European Community Discourse," in *Cultural Identity and Archaeology: The Construction of European Communities*, ed. P. Graves-Brown, S. Jones, and C. Gamble (London; New York, 1996).

CHAPTER 5

Slovenian Identity and the Early Medieval Past

Slovenian history started when our Slavic ancestors came from behind the Carpathi [sic] Mountains and proclaimed the principality of Carantania in the 7th century. Historians believe it was one of the most democratic and modern states at that point in history. So it is no surprise that even Thomas Jefferson took the example of Carantania when founding the modern American state.

— Website for the Embassy of the Republic of Slovenia in Tokyo

The Early Medieval Eastern Alps: A Slavic Narrative

The above quote, taken from the website of the Slovenian Embassy in Tokyo, reveals how important the early Middle Ages are to the historical identity of the Slovenian people. Since the eighteenth century, Slovenians have traced their national origins to the arrival of Slavic-speaking peoples in the Eastern Alps during the early Middle Ages. Although the narrative advanced by Slovenian historians covers roughly the same time and place as the German version introduced in the previous chapter, it departs from the latter in a number of key ways:

Notes for this section begin on page 105.

Less than a century after the last Roman Emperor in the West was deposed by Odoacer, the Slavic-speaking ancestors of modern Slovenians migrated from their homeland in Eastern Europe to the former imperial province of *Noricum mediterraneum*, populating the numerous river valleys of the Eastern Alpine region abandoned by the earlier Romanized population.[1] Their migration and settlement is marked archaeologically by the spread of small rectangular houses and coarse-ware ceramics.[2] While their initial colonization occurred under the auspices of the Avar Empire, the Alpine Slavs enjoyed a great degree of independence, since the topography of their new home was not amenable to nomadic steppe people.[3] They soon joined a regional rebellion against the Avars led by a Frankish merchant named Samo. According to the Chronicles of Fredegar, after a series of military victories over the Avars and Franks, Samo was declared king of a new union of Slavic tribes that stretched from Silesia (modern Poland) to the Eastern Alps.[4] Although Samo's realm did not survive long after his death around 660 CE, the Alpine Slavs managed to retain their political autonomy, establishing some of the earliest "Slavic states" in history: Carantania in what is today southern Austria and northern Slovenia, and Carniola in the Karawank Mountains to the south. The former polity is mentioned in Paul the Deacon's *History of the Lombards* as "a nation of the Slavs" called "Camuntum, which they mistakenly call Carantanum," while the latter is identified as "Carniolenses" in the *Royal Frankish Annals*.[5]

During the late seventh and early eighth centuries, these Slavic-controlled duchies managed to remain independent from Franks and Bavarians in the north, the Lombards further west, and an ever-present Avar threat to the east.[6] Although neither textual nor material evidence provides much insight into their sociopolitical structure, Carantania and Carniola were ethnically diverse and unusually egalitarian in nature; the latter fact is evidenced by the "Ducal Inauguration Ceremony," in which a free peasant sat on an inverted ionic pillar known as the *Fürstenstein* (Duke's Stone) and led the rite in the local Slovene language. Then the new duke, dressed in peasant's clothes, promised to rule justly and uphold the Christian religion, as a symbolic recognition that he only ruled with the consent of the governed. Established at some point in the early Middle Ages, this proto-democratic ritual continued to be regularly performed in the region until the fifteenth century, inspiring modern political thinkers such as Jean Bodin and Thomas Jefferson.

However, in the mid eighth century, the Slavic dukes were forced to submit to Bavarian rule in exchange for aid against a renewed Avar threat. Ensuing political and religious colonization by Germanic-speaking peoples was fiercely resisted; early Christian missionaries from the Archbishopric of Salzburg were expelled and the Carantanian leaders later joined Pannonian Duke Ljudevit's rebellion against the Franks in 818 CE. Ultimately, such efforts proved futile, and the Alpine Slavs were forced to submit to Carolingian authority. Yet, even as Germans assumed most positions of political and economic power in the High Middle Ages, Slovenian peasants fought to maintain their distinct cultural identity. Centuries of oppression and subjugation under a harsh foreign yoke only stoked a desire for independence. This fire was reignited during the national awakening in the mid nineteenth century, but only came to fruition with the formation of the Republic of Slovenia in 1990. For the first time in 1,200 years, Slovenians, the Alpine Slavs, had a state of their own.

This chapter continues our exploration of the ways in which historical narratives of the early Middle Ages have been appropriated by modern political agendas in the Eastern Alpine region. While the previous chapter examined how German and Austrian imperialist historians exploited the medieval past to justify Germanic control of this region, this chapter investigates the Slavic counter-narrative sketched above that invented a shared past for Slovene-speaking communities. As with many aspiring nations in late eighteenth-century Europe, historical narratives played a critical role in nurturing a distinctly Slovenian identity. They provided the Slavic-speaking communities of the Eastern Alps with an origin story, a set of collective memories and national heroes, and a common historical destiny. Slovenian nationalist historians and archaeologists (not unlike their German counterparts discussed in Chapter 4) were eager to collapse the distance between past and present in order to make the individuals and events of the Middle Ages relevant for—indeed, inseparable from—contemporary political concerns. Ironically, we will see that Slovenian historians not only adopted the same intellectual framework as their German political adversaries, but internalized and reproduced many of the same stereotypes advanced by German colonialist histories.

According to Irish political scientist John Coakley, ethno-nationalist histories can be divided into three main categories: (1) Myths of Origin are narratives that describe the "birth" of a particular ethno-nationalist group; (2) Myths of Development explain how an early "golden age" of national flourishing was followed by a tragic "fall" and prolonged period of suffering and/or subjugation; and (3) Myths of Destiny are future-oriented narratives that help inform a group's "national mission" and collective destiny.[7] We will see in this chapter that Slovenian nationalist histories fit quite nicely into this taxonomy. The first section investigates the role Slovenian Myths of Origin played in the emergence of a distinct national identity in the late eighteenth century. The second section then reveals how the traditional Slovenian narrative of the medieval past closely follows the "golden age, followed by a fall" historical arc typical of Myths of Development. The third section traces the debates over Myths of Destiny that have re-emerged in the decades following Slovenian independence, which have had significant consequences for conceptions of the medieval past, as well as questions of what it means to be authentically Slovenian. The chapter concludes by considering how German stereotypes continue to manifest themselves in contemporary debates on Slovenian origin myths and national identity

Myths of Origin: The Rise of Slovenian Nationalism

The emergence of a distinctly Slovenian identity can be traced to the late eighteenth and early nineteenth centuries, a period—sometimes referred to as the Spring of Nations—culminating in the political upheavals of 1848.[8] Nationalist ideologies during that era were deeply informed by the romanticism of German philosophers Herder and Fichte, which posited that every people (i.e. ethnic group) possessed a unique national "soul" (*Geist*).[9] Since language was widely presumed to be the purest expression of this collective spirit, nationalists stressed the importance of literary traditions in group identity and also searched for the most primordial forms of modern languages.[10] Although the Slovene language did not possess a particularly long or distinguished literary tradition, an emphasis on language proved well suited to the rise of Slovenian nationalism, since a shared tongue offered a point of common identity among Slovene speakers scattered across the Austro-Hungarian Empire (with communities in Gorizia, Istria, Carinthia, Styria, Carniola, and Vas). For this reason, Slovenian nationalists were eager to show that language was not just a means of communication, but reflected a profound social bond more primordial than religious, regional, feudal, or other dimensions of social identity.[11] However, in order to show that language reflected a deeper kinship—one based on "blood" and ancestry—what the Slovenian nation needed was a shared past, a Myth of Origins.

The first person to craft this shared past for Slovene speakers was the Carniolan playwright and historian Anton Tomaž Linhart (1756–1795). An enthusiastic disciple of Herderian romanticism, Linhart saw language as the essence of the Slovenian national spirit. His 1791 work *Versuch einer Geschichte von Krain und den übrigen Ländern der südlichen Slaven Oesterreichs* ("An Essay on the History of Carniola and Other South Slavs") traced the origins of contemporary Slovene-speaking peoples to the Slavic settlement of the Eastern Alps during the centuries following the dissolution of the western Roman Empire. Linhart's narrative laid the foundation for what remains today a key component of Slovenian identity: their affinity and kinship with other Slavic-speaking peoples (as opposed to other non-Slavic populations in their region). This origin story, which located the moment of Slovenian "ethnogenesis" in the early Middle Ages, was later adopted into academic historiography primarily through the influence of Slovenian medievalist Franc Kos (1853–1924). Around the same time, this narrative would enter the public's historical consciousness through popular literature like F. S. Finžgar's 1907 novel *Pod svobodnim soncem* ("Under the Free Sun"), which ends with the triumphant arrival of Slavic groups at the gates of the Roman city of Tergeste (today Trieste) in the sixth century.[12] Locating the birth of their nation in the early Middle Ages remains, even today, "almost a patriotic duty for Slovenes," as Luka Gabrijelčič has argued.[13]

The historian Peter Štih has written extensively about how contemporary Slovenian identity has been, and continues to be, informed by particular narratives and images of the Middle Ages.[14] Štih has shown how, for decades, Slovenian historians and archaeologists explicitly described the late sixth-century settlement of the Eastern Alps as carried out not by generic Slavic-speaking peoples, but *Slovenians* specifically, even though philological evidence suggests that the ethnonym "Slovene" did not appear until at least four centuries later.[15] While criticizing the use of the phrase "early medieval Slovenes" may seem like nit-picking, such a conflation of early medieval and modern identities reveals the central place of this Myth of Origins in the Slovenian historical imagination. It should be noted that while many Slovenian medievalists today consciously avoid such anachronistic phraseology, the assumption that a distinctly Slovenian people has continuously inhabited the Eastern Alps for the past 1,400 years is still frequently found in journalism, tourist guides, official government websites (see opening quote), amateur histories, and even some scholarly publications.

Indeed, not all contemporary Slovenian academics are as eager as Štih to dissociate early medieval Slavs from modern Slovenians. Perhaps the most vocal opponent of this perspective is medieval historian and archaeologist Andrej Pleterski, who has railed against the historiographical trend of "denying the identity connections between the past and the present." The problem, according to Pleterski, is that historians who emphasize discontinuity rely exclusively on the written sources, which reveal only the ever-changing tastes of an elite minority. The "invisible masses," on the other hand, "maintain the tradition as a structure of long duration." In his recent study of the region around Lake Bled in Slovenia, Pleterski uses archaeological, historical, linguistic, and folkloric evidence to argue that the organization of space in these villages and agricultural fields has remained essentially unaltered since the seventh century. Furthermore, his conclusion seems to

endorse the very idea that Štih criticizes above: "All these are the components of the identity of the present-day local inhabitants—Slovenes, clearly
telling them that they have not been here only since now or the recent
past."[16]

Pleterski's work further reveals (despite claims to the contrary[17])
how archaeology has played, and continues to play, an important role in
Slovenian nationalist ideology, particularly in terms of the Myth of Origins.
Since the textual record provides little reliable information on the Eastern
Alpine region during the sixth and seventh centuries, Slovenian archaeologists have long sought to complement the written evidence by tracking the
migration of Slavic-speaking populations during this enigmatic period with
specific categories of material culture (particularly low-fired, wavy-banded
pottery known as the Prague Type).[18] Even though this assumption of a one-
to-one relationship between artifact styles and past ethno-linguistic groups
is riddled with a host of methodological and theoretical shortcomings, the
culture-history approach has long been the dominant theoretical paradigm
of medieval archaeology across Central Europe, and in many ways continues to subtly underwrite interpretations of material culture (see Chapter 6).
Particularly relevant to the discussion here is medieval scholar Florin Curta's
provocative claim that neither textual nor archaeological nor toponymical
data provide compelling evidence of what language the inhabitants of the
Eastern Alpine and Northern Adriatic regions spoke during the sixth and
seventh centuries.[19] The idea that the earliest settlers in the post-Roman
Eastern Alps spoke a Slavic tongue is simply a longstanding assumption,
Curta notes, and it is equally possible that the Slavic language only arrived
in the region several centuries later. While this hypothesis remains highly
controversial, the complete omission of debate on this issue attests to the
continuing power of this Origin Myth.

Myths of Development: A Golden Age before the Fall

Early Medieval Carantania

The Middle Ages have played a crucial role in the Slovenian Myth of
Development, which usually posits a "golden age" of collective prosperity
followed by a "dark age" of collective misery and/or subjugation. As evident
from the narrative articulated above, the enigmatic early medieval polity
known as Carantania fits the typical profile of an ancient "golden age."[20]
Although the textual evidence does not provide much reliable information
on the nature or scope of this political entity, Slovenian historians have long
asserted that it was a Slavic-led principality that enjoyed a period of political

independence from 658 CE (with the end of Samo's realm) until its annexa-tion by the Agilolfing dukes in 743 CE. Carantania is also commonly claimed to have been the first Slavic state in history, predating even Great Moravia, the ninth-century polity centered on the Morava River (today in the Czech Republic and Slovakia) that also frequently claims that title.[21]

The historical origins of this early medieval "golden age" narrative, like the Myth of Origins, can be traced to A. T. Linhart, who viewed the Carantanian state as a powerful historical argument for a modern Slovenian right to political sovereignty.[22] Carantania would later be idealized in Slovenian historiography as "the pivotal axis of the evolution of the Eastern Alpine Slavic communities during the Middle Ages" when the nascent Slovenian nation expressed itself in its finest form.[23] Even after this principal-ity was absorbed into the expanding Carolingian Empire during the ninth century, some Slovenian historians maintained that it continued to be "an internally independent semi-vassal principality."[24] Tellingly, the term *Velika Karantanija* ("Great Carantania") was often used in the scholarly literature, even though it does not appear anywhere in the early medieval sources.[25] Furthermore, Carantania became an important ideological tool for Slovenian nationalists in the early twentieth century, For example, Anton Korošec, the first head of the National Council for Slovenia and Istria, alluded to this early medieval state in a 1918 statement: "The state rights that the Slovene people had exercised and fulfilled in its own state passed into foreign hands for over a thousand years, (but) the self-determination of the peoples will restore them to it and unite all the Slovenes, Croats, and Serbs in an independent Yugoslav state."[26]

Archaeologists have also sought to use material culture to fill in the gaps of the fragmented textual evidence, particularly in determining the territo-rial extent of this early medieval polity. The archaeologist Walter Schmid (1875–1951) was perhaps the first to connect archaeological materials to this "golden age" of the Slovenian past, arguing that the distribution of the *Köttlach* style of early medieval jewelry and dress ornamentation could be used to reconstruct the boundaries of Carantania, which extended far beyond the Slovenian "homeland" of the Eastern Alps into the Danube basin and areas further westward.[27] To emphasize the connection between arti-fact style and political boundaries, Schmid rebranded this artifactual style the "Carantanian Culture," which (predictably) infuriated German imperialist archaeologists like Karl Dinklage, whom we met in Chapter 4.[28] While the hyphenated term *Karantanisch-Köttlacher Kulturkreis* (Carantanian-Kettlach Cultural Circle) became common parlance among Slovenian early medieval archaeologists,[29] it was (unsurprisingly) not widely adopted by Austrian and German scholars, who tended to stick with the original *Köttlach*.[30]

However, drawing a direct line from early medieval Carantania to modern Slovenia or the province of Carinthia "does not work politically or geographically," as Patrick Geary has pointed out.[31] In other words, the territory that Carantania probably covered does not line up with the boundaries of the modern Slovenian nation. Indeed, much of early medieval Carantania likely lay in modern Austria, a fact that has occasionally led to tensions between the two neighboring nations. Moreover, not only has the term "Carantania" held several different historical meanings (the seventh-century polity, a duchy within the Carolingian Empire, the modern province), but there is no reason to believe that the people inhabiting the *dux Carinthiae* constituted an ethnically homogeneous group.

The Servility Myth

In Slovenian historiography, the brief "golden age" of the Carantanian state was followed by a much longer epoch of suffering and oppression that Peter Štih has termed the "Servility Myth."[32] This narrative, which arguably occupies a more prominent place in the Slovenian collective memory than the preceding "golden age," details how their ancestors toiled under the German "foreign yoke" for over a millennium. As the great Slovenian poet France Prešeren (1800–1849) wrote in his *Wreath of Sonnets*:

> Where tempests roar and nature is unkind:
> Such was our land since Samo's rule had passed
> With Samo's spirit—now an icy blast
> Sweeps o'er his grave reft from the nation's mind
> Our fathers' bickerings let Pepin bind
> His yoke upon us, then came thick and fast
> Bloodstained revolts and wars, the Turk at last
> With woes our history is deeply lined.[33]

Far more than just a fanciful literary trope, the Servility Myth came to occupy a prominent place in Slovenian historiography under the influence of Ljudmil Hauptmann (1884–1968), who imagined the Slovenian medieval past as a story of continuous subservience to powerful outside forces, such as the Avar and German Empires. Contrary to the dominant narrative above, Hauptmann dismissed a century of Slovenian autonomy in the early Middle Ages, curiously claiming that the political elites in Carantania were Croats, not Slovenians.[34] While Hauptmann's servility thesis never garnered much support among other Slovenian medievalists, the underlying idea that their medieval ancestors were poor farmers, not urban elites, is deeply ingrained in the historical consciousness of academics as well as the general public. For example, the "Slovenes = peasants, Germans = nobility" binary was dramatically illustrated by the systematic destruction of medieval castles by the Yugoslav state in the decades after World War II, because they were seen as symbols of German oppression. It may also explain why many Slovenian historians have been more interested in studying the peasantry rather than nobility, with the latter group being virtually ignored in the scholarly literature until quite recently.[35] Furthermore, it is surely not coincidence that one of the most prominent aspects of Slovenian medieval history is the investiture ceremony of the Carantanian dukes, which was known from the early modern period, but is claimed to have begun in the early Middle Ages.[36] The idea that a peasant was given the power to invest the new duke with his authority, as well as the duty to remind him of his responsibilities to his people, clearly suggests an affinity with the peasantry.

The association of Slovenes with the poor, downtrodden peasants suggests that nationalist historians internalized some of the German colonial tropes outlined in the previous chapter. Indeed, Hauptmann's "Servility Myth" could have been lifted right from the German imperial agenda, the only difference being that Slovenian historians inverted the moral of this historical narrative, imagining their medieval ancestors as righteous victims of German aggression rather than as a culturally or racially inferior people. Furthermore, a longstanding scholarly interest in the mythology and spirituality of the rural peasant indicates that the "noble savage" trope may still subtly shape the agenda of Slovenian historiography. For example, the journal *Studia mythologica Slavica*, which is dedicated to "the mythology, spiritual culture and tradition of Slavic and also other nations and peoples," is published by the Slovenian Academy of Arts and Sciences.[37] Similarly, the ideological association of the early medieval Church with German imperialism may even explain the widespread interest among historians, archaeologists, folklorists, and ethnographers in recovering aspects of pre-Christian beliefs and rituals (i.e. "Slavic paganism").[38]

Myth of Destiny: History and Identity in an Independent Slovenia

One of the central questions for nationalist ideology is: what exactly makes one an authentic member of a particular nation? As outlined above, eighteenth- and nineteenth-century nationalists across Europe focused on language and ethnicity as an expression of deeper primordial ties of kinship, "blood," and shared ancestry. This framework encouraged Slovenian historians and archaeologists to trace their ethnic origins to the settlement of the Eastern Alps by Slavic-speaking groups during the early Middle Ages; this, in turn, fostered a sense of kinship with other South Slavic peoples, eventually becoming an intellectual cornerstone in the justification for the creation of Yugoslavia after World War I. For over seventy years, Slovenians remained a part of this multi-ethnic nation, although their relationship with other ethnic communities in the Balkan states was not always harmonious.

Then, in 1991, the longstanding nationalist dream of political sovereignty was finally realized when the Republic of Slovenia declared its independence from Yugoslavia. While this was a celebratory moment for many Slovenians, independence would ultimately force this young nation to revisit several key assumptions about the fundamental nature of Slovenian national identity. The dominant ethno-linguistic conception of national identity was explicitly written into the Slovenian constitution, which asserted "the fundamental and permanent right of the Slovene nation to self-determination; and from the historical fact that in a centuries-long struggle for national liberation we Slovenes have established our national identity and asserted our statehood."[39] However, as Veronika Bajt has noted, since the Republic of Slovenia was established as a state *of* and *for* ethnic Slovenians, over 25,000 permanent residents who did not fit into this category were denied citizenship, effectively rendering them "stateless" peoples. The deliberate and systematic exclusion of certain ethnic groups (primarily Serbs, Croats, Bosnian Muslims, Kosovoans, and Roma) from the Slovenian national community exposed the traditional understanding of Slovenian identity to be incongruous with the modern conception of nation-states as organized around "civic elective membership in a community of multiethnic and multicultural solidarity."[40]

Moreover, as their national independence coincided with the end of the Cold War, Slovenians were also granted an opportunity to rekindle their political, economic, and cultural relationship with Western Europe. Even before the disintegration of Yugoslavia, many had already begun to see their membership in the South Slavic state as a detriment to economic growth and development. Some Slovenian politicians positioned their country as a "lost child" that was finally "coming home" to Europe after decades of unwanted Yugoslav domination behind the Iron Curtain.[41] In the early 1990s, representations of other South Slavic peoples, and even the term "Balkan," were increasingly saddled with negative connotations in Slovenian media and political discourse.[42] In some ways, this so-called "return to Europe" might be seen as a revival of early twentieth-century debates over whether Slovenians should align themselves with the Austro-German or Balkan spheres of influence (see Chapter 3).

Renewed debates over the nature of Slovenian identity have reshaped their collective historical consciousness in a number of important ways. First, there has been a subtle but revealing shift in historical descriptions of early medieval Carantania: once perceived as a "Slavic" state, scholars have increasingly characterized it as a culturally heterogeneous society comprised by various ethno-linguistic groups.[43] Second, the aforementioned

ritual concerning the installation of medieval dukes has been used to illustrate Slovenia's ancient democratic pedigree, specifically as a way to make
their case for admittance into the European Union.[44] In fact, some historians even suggested that this medieval political ceremony inspired none
other than Thomas Jefferson, since he supposedly marked this ritual in his
personal copy of Jean Bodin's 1576 *Treatise on Republican Government.*

The third, and most significant way in which this new conception
of Slovenian identity has become manifest in their collective historical
imagination is the growing popularity of the so-called "Venetic Theory"
of Slovenian origins, which offers a striking alternative to the early medieval Myth of Origins that has dominated the Slovenian history since the
late eighteenth century. This theory argues that contemporary Slovenians
are not descended from early medieval Slavs, but rather the Veneti, an
Indo-European people who first appeared in the Eastern Alps around 1200
BCE.[45] According to the proponents of this theory (sometimes described as
Venetologists), Venetic culture exerted a profound influence on contemporaneous Iron Age societies across Central Europe, making the ancestors of modern Slovenians one of the most culturally significant groups in
European prehistory. Of course, nearly all professional historians, archaeologists, and linguists reject the validity of the Venetic Theory due to its
sloppy use of cross-cultural comparison, dubious place-name etymologies,
inconsistent application of historical and linguistic methods, conspiratorial suspicion of mainstream scholarship, and other typical characteristics
of pseudo-historical and pseudo-archaeological thinking.[46] Nevertheless,
despite the concerted efforts of academics to debunk this deeply flawed
version of the past, it continues to be remarkably popular among the
Slovenian public, particularly among the political Right and members of
the Slovenian diaspora in Australia and North America.[47] The surprising
but undeniable appeal of this theory must be understood in the context of
the shifts in Slovenian politics and identity in the quarter-century since its
independence. That is to say, in light of the dissolution of Yugoslavia and
expansion of the European Union, the Venetic Theory can be seen as an
overt attempt to reorient "Slovenian-ness" away from a specifically Slavic
identity and toward a broader pan-European one. To wit, the English
translation of the title of one of its seminal books is *Veneti: First Builders
of European Community.*[48] This theory also shares some intriguing parallels
with the recent archaeological attempts to create a shared "Celtic" past for
contemporary Europe.[49]

The Venetic Theory must also be understood in terms of the failure of
ethnicity (as specifically tied to language) as the essence of a Slovenian identity. To insist that Slovenians are not Slavs, but rather the autochthonous
population of the Eastern Alps, prioritizes territory over language when it

comes to the authenticity of national identity. As Gabrijelčič has argued, the Venetic Theory constitutes "the replacement of an ethnicist model of identity based on natural right and supported by an exclusivist demotic-genealogical treatment of history with one based on historic rights and supported by an incorporative, territorial and historicist vision of the past."[50] In other words, one could argue that Venetic Theory is actually more aligned with the multicultural, territorial-based model of the nation–state than the longstanding early medieval Slavic narrative.

Finally, in light of some of the themes discussed in the previous two chapters, it is clear that the Venetic Theory is, in some sense, both a fulfillment of and a reaction against German imperialist tropes concerning Slovenian history and identity. The Venetic Theory's rejection of Slovenians as Slavs can be understood as an internalization of the longstanding negative German portrayals of Slavs, who were not only constructed as backwards and uncivilized, but not even truly Europeans.[51] However, according to the Venetologists, Slovenians can claim a more cultured Latin (i.e. European) heritage, unlike the more backwards and vaguely un-European Balkan Slavs, who arose from the "Trans-Carpathian swamps."[52] Venetologists have even accused mainstream Slovenian historians of perpetuating "a fabrication and conspiracy designed initially by German nationalist historians ... to deprive Slovenes of their rightful status as Europeans par excellence and to keep them in their superficial political union with other Balkan Slavs."[53]

Chapter 4 demonstrated that a central objective of German imperialist history was the denial of any meaningful Slovenian "history" or "culture" by portraying medieval Slovenians as serfs who relied on the German nobility for leadership. It seems clear that the Venetic Theory seeks to fill this perceived void, offering Slovenian nationalists "a narrative about his/her nation as a nation with dignity, history, heroic tradition and rich culture."[54] In an intriguing inversion of this colonial stereotype, the Venetic "myth of origins" suggests that it was actually *Slovenians* who formed the basis for other European cultural traditions, including prehistoric Germans. In stark contrast to Hauptmann's Servility Myth described above, leading Venetologist Jožko Šavli has interpreted early medieval Carantania as the reincarnation of the Venetic Iron Age kingdom of Noricum, noting that while the upper social strata may have embraced German traditions, the "infrastructure" of the territory was decidedly Slovenian/Venetic.[55] Venetologists have also echoed (but inverted) mainstream scholarly interest in the ancient religion and spirituality of Slovenians. While we saw above how medieval archaeologists have sought to identify remnants of Slavic pagan ritual and belief in the Christian era, the Venetologists have instead claimed that the pre-Christian religion of the Veneti contained elements that resembled and foreshadowed the tenets of Christianity.[56]

Conclusion

The Eastern Alpine region provides a fascinating glimpse into the Western historical imagination at a number of levels. We have seen how colonial-ist tropes were adopted by German medieval historians seeking to justify German expansion in this region, as well as how the Middle Ages were essen-tial to the construction of a shared Slovenian past. More importantly, despite the opposing overall goals of German imperialists and Slovenian nationalists, we can see how they utilized basically the same theoretical framework that collapsed the distance between the past and present in order to include medi-eval peoples within their imagined communities. In other words, underlying assumptions of Western historical thinking—specifically in terms of identity and temporality—allowed the medieval past to become a blank canvas upon which they could write their own political agendas. In the next two chapters of this book, we will consider how to develop an alternative approach to the medieval past that can prove more resistant to this kind of blatant political appropriation.

Notes

1. Franc Kos, *Izbrano delo* (Ljubljana, 1982).
2. M Guštin, ed., *Zgodnji Slovani: zgodnjesrednjeveška lončenina na obrobju vzhodnih Alp (Die frühen Slawen: frühmittlalterliche Keramik am Rand der Ostalpen)* (Ljubljana, 2002).
3. Peter Štih, "The Slavic Settlement and Ethnogenesis," in *The Land Between: A History of Slovenia*, ed. O. Luthar (New York, 2008), 85–86.
4. Ibid.
5. Peter Štih, "The Carolingian Period of the 9th Century," in Luthar, *The Land Between*, 94; Rajko Bratož and H.-D. Kahl, eds, *Slovenija in sosednje dezele med antiko in karolinsko dobo: zacetki slovenske etnogeneze = Slowenien und die Nachbarländer zwischen Antike und karolingischer Epoche: Anfänge der slowenischen Ethnogeneseslovenske etnogeneze* (Ljubljana, 2000).
6. Hans Dietrich Kahl, *Der Staat der Karantanen. Fakten, Thesen und Fragen zu einer frühen slawischen Machtbildung im Ostalpenraum (7.-9. Jh.)* (Ljubljana, 2002).
7. John Coakley, "Mobilizing the Past: Nationalist Images of History," *Nationalism and Ethnic Politics* 10 (2004); see also Matthew Levinger and Paula Franklin Lytle, "Myth and Mobilisation: The Triadic Structure of Nationalist Rhetoric," *Nations and Nationalism* 7 (2001).
8. E. J. Hobsbawm, *Nations and Nationalism since 1780: Programme, Myth, Reality* (New York, 1990); for Slovenian nationalism specifically, see Veronika Bajt, "Slovenian Nationalism," *Sprawy Narodowościowe* 24/25 (2004).
9. See Chapter 3.
10. Patrick J. Geary and Gábor Klaniczay, eds, *Manufacturing Middle Ages: Entangled History of Medievalism in Nineteenth-Century Europe* (Leiden, 2013), 2.

11. Peter Thaler, "The Discourse of Historical Legitimization: A Comparative Examination of Southern Jutland and the Slovenian Language Area," *Nationalities Papers* 40 (2012): 12.

12. Luka Gabrijelčič, *The Dissolution of the Slavic Identity of the Slovenes in the 1980s. The Case of the Venetic Theory* (Budapest, 2008).

13. Ibid., 37.

14. Indeed, much of the analysis in this chapter is both inspired by, and indebted to, Štih's work over the past several decades; Peter Štih, *The Middle Ages between the Eastern Alps and the Northern Adriatic: Select Papers on Slovene Historiography and Medieval History* (Leiden, 2010).

15. Ibid., 13; Veronika Bajt, "Myths of Nationhood: Slovenians, Caranthania and the Venetic Theory," *Annals for Istrian and Mediterranean Studies. Series historia et sociologia* 21 (2011): 254.

16. All quotes from Andrej Pleterski, *The Invisible Slavs: Župa Bled in the "Prehistoric" Middle Ages* (Ljubljana, 2013).

17. For example, Predrag Novaković has claimed that "[a]cademic historiography and archaeology in Slovenia succeeded in avoiding the major pitfalls of nationalism in the 1980s and 1990s." Novaković, "Archaeology in Five States—A Peculiarity of Just Another Story at the Crossroads of 'Mitteleuropa' and the Balkans: A Case Study of Slovene Archaeology," 344. B. Slapšak and Predrag Novaković, "Is There National Archaeology without Nationalism? Archaeological Tradition in Slovenia," in *Nationalism and Archaeology in Europe*, ed. M. Diaz-Andreu and T. Champion (London, 1996), draw a distinction between "national" and "nationalist" archaeology.

18. Guštin, *Zgodnji Slovani*.

19. Florin Curta, "The Early Slavs in the Northern and Eastern Adriatic Region: A Critical Approach," *Archaeologia Medievale* 37 (2010): 322.

20. In German, this state is called *Karantanien*, while in Slovene it is called *Karantanija*

21. On Carantania as the first Slavic state, see Bogo Grafenauer, *Ustoličevanje koroških vojvod in država karantanskih Slovencev* (Ljubljana, 1952); for a recent overview of the debates surrounding Great Moravia, see Jiří Macháček, "Disputes over Great Moravia: Chiefdom or State? The Morava or the Tisza River?" *Early Medieval Europe* 17 (2009).

22. Slapšak and Novaković, "Is There National Archaeology without Nationalism?" 266.

23. As quoted in Rado L. Lencek, "Carantania," *Slovene Studies Journal* 15 (1993): 191; for a critique, see Bajt, "Myths of Nationhood," 254.

24. Bogo Grafenauer, *Zgodovina Slovenskega Naroda* (Ljubljana, 1954), 391.

25. For uses of this phrase, see Bogumil Vošnjak, *A Bulwark against Germany; the Fight of the Slovenes, the Western Branch of the Jugoslavs, for National Existence* (New York; Chicago etc., 1919).

26. As quoted in Dusan Necak, "The 'Yugoslav Question': Past and Future," in *State and Nation in Multi-ethnic Societies: The Breakup of Multinational States*, ed. U. Ra'anan, M. Mesner, K. Armes, and K. Martin (Manchester, 1991), 131.

27. Šmid, "Südsteiermark im Altertum."

28. Dinklage, "Frühdeutsche Volkskultur der Ostmark"; see Chapter 4.

29. Valter Šmid, "Südsteiermark im Altertum"; Z. Vinski, "Köttlacher Kultur"; Paola Korošec, *Zgodnjesrednjeveška arheološka slika karantanskih Slovanov*; V. Šribar, "Der Karantanisch-Köttlacher Kulturkreis, Aquileja und Salzburg,"; Walter Modrijan, "Der Forschungstand zum Karantanisch-Köttlacher Kulturkreis"; V. Šribar and V. Stare, "Das Verhältnis der Steiermark zu den übrigen Regionen der Karantanisch-Köttlacher Kultur."

30. See, for example, F. Hampl, "Funde der Köttlacherkultur aus Kaiserbrunn, Krumbachgraben, NÖ," *Nachrichtenblatt für die Österreichische Ur- und Frühgeschichtsforschung* 2 (1953); S. Denk, "Neue Funde der Köttlacher Kultur im Erlauf-Gebiet 1953–1956," *Unsere Heimat, Monatsblatt des Vereines für Landeskunde von Niederösterreich und Wien* 28 (1957); Jochen

Giesler, "Köttlachkultur," in *Reallexikon der Germanischen Altertumskunde. 17: Kleinere Götter—Landschaftsarchäologie*, ed. J. Hoops (Berlin, 2001). It should also be noted that some scholars, such as Paola Korošec, would later distinguish between earlier Slavic (*Karantanisch*) and later Germanic (*Köttlach*) phases of this material.

31. Patrick J. Geary, "Slovenian Gentile Identity: From Samo to the Fürstenstein," in *Franks, Northmen, and Slavs: Identities and State Formation in Early Medieval Europe*, ed. I.H. Garipzanov, P.J. Geary, and P. Urbańczyk (Turnhout, Belgium, 2008), 254.

32. Štih, *The Middle Ages between the Eastern Alps and the Northern Adriatic*.

33. France Prešeren, Miha Maleš, and Niko Grafenauer, *Sonetni venec* (Ljubljana, 1995, [orig. 1834]); translation from http://www.preseren.net/ang/3_poezije/76_sonetni_venec-08.asp.

34. Gerhart Hauptmann, *Winckelmann, das Verhängnis, Roman* (Gütersloh, 1954); see also Anton Melik, *Planine v Julijskih Alpah* (Ljubljana, 1950).

35. Štih, *The Middle Ages between the Eastern Alps and the Northern Adriatic*.

36. Ibid.

37. The website for this journal can be found at: http://sms.zrc-sazu.si/En/Studia_predstavitev.html.

38. For example, a number of medieval archaeologists have argued that aspects of the Slavic pagan landscape were retained well after Christianization in the eighth century CE (see Chapter 7). Even more provocatively, a recent ethnography by Boris Čok has contended that non-Christian rituals continued to be covertly practiced in areas of southwest Slovenia at least into the late nineteenth century. Boris Čok, *V siju mesečine: ustno izročilo Lokve, Prelož in bližnje okolice (Outlines of Mythic Characters in the Villages of Lokev and Prelože in the Context of Slavic Mythology)* (Ljubljana, 2012).

39. Preamble to the Slovenian constitution, as quoted in Bajt, "Myths of Nationhood," 253.

40. Ibid., 253, 250; this is sometimes referred to as the "Erasure."

41. Sabina Mihelj, "To Be or Not to Be a Part of Europe: Appropriations of the Symbolic Borders of Europe in Slovenia," *Journal of Borderlands Studies* 20 (2005): 111; see also Nicole Lindstrom, "Between Europe and the Balkans: Mapping Slovenia and Croatia's 'Return to Europe' in the 1990s," *Dialectical Anthropology* 27 (2003).

42. Karmen Erjavec, "Discourse on the Admission of Slovenia to the European Union: Internal Colonialism," *Journal of Multicultural Discourses* 3 (2008); Ljiljana Šarić, "Balkan Identity: Changing Self-Images of the South Slavs," *Journal of Multilingual and Multicultural Development* 25 (2004).

43. Kurt Karpf, "Slawische Fürsten und Bairischer Adel: Das Frühmittelalterliche Karantanien am Schnittpunkt Zweier Kulturen," *Hortus artium medievalium: Journal of the International Research Center for Late Antiquity and the Middle Ages* 8 (2002); Hans Dietrich Kahl, "Slovenci in Karantanci. Evropski problem identitete / Slowenen und Karantanen. Ein europäisches Identitätsproblem," in *Slovenija in sosednje dežele med antiko in karolinško dobo*, ed. R. Bratož and H.-D. Kahl (Ljubljana, 2000); Stefan Eichert, "Karantanische Slawen—slawische Karantanen. Überlegungen zu ethnischen und sozialen Strukturen im Ostalpenraum des frühen Mittelalters," in *Der Wandel um 1000: Beiträge der Sektion zur slawischen Frühgeschichte der 18. Jahrestagung des Mittel- und Ostdeutschen Verbandes für Altertumsforschung in Greifswald, 23. bis 27. März 2009*, ed. F. Biermann, T. Kersting, and A. Klammt (Langenweißbach, 2011).

44. Lindstrom, "Between Europe and the Balkans."

45. The primary work on this hypothesis is Joško Šavli, Matej Bor, and I. Tomažič, *Veneti: First Builders of European Community: Tracing the History and Language of Early Ancestors of Slovenes* (Vienna, 1996).

46. For a critical perspective on the Venetic Theory, see Tom Priestly, "Vandals, Veneti, Windischer: The Pitfalls of Amateur Historical Linguistics," *Slovene Studies Journal* 19

(2002); for a more general overview of the common characteristics of pseudo-historical and pseudo-archaeological work, see Kenneth L. Feder, *Frauds, Myths, and Mysteries: Science and Pseudoscience in Archaeology* (New York, 2011).

47. Zlatko Skrbiš, "The Emotional Historiography of Venetologists: Slovene Diaspora, Memory and Nationalism," *Focaal: European Journal of Anthropology* 39 (2002).

48. Šavli, Bor, and Tomažič, *Veneti*; its original Italian title (*I Veneti: progenitori dell'uomo europeo*) carried the same connotation.

49. Michael Dietler, "Celticism, Celtitude, and Celticity: The Consumption of the Past in the Age of Globalization," in *Celtes et Gaulois dans l'histoire, l'historiographie et l'ideologie modern*, ed. S. Rieckhoff (Glux-en-Glenne, 2006); P. Graves-Brown, S. Jones, and Clive Gamble, *Cultural Identity and Archaeology: The Construction of European Communities* (London; New York, 1996).

50. Gabrijelčič, *The Dissolution of the Slavic Identity*, 96.

51. Carmichael, "Ethnic Stereotypes in Early European Ethnographies."

52. Bajt, "Myths of Nationhood," 255.

53. Skrbiš, "The Emotional Historiography of Venetologists," 43.

54. Zlatko Skrbiš, "The First Europeans: The Case Study in Slovene National Imagining in Diaspora," in *TASA 2001 Conference* (Sydney, 2001), 4.

55. Šavli, Bor, and Tomažič, *Veneti*; cf. Gabrijelčič, *The Dissolution of the Slavic Identity*, 91.

56. Skrbiš, "The First Europeans," 5; here too we can see why this theory appeals to the more conservative elements of Slovenian society.

CHAPTER 6

Beyond Ethnicity

Technological Choice and Communities of Practice

> [B]y establishing sex, class and ethnicity as foundational axes of
> identity, we construct archaeological analysis as a tautology whereby
> the discovery of historical modes of constituting subjects is in fact
> already given by the overly burdensome theoretical apparatus.
> —Adam T. Smith, "The End of the Essential
> Archaeological Subject"

Barbarians and the Fall of Rome

From their earliest history, Romans traded with, fought against, and
defined themselves in contrast to their "barbarian" neighbors.[1] However,
by the later imperial period, increasing militarization of the empire pre-
cipitated a fundamental change in the nature of this longstanding intercultural relationship. The accelerated growth of the Roman army under
Diocletian and Constantine—to the point where it consumed two-thirds
of the entire imperial budget[2]—not only encouraged the recruitment
of more barbarian soldiers to fill its ranks, but also required the settlement of barbarian *foederati* onto Roman territory in order to expand the
empire's tax base.[3]

It was under such conditions that Roman Emperor Valens in 376
CE invited tens of thousands of Gothic-speaking Tervingi to cross the
Danube and settle in the province of Thrace. However, an administrative

---

bungling of the resettlement process led to food shortages, resent-
ment, and eventually an armed uprising. The conflict would come to a
head several years later at the Battle of Adrianople, where the Roman
army experienced a stunning defeat at the hands of Gothic forces that
included the death of the emperor himself. While subsequent negotia-
tions would allow the Goths to settle peacefully within imperial borders,
Rome's aura of military invincibility had been shattered, emboldening
other barbarian groups to challenge Roman power.

By the early fifth century CE, increasing numbers of barbarian peoples
made aggressive incursions into imperial territory, and internal political
turmoil severely hindered the empire's ability to adequately respond to
this potentially existential threat. Gothic tribes invaded the Italian peninsula under Radagasius in 405 CE, later joining in Alaric's infamous sack
of Rome. The same year, a group of Alans, Sueves, and Vandals crossed
the Rhine and effectively ended Roman control of Gaul. Further east, in
the province of Noricum along the Danube, historical sources suggest
that the military garrisons protecting the borders no longer received
regular pay, leaving the imperial *limes* virtually undefended.[4] Within
just a few decades, Childeric I had consolidated Merovingian power in
northern France, Gaiseric established a Vandal kingdom in North Africa,
and Roman Britain was left exposed to raiding Angles, Saxons, and Jutes
from across the North Sea. In less than half a century, the western half
of the empire disintegrated into a patchwork of barbarian kingdoms,
setting the stage for the emergence of the early medieval world.

This narrative demonstrates that no account of the transformation of the
late Roman world is complete without considering the role played by the
diverse social groups often referred to as the "barbarian tribes." Goths,
Angles, Saxons, Huns, Gepids, Scalvenes, Vandals, Alans, Thuringians, and
the list goes on; in the fifth and sixth centuries, the Roman world seems
overrun by a dizzying array of these exotic and enigmatic peoples. Some
appear abruptly on the historical stage, only to later vanish without a trace,
while others formed the basis of many early medieval societies that emerged
out of the ashes of imperial provinces. Despite an enduring fascination with
these barbarian tribes, historians and archaeologists continue to debate their
origins, composition, and purpose: were they large, homogeneous, and stable
communities bound together by common language, culture, and kinship?
Or were they ethno-linguistically diverse, ephemeral political associations
that had coalesced around a small core of elites? How reliable are the textual
accounts of such groups, since nearly all were written from an outsider's
point of view? What can the archaeological record tell us about the genesis,
movement, and interaction of these peoples?

Scholarly inquiry into such critical questions is further complicated by the blatant manner in which many of these early medieval "barbarian" groups have been co-opted in the service of modern political agendas. Ethno-nationalist movements have often sought to stretch their "imagined communities" deep into the early Middle Ages, encouraging their members to identify with the triumphs and tragedies of these long-dead "ancestors." As argued in Chapters 4 and 5, historians' assumptions about the nature of group identity not only shape our images of the early medieval past, but determine the degree to which this period can be appropriated for modern political concerns. Since nationalists have shown an ability to appropriate (and distort) even the work of scholars who are unsympathetic to their political causes, this chapter argues that it is only through a radical rethinking of group identity that historians and archaeologists can effectively deplete the early Middle Ages of its current political potency.

The goal of an anthropology of historicity is not only to examine the sociopolitical context of historical narratives, but also to develop a more sophisticated way to study the past, so this chapter attempts to move beyond the ethnicity paradigm that dominates contemporary approaches to group identity in early medieval history and archaeology. Since debates over ethnicity have proven to be complicated and contentious, it is important to begin by precisely identifying the three central claims of the argument that will be developed below:

(1) One of the principle underlying problems with current academic discourse on early medieval ethnicity is the inconsistent and/or imprecise use of this term in the historical and archaeological literature.

(2) If one accepts the dominant understanding of ethnicity in contemporary social theory—which emphasizes its fluid, situational, and subjective nature—then neither the written nor archaeological evidence is particularly well suited to providing reliable data about its expression in the early medieval world.

(3) The current preoccupation with ethnicity in early medieval archaeology has diverted scholarly attention away from other equally significant, if historically invisible, manifestations of group identity. One promising candidate in this arena is the "community of practice" informed by technological choices.

The remainder of this chapter will flesh out these assertions in greater detail. It begins by reviewing several paradigmatic shifts in the study of group identity in the social sciences, followed by an examination of recent debates over the significance of ethnic identity in late antique and early medieval Europe and its potential manifestation in the archaeological record. The following section then sketches out an alternative framework for studying early medieval group identity, specifically arguing that archaeological investigations of technological choice can reveal manifestations of group identity otherwise outside the scope of the fragmented written record. Finally, an examination of changes in coarse-ware pottery technology in the Eastern Alps will show the potential of this new approach for investigating such localized manifestations of group identity.

Group Identity in Anthropology, Archaeology, and History

Early Approaches

The recent preoccupation with identity in social science research makes it easy to forget that before the mid twentieth century scholars were far more interested in establishing group taxonomies than in understanding social identity. In other words, most scholarship was concerned with determining the proper scientific classification of human physical and cultural variation, not studying individuals' subjective or psychological experiences of group belonging. For example, in the eighteenth and nineteenth centuries, it was widely believed that humans could be meaningfully divided into a few broad categories based on a defined set of physical, behavioral, and/or cultural characteristics. The famous Swedish biologist Carolus Linnaeus used an array of physical and cultural traits (including hair color, facial structure, dress, personality, form of government) to identify five "subspecies" of humans, while the German physician Johann Blumenbach relied exclusively on physical appearance and skull shape to distinguish four racial categories. Although there was never a consensus on how many races existed, or which specific traits should be given taxonomic priority, the existence of biological races (as subspecies of *Homo sapiens*) and the inherited and immutable nature of racial characteristics was taken for granted by most scholars of that era.[5] However, by the late nineteenth century, discontent with this singular focus on biology led some anthropologists to place greater emphasis on cultural behaviors, customs, and attitudes in establishing social categories. Nevertheless, most of these early schools of ethnology still assumed that people could be sorted into a finite number of homogeneous, bounded, and discrete cultures based on a defined set of empirical data.[6]

Medieval historians in the eighteenth and nineteenth centuries similarly imagined barbarians to be organized into relatively homogeneous and stable communities bound by shared language, culture, and kinship (i.e. "blood"). Not only did this view fit with the aforementioned ethnological approaches, but it seemed to be further corroborated by ancient sources that typically distinguished these groups by physical appearance, language, customs, dress, or other cultural behaviors.[7] When medieval archaeology emerged as a distinct field of study in the early twentieth century, the notion that artifacts constituted a passive reflection of social traditions and "ways of doing" allowed archaeologists to match up patterns in the material record with barbarian tribes identified in written sources. In this way, archaeology emerged as a powerful new tool for tracing the origin, movement, and interaction of barbarian tribes beyond the purview of the historical record.

The Rise of Ethnicity

Western scientists' confidence in their ability to establish a valid racial taxonomy began to wane in the early twentieth century. Rather than moving closer to an objective list of "diagnostic" racial characteristics, physical anthropologists like Franz Boas recognized that supposedly immutable physical features like skull shape could change within just a few generations under new environmental conditions.[8] A few decades later, ethnologists came to realize that their scientific classification of cultural groups often did not align with individual perceptions of social difference.[9] Such realizations would ultimately shift the anthropological study of human groups from an "etic" (outsider) to "emic" (insider) perspective. This meant that the ethnographers could no longer establish isomorphic groups through some "checklist" of cultural traits, but had to account for group members' subjective perceptions of sameness and difference.[10]

The rise of the term "ethnicity"—broadly defined as individual perceptions of cultural differentiation and shared descent—marked this epistemological shift in anthropological research during the second half of the twentieth century. But even as this paradigm allowed scholars to sidestep the previous challenge of "objectively" categorizing social groups, the realization of the multifaceted, fluid, and even contradictory nature of human identity raised a host of thorny questions. From where precisely do the bonds of ethnic identity draw their power? Is ethnicity an expression of an intrinsic psychological need for belonging, or is it an invention of elites to further their political or economic goals? Which cultural traits, if any, are essential to the construction of ethnicity? How does ethnicity intersect with other identities such as race, nationality, class, gender, and kinship? While such issues, and many others, continue to be debated across the social sciences, there remains widespread agreement that social identity is not, as once believed, a passive reflection of pre-existing social categories, but rather the very mechanism through which such categories are created and defined.[11]

How was this new understanding of group identity incorporated into the study of early medieval Europe? While some early historians had questioned whether barbarian groups were really as bounded and homogeneous as the written sources claimed,[12] it is the work of German philologist Reinhard Wenskus and his followers that gets the lion's share of credit for fundamentally changing how medieval historians approached this topic. In his 1961 book *Stammesbildung und Verfassung; das Werden der frühmittelalterlichen Gentes*, Wenskus argued that barbarian groups were not large and stable populations that migrated *en masse* from Northern Europe or Central Asia, but rather conglomerates of culturally and linguistically diverse "recruits" that had formed around a small core of political-military elites, which he called the *Traditionskern* ("kernel of tradition").[13] Although Wenskus preferred the term *Stamm* (tribe) over "ethnic group," later historians like Patrick Geary, Herwig Wolfram, and Walter Pohl would combine Wenskus's ideas with social science research to establish the so-called "Ethnogenesis Model." This model contends that ancient barbarian groups were invented rather than *a priori* social categories, and that ethnic identity was not based in deep, primordial bonds of culture or kinship, but rather served political purposes such as providing the "opportunity to reinforce loyalties and facilitate integration" within such groups.[14]

While the concept of ethnogenesis has proven tremendously influential among historians of late and post-Roman Europe,[15] some scholars have claimed that it overstates the role of barbarian (specifically Germanic) peoples in the transformation of the western Roman Empire, and places undue emphasis on ethnic identities at the expense of other important political or religious processes during this period. For example, Walter Goffart has claimed that the traditional image of the western Roman Empire being overrun by barbarian groups is, more than anything else, a legacy of Byzantine propaganda, while Patrick Amory has used prosopographical techniques to show that Gothic identity was less important to social elites in sixth-century Italy than regional, professional, and institutional loyalties.[16] It should be noted that these critics do not deny the existence of ethnic identity during this period, nor do they disagree with the central tenet that social identities are fluid, situational, and multifaceted. If anything, they tend to embrace an even more subjectivist stance, criticizing Wenskus and his followers for implicitly retaining an essentialist (or racialized) conception of ancient Germanic tribes.[17]

Debating Ethnicity in Early Medieval Archaeology

While historians continue to debate the role of barbarian groups in the collapse (or, as some prefer, *transformation*) of the western Roman Empire, the subjective and multifaceted nature of ethnicity has achieved paradigmatic status. Yet this dominant understanding of group identity poses theoretical and methodological challenges for the historical and archaeological investigation of this social phenomenon. The aforementioned "culture-history" framework of archaeology, in which artifacts are understood to passively reflect group identities, once offered an ideal framework for matching patterns in the material record to groups identified in the written sources. That is, if we assume that barbarian tribes were expansive, stable, and culturally coherent communities moving around the late Roman and early medieval landscape, these groups surely would have left identifiable traces in the archaeological record. On the other hand, if barbarian groups were ephemeral, volatile, and culturally diverse social entities, then making such inferences with material data becomes far more tenuous.

Perhaps this is why many early medieval archaeologists continue to employ (at least implicitly) a traditional culture-history framework that has long fallen out of favor in the broader archaeological community. This is most clearly seen in the classificatory schemes of site reports and monographs, where terms like "Slavic house," "Lombard pottery," and "Avar arrowhead" subtly suggest that ethnic or cultural identity can be easily discerned from particular styles of artifacts. Although some might protest that these terms are employed only as handy conventions that no longer carry specific ethnic connotations, there is no doubt that the distinction between "archaeological cultures" and past ethnic groups remains far blurrier in early medieval archaeology than prehistoric archaeology, in large part due to the seductive nature of the historical record. That is to say, it is much easier to recognize that archaeological terms like "Bell Beaker" and *Linearbandkeramik* are modern conventions with no relationship to past political or ethnic units than to dissociate "Frankish brooches," "Saxon longswords," or "Slavic fibulae" from those groups of the *same name* found in written accounts.

Further evidence of this conflation of "pots" and "peoples" comes from the number of influential early medieval archaeologists who continue to defend a culture-history approach. For instance, the German archaeologist Frank Siegmund has asserted that "our knowledge about the distribution of early medieval ethnic groups derived from written sources ... allows us to combine these purely archaeological defined 'culture-groups' with early medieval ethnic groups,"[18] while French archaeologists Michel Kazanski and Patrick Périn have similarly claimed that, "in most cases the geographical coincidence of archaeological cultures with named historical 'peoples' (that is to say groups recognizing themselves under a single name) does allow us to link the two of them ... All these groups present a number of common archaeological traits."[19]

If one sees through the updated terminology (i.e. "ethnic groups" rather than "tribes" or "peoples"), it is clear that the underlying assumption of a straightforward correlation between artifact styles and past social groups remains essentially unchanged from the traditional culture-history model.[20] While there is no need to revisit in detail the innumerable critiques of this interpretive framework made over the past five decades,[21] a few obvious objections are worth mentioning. First, using artifacts to establish the "ethnic identity" of a burial is highly problematic because numerous other factors (e.g. trade, gift exchange, local customs, etc.) could also explain why particular artifacts end up in a grave.[22] Secondly, from a historiographical perspective, virtually all our knowledge of these barbarian groups comes from outside (Roman) perspectives that were not only shaped by their own cultural biases and political agendas, but were often inconsistent in how they applied these ethnonyms.[23] Therefore, using historical evidence to ascertain the "ethnicity" of early medieval barbarians is deeply problematic, since the written sources provide precious little (if any) reliable insight into the *self-perceptions* of the members of these groups.

In recent decades, a number of archaeologists have sought to address these theoretical and methodological complications by developing more sophisticated conceptual frameworks for studying ethnicity in the material record. Many of these "interpretive" approaches (as I will refer to them here) emphasize that material culture is not a passive reflection of group identity, but is intentionally used to create, negotiate, or destabilize social categories.[24] This framework entails seeing artifacts as "part of a symbolic system and largely encodes ideas or general social behavior" in the sense that material culture is a "text" that can be "read."[25] Borrowing from structuralism and semiotic theory, material culture is understood to participate in a complex system of information exchange by "encoding" particular sociocultural meanings. Therefore, the goal for archaeologists, as the Austrian medievalist Falko Daim has argued, would be to decode such meanings in order to determine "the nature of the group to which the symbol is referring."[26] Not coincidentally, the concept of identity as stemming from self-conscious "strategies of distinction" involving symbolic communication within and among social groups is also increasingly popular among historians of the early Middle Ages.[27]

While these semiotic approaches are unquestionably more successful in applying current theoretical understandings of ethnicity to the interpretation of archaeological data, not all scholars have been convinced of their efficacy. One common objection is that ethnicity cannot be meaningfully distinguished from other manifestations of identity (e.g. gender, class, status, age, faction, etc.) that may also have been part of this socio-semiotic system of communication. Skeptics like Sebastian Brather do not deny that material culture *could* have been used to signal ethnic identities in the early Middle Ages, but point out that "it is possible that no material sign was important; *habitus* and people's actions could have been the only relevant way that an *ethnos* differentiated itself from its neighbors."[28] The validity of this interpretive concern is further corroborated by numerous ethno-archaeological studies showing that without the advantage of direct observation of behavior, there is no reliable way to determine which kind of identity is being "signaled" in material culture.[29]

Group Identities beyond Ethnicity

Towards an Alternative Theoretical Framework

The question of how to effectively study early medieval ethnicity in the archaeological record (or whether this is even possible) remains unsettled. Some scholars remain adamant that archaeology has little to contribute to the study of early medieval ethnicity, and should stick to investigating aspects of the past better suited to its unique dataset, like settlement patterns, trade, technology, or environmental conditions.[30] Others insist that—at least under the right circumstances—material culture can indeed provide an important complement to historical sources in understanding the nature and expression of barbarian ethnicity.[31] While both of these positions make valid points, the fruitfulness of this debate has been hampered by the semantic slipperiness of the concept of ethnicity itself. A careful reading of the relevant literature reveals not only a lack of consistency in employing this term, but also that many scholars fail to define exactly what they mean by "ethnic identity."[32] As evident from the discussion above, some archaeologists use the term synonymously with "tribe" or "cultural group," while others employ a more anthropologically informed definition of "perceptions of social differentiation or common descent"[33]; no wonder that the two sides cannot seem to find common ground.

The problem for archaeologists following the latter (more widely accepted) definition of ethnicity is the inherent difficulty of recovering individual perceptions in the material record. Even if we assume that such perceptions were "encoded" in particular artifactual styles, there is currently no reliable way of distinguishing ethnic differences from other aspects of social identity without the benefit of ethnographic observation. But while skepticism about the utility of an "archaeology of ethnicity" is understandable, this does not mean that archaeologists must abandon questions of identity to ethnographers and historians, and turn their attention to patterns and processes farther down the "Hawkesian ladder"[34] (settlement, economy, environment, and technology). The problem with this conclusion, as reasonable as it may sound, is that it assumes a hierarchical and unidirectional relationship between the "social" and "technological" worlds, where the latter merely *represents* the former. In other words, identity is understood to exist first and foremost in a purely "mental" realm, which can be (at least potentially) expressed in the material world. Interestingly, whether one follows a traditional culture–history model (where artifacts passively reflect a shared identity) or interpretive approaches (that focus on the intentional manipulation of material culture by individuals), the underlying assumption is essentially the same: artifacts serve only as vehicles of symbolic meaning. The object world merely provides a blank canvas upon which cultural, ethnic, or other forms of human identity can be inscribed; this is why archaeologists are always searching for ethnic "markers," that is, some stylistic quality of an artifact (like decoration or form) that reveals its meaning as a cultural symbol.[35]

However, what if we begin from an entirely different theoretical starting point by positing that artifacts do not only mediate our experiences of the world as carriers of meaning, but their very *materiality* also shapes and directs our intentions and actions? A wealth of recent scholarship in anthropology, sociology, and archaeology has demonstrated that the "purification" of an active realm of (human) subjects from a passive realm of (material) objects is deeply inadequate for tracing the complex, intimate, and dynamic relationships between the human and nonhuman worlds. Bruno Latour has famously argued that the material world simultaneously stabilizes and "translates" human agency. In his actor-network theory, objects can redirect, encourage, block, inhibit, suggest, forbid, or render possible human intentions and actions, making them durable in time and space.[36] Agency is therefore not the sole possession of individual free will or deterministic technologies, but is always distributed throughout relational networks comprised of human and

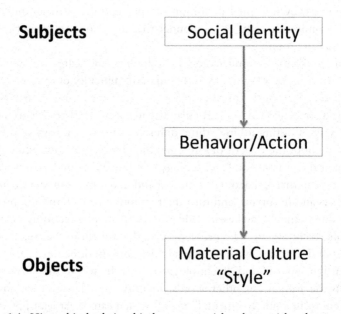

Figure 6.1. Hierarchical relationship between social and material realms.

nonhuman actors. Indeed, it is our immersion in a world of technologies that distinguishes human social relationships from those of all other animals.[37] Therefore, to assume that material cultures simply express aspects of social identity falls into a modernist fallacy that humans remain ontologically independent of the material world, when in fact we are deeply enmeshed in this technological milieu. Put another way, the aforementioned studies of ethnicity in the early Middle Ages have focused exclusively on what artifacts *mean*, but we need to give more consideration to what they *do*.

Skilled Craftsmanship, Technological Choice, and Communities of Practice

For the moment, we can leave aside this complex and rather abstract philosophical debate over which of these two competing social ontologies (substantivism or relationality) is the more compelling approach to studying human society. The germane point here is that scholars of early medieval Europe (and archaeologists in particular) should give greater consideration to how they might examine other manifestations of group identity beyond ethnicity.[38] The fact that ethnicity continues to dominate the archaeological literature despite the numerous conceptual and methodological limitations described above can be attributed to the power of the written sources in shaping our historical imaginations of the late and post-Roman world. To escape this "tyranny" of the historical record, archaeologists would do well to follow the advice of the British historian Peter Heather, who recently observed:

> Concentration upon the question of whether or not any particular collection of human beings is an ethnic group—with the implicit assumption that if you cannot prove it to be one, it cannot have a grouping worth worrying about—is thus an argument which in most cases will quickly end up going nowhere. It might even draw attention away from more answerable questions ... thinking about dimensions of the identity question beyond the ethnicity issue might well open up more productive areas for research.[39]

If we take seriously the possibility of a "relational" social ontology, then archaeologists can investigate aspects of social identity that are far more amenable to their dataset than ethnicity. One expression of social identity that will be further pursued below lies at the intersection of skilled practice and technological choice. Ethnographic research has shown, for example, that individuals form powerful bonds of social identity within groups of craft specialists. For example, potters who serve as part-time specialists in modern rural, small-scale societies (not unlike those of early medieval Europe[40]) have been shown to maintain a distinct sense of social identity through their craftsmanship.[41] The anthropological concept of "communities of practice"—which emphasizes that skill acquisition is a socially embedded process whereby the learner is initiated into a distinct community that shares knowledge, material resources, and an identity[42]—provides an ideal lens through which to investigate these local expressions of social identity. In other words, learning to become a master potter requires the apprentice not just to acquire informational knowledge (e.g. where to find the best clays, how long to let the pots dry before firing, etc.), but also to continually re-enact a particular sequence of bodily gestures and motor habits (e.g. the right amount of pressure to shape the wet clay spinning on the wheel) that are learned through habitual practice rather than communicatively. In this way, social identity in a community of practice derives not just from a shared set of perceptions, beliefs, and worldviews, but also a fundamentally non-discursive sense of being-in-the-world. In fact, the British ethnographer Tim Ingold has suggested that this process of "enskilment" is even more important in the transmission of cultural lifeways than language or propositional knowledge.[43] Florin Curta has recently made a similar point in a slightly different way, noting: "What should concern medieval archaeologists is not so much what people do, what kind of pots or brooches they make, what shape of houses they build, but the 'way they go about it'."[44]

Furthermore, technological choices made during pottery production do not just reflect aspects of group identity, but actually help to create and maintain such social bonds. Like riding a bicycle, playing a musical instrument, or even learning how to walk, the continual repetition of particular physio-motor habits is enacted at a non-discursive, preconscious level that becomes part of the very core of our identity.[45] In this sense, Sandy Budden and Joanna Sofaer's claim that "potters literally came into being as potters through those techniques of the body learnt through repeated bodily enactment of potting skills and their engagement with material and tools" is not mere rhetorical flourish.[46] For this reason, members of a community of practice not only perceive but also *inhabit* their world differently from other social groups who may even be otherwise (socially, politically, linguistically, or ethnically) indistinguishable. Interestingly, recent advances in neuroplasticity have given further support to this theoretical insight by showing how motor skill learning, even in adults, causes structural changes in the neural substrates of the brain.[47]

But how can we investigate communities of practice that would have existed in rural post-Roman Europe, far beyond the purview of historical sources? Fortunately, archaeologists working in various regions and periods have demonstrated that communities of practice leave discernable patterns in the material record because members of these communities tend to make the same technological choices during the production process.[48] In other words, being part of a community of practice means having the same general concept of the "proper way" to make a pot, which can be measurably distinct from nearby communities.[49] Here the concept of *chaîne opératoire*—a strategy for tracing the sequence of choices that a potter makes at each step of the production process[50]—is quite useful because it allows us to consider the entire process of creating an artifact, rather than focusing only on the finished product (like most archaeological investigations of ethnicity, which are primarily concerned with visible forms or decorations).[51] Of particular interest, given the way that most archaeologists conceptualize ethnicity as being communicated through visible decorations on an artifact, are ethnographic studies like Olivier Gosselain's work on contemporary African pottery, which have shown that visible decorations on the finished vessel actually reflected the most superficial, situational, and temporary facets of identity, while those steps along the *chaîne opératoire* requiring specialized gestures (e.g. clay selection, processing, firing, and primary forming) tended to "reflect those most rooted and enduring aspects of social identity."[52]

Pottery Technology in the Late Antique and Early Medieval Eastern Alps

The enigmatic transition from late antiquity to the early Middle Ages in the Eastern Alps provides an illustrative case study for approaching social identity (broadly defined here as "feelings of association with or attachment to someone else"[53]) through technological practice rather than ethnic categories derived from written sources. The traditional historical narrative for this period—and hence most archaeological interpretation—has focused on presumed changes among ethno-linguistic groups, despite the fact that the written sources have almost nothing to say regarding questions of group identity during this period.[54] Not long ago, the shift from the late classical to early medieval world in the Eastern Alpine region was assumed to be relatively straightforward: in the century following the collapse of Roman political authority, most of the indigenous "Romanized" population either fled or perished, leaving a vacant landscape subsequently colonized by Slavic-speaking peoples in the late sixth century.[55]

However, archaeological research in recent decades has painted a far more complex and interesting picture, as a growing number of discoveries suggest that a distinctly "Roman" way of life continued in this region into at least the seventh century.[56] The cemetery at Kranj in central Slovenia not only appears to have been in continuous use from late antiquity through the early Middle Ages, but also contains graves that are characteristic of an indigenous Romanized population as well as recent Slavic-speaking immigrants.[57] Similarly, recent excavations in the Gorenji Mokronog region of southeastern Slovenia have uncovered a sixth- to seventh-century cemetery with a small Christian chapel, suggesting the presence of a Romanized Christian population, yet the ceramic finds were typical of what is usually found at "early Slavic" sites.[58] Such discoveries suggest that, contrary to the traditional narrative, Romanized, Slavic, and Germanic peoples coexisted and interacted for several centuries in this region. They have also reopened important questions about the manner in which people in the post-Roman eastern Alps articulated and negotiated their sense of social belonging in a culturally, linguistically, and religiously diverse milieu. However, at the same time, the traditional method of using particular artifact types as evidence for the presence of certain ethno-linguistic groups (e.g. low-fired undecorated pottery = Slavic; Christian symbolism = Romanized; black burnished pottery = Lombard, etc.) is becoming increasingly difficult to sustain. In fact, as noted in Chapter 4, even the longstanding assumption that the sixth- and seventh-century populations in the southeastern Alps spoke a Slavic language is not directly supported by any archaeological or toponymical evidence.[59]

With this in mind, perhaps it is time to set aside our fixation on ethno-linguistic groups and consider what other manifestations of social identity were present during this period. Here, we can turn to one category of evidence—locally manufactured coarse-ware pottery—that has largely been ignored in studies of identity because its relatively homogeneous and undecorated nature has not proven very useful for an approach to ethnicity based on symbolic communication. However, coarse-ware pottery provides an excellent opportunity to examine aspects of group identity within the aforementioned "communities of practice" framework. The following case study set out to investigate changes in communities of practice across the late antique–early medieval transition by reconstructing the technological choices made in the manufacture of coarse-ware pottery at four settlements in the eastern Alpine region: (1) the port site of Koper on the North Adriatic coastal; (2) the upland fortified settlement of Tonovcov grad by Kobarid; (3) the small upland settlement of Tinje by Loka pri Žusmu; and (4) the upland fortified settlement at Rifnik (Map 6.1). Selecting sites with evidence of settlement during both late antiquity and the early Middle Ages (Figure 6.2) provides a window into changes in local ceramic production traditions during this poorly understood historical transition.[60]

Coarse-ware pottery from these sites was subject to compositional analyses using a combination of macroscopic fabric analysis and ceramic petrography, methods that allow us to reconstruct those critical technological choices made during the pottery production process.[61] Compositional analyses allowed for the identification of a variety of distinct fabric types at the four sites examined in this study. As noted above, each fabric type is the result of a unique combination of technological choices made during the manufacturing process: the utilization of clay sources, tempering agents, throwing techniques, and/or firing atmospheres. While it is not always possible to

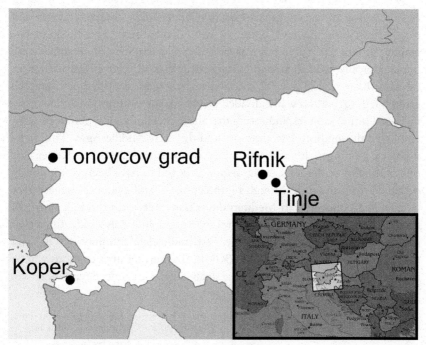

Map 6.1. Location of sites discussed in chapter.

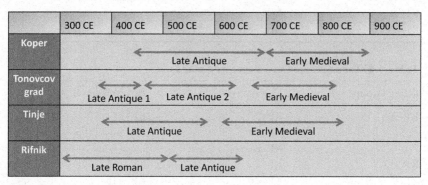

Figure 6.2. Chronology of sites discussed in chapter.

precisely identify the exact technological choices behind these differences, comparing how these fabric groups were divided between late antique and early medieval contexts indicates whether ceramic technological traditions at each site were broadly characterized by continuity or change. Overall, the results from this mineralogical analysis revealed a previously unknown degree of local variability across the Eastern Alps in terms of continuity and change in ceramic traditions that will be briefly outlined here.[62]

The site of Koper on the Adriatic coast exhibited the greatest degree of technological continuity between late antiquity and the early Middle

Ages. Twenty-three ceramic samples (twelve from late antique contexts and eleven from early medieval contexts) were divided into three broad petrographic groups. As Table 6.1 indicates, the vast majority of ceramics were mineralogically indistinguishable, suggesting that all were manufactured in the same basic way. Table 6.2 shows that the largest identified petrographic group (KP—A) was evenly divided between late antique (ten) and early medieval (nine) samples, indicating that similar technological traditions were employed during both late antiquity and the early Middle Ages. This technological homogeneity and continuity is not surprising, since Koper was one of the few settlements in the region believed to have been continuously occupied from the fifth through ninth centuries, and evidence suggests that it remained connected to Mediterranean trade networks through much of this period.[63] It should be noted that the petrographic analyses identified two additional distinct fabric styles—one restricted to late antiquity (KP–C) and the other to the early Middle Ages (KP–B), but further investigations will be necessary to determine whether these small samples are indeed representative.

Table 6.1. Fabric groups from Koper.

Group	# Samples	Quartz %	Carbonate %	Carbonate Character	Mica %
KP–A	19	1–5%	20–25%	Sparry	0–2%
KP–B	2	10%	0%	n/a	2%
KP–C	2	10%	20%	Sparry	1%

Table 6.2. Fabric groups from Koper by period.

Fabric Group	Late Antique	Early Medieval
KP–A1	KP–2	KP–21
	KP–12	KP–16
	KP–8	
KP–A2	KP–5	KP – 13
	KP – 6	KP – 15
	KP – 10	KP – 18
	KP – 9	KP – 20
	KP – 3	
KP – A3	KP – 7	KP – 14
	KP – 4	KP – 17
		KP – 23
KP – B		KP – 19
		KP – 22
KP – C	KP – 1	
	KP – 11	

Secondly, at the upland fortified settlement of Tonovcov grad, ceramic analyses revealed a similar, though not quite as extensive degree of technological continuity from late antiquity to the early Middle Ages. Here, twenty-three samples were selected for analysis (sixteen from late antique contexts and seven from early medieval contexts), and were divided into four different fabric types (see Table 6.3). Similar to Koper, the two largest fabric types, representing nearly 80% of the samples, were found in similar proportions in each period (Table 6.4). However, two distinct petrographic groups also suggest a degree of discontinuity in ceramic technological traditions, as one is only present in late antique contexts (TG – A) and the other only in early medieval contexts (TG – C).[64] The degree of technological continuity at Tonovcov grad is somewhat more surprising than at Koper, since archaeological evidence suggests at least a fifty-year abandonment of the settlement (c. 625–675 CE).[65] Nevertheless, we see that much of the pottery manufactured in the early Middle Ages followed similar technological choices to late antique traditions, suggesting broad similarities in the communities of practice during this period.

Finally, we find a markedly different situation at the upland settlement of Tinje at the eastern end of the region. Here, a total of sixteen

Table 6.3. Fabric groups from Tonovcov grad.

Group	# Samples	Quartz %	Carbonate %	Mica %
TG – A	3	0–<1%	20–25%	0–1%
TG – B	4	2–5%	0–5%	0–2%
TG – C	2	8%	20%	<1–1%
TG – D	14	2–6%	15–30%	1–3%

Table 6.4. Fabric groups from Tonovcov grad by period.

Group	Late Antique 1	Late Antique 1/2	Late Antique 2	Early Medieval
TG – A	TG – 14	TG – 18	TG – 15	
TG – B		TG – 21		TG – 11
		TG – 16		TG – 17
TG – C				TG – 12
				TG – 13
TG – D1	TG – 23	TG – 1	TG – 2	
TG – D2	TG – 7		TG – 9	TG – 20
	TG – 19		TG – 8	TG – 10
TG – D3		TG – 22	TG – 6	TG – 5
			TG – 3	
			TG – 4	

samples (six from late antique houses and ten from early medieval houses) were divided into four fabric groups, each of which was restricted to a single chronological period. In other words, as Table 6.6 shows, three of the fabric types were uniquely early medieval, while one was uniquely late antique. These results suggest that, unlike Koper and Tonovcov grad, ceramic technological traditions at Tinje demonstrated significant discontinuity across this transition. It is also interesting to note that this coarse-ware pottery does not exhibit significant decorative differences between the two contexts.[66] Moreover, analyses of ten additional ceramic samples at the late Roman fortified settlement of Rifnik (only a few kilometers from Tinje) reveal strong parallels with the late antique, but not early medieval material at Tinje, further indicating a rupture in ceramic traditions in this part of the Eastern Alps between late antiquity and the early Middle Ages (Table 6.7).

Table 6.5. Fabric groups from Tinje.

Group	# Samples	Quartz %	Carbonate %	Carbonate Character	Mica %
TI – A	3	10–15%	0%	n/a	2–6%
TI – B	4	10–15%	5–10%	Micritic/rounded	<1–2%
TI – C	5	5–6%	10–15%	Sparry/angular	1–2%
TI – D	4	6–8%	15–30%	Sparry/angular	2–4%

Table 6.6. Fabric groups from Tinje by period.

Group	Late Antique (House 4)	Early Medieval (House 5)
TI – A		TI – 5
		TI – 6
		TI – 7
TI – B		TI – 1
		TI – 2
		TI – 3
		TI – 16
TI – C	TI – 8	
	TI – 9	
	TI – 10	
	TI – 11	
	TI – 13	
TI – D	TI – 12	TI – 4
		TI – 14
		TI – 15

Table 6.7. Fabric groups from Rifnik.

Group	# Samples	Quartz %	Carbonate %	Carbonate Character	Mica %
RF – A	4	5–6%	20–30%	Sparry/mixed	1–3%
RF – B	2	6–9%	10–15%	Sparry/rounded	1%
RF – C	4	3–4%	20%	Sparry/mixed	1–2%

Technological Choices and Social Identity: Some Preliminary Conclusions

Compositional methods not only allow us to identify change and continuity in ceramic traditions, but also provide some insight into which technological choices are causing such differences. However, it is important to note that particular choices along the *chaîne opératoire* are not always easy to discern, due to the palimpsesting nature of the ceramic manufacturing process; in other words, later choices (e.g. firing) can erase evidence of previous ones (e.g. tempering). Nevertheless, educated guesses about technological choices are worth pursuing, and reveal some interesting patterns across the region.

When examining the significant technological changes evident at Tinje, for example, the most conspicuous difference between late antique and early medieval ceramics is the quantity of calcium carbonate (limestone) present. All the late antique fabrics at Tinje and nearby Rifnik contain significant quantities of limestone inclusions, mirroring the underlying geology of this region.[67] However, limestone is noticeably absent from early medieval samples, which suggests that they are being purposefully removed during the production process. Moreover, the early medieval ceramics contain markedly higher proportions of coarse quartz, which possibly indicates the addition of sand as a tempering agent during the production process, or a shift in the clay sources being used for the coarse-ware pottery. Interestingly, this general pattern of higher proportions of quartz in early medieval ceramics than their late antique counterparts seems to be generally true across the region, although whether this is a meaningful pattern or merely coincidence remains unclear.

What do these shifts in technological choices during this tumultuous sociopolitical transition suggest about social identity in the post-Roman Eastern Alps? As outlined above, the results from the compositional analyses reveal a pattern of significant local variability in which ceramic technological traditions underwent a major shift at Tinje in the eastern portion of the study region, a minor shift at Tonovcov grad in the northwest, and almost no changes on the coastal site of Koper. At Tinje, in particular, we have strong evidence that the *chaîne opératoire* underwent significant changes from the late antique to early medieval phases, suggesting that social identity related to the community of practice would also have undergone significant shifts. In other words, this reveals a meaningful change in the habituated, embodied practices and social knowledge of the "communities of practice" responsible for the production of this material. These technological shifts represent a change in the way that potters at Tinje inhabited their worlds. In contrast, at Koper and Tonovcov grad there appears to be much stronger continuity in technological choices, reflecting the persistence of ceramic traditions at this site over the course of many generations.

One is tempted to speculate about whether such technological shifts in ceramic manufacture indicate the presence of a new ethno-linguistic population at sites like Tinje; that is, were these new pottery traditions brought by Slavic-speaking populations? Although this possibility cannot be discounted, the whole point of the alternative approach to early medieval group identity outlined above is to avoid always falling back on such "ethnic" interpretations—admittedly, not an easy task due to the power that the written sources hold over our historical imaginations. Ethno-archaeological work has shown that changes in communities of practice do not necessarily overlap with ethnic, linguistic, political, religious, or other dimensions of social identity. Although this localized expression of identity remained beyond the purview of the written sources, this should not allow us to assume that it was unimportant. One of the main challenges of this new approach is to figure out how to even "talk" about these identities, since (unlike ethnicity) we do not have an existing template of categories to draw upon.

At the same time, we must avoid the urge to interpret changes in coarse-ware pottery traditions as reflecting only shifts in technical, material, or environmental variables (having nothing to do with identity). The relational framework sketched above demonstrates why identity can no longer be understood simply as something "added on" after all other factors in the production process (i.e. resource acquisition, technological constraints, performance characteristics) have been addressed. To reiterate, social identity is deeply entangled at every step of the operational chain, and not only in the formal or design properties of the pottery.[68]

To be sure, this case study only begins to scratch the surface of what an investigation into early medieval communities of practice might yield. Future research should not only expand the dataset of coarse-ware pottery— including greater sample sizes and additional sites—but also incorporate other types of technologies (e.g. metalworking, glass production, house construction, etc.), which, if mapped on to one another, would generate a far more detailed and nuanced picture of local expressions of identity than would be possible by looking at ethnicity alone.

Notes

1. Portions of this chapter previously appeared in K. Patrick Fazioli, "Rethinking Ethnicity in Early Medieval Archaeology: Social Identity, Technological Choice, and Communities of Practice," in *From West to East: Current Approaches to Medieval Archaeology*, ed. Scott Stull (Newcastle upon Tyne, 2014).

2. Stephen Mitchell, *A History of the Later Roman Empire, AD 284–641: The Transformation of the Ancient World* (Malden, MA, 2007), 53.

3. Walter Goffart, *Barbarian Tides: The Migration Age and the Later Roman Empire* (Philadelphia, PA, 2006).

4. Friedrich Lotter, *Severinus von Noricum, Legende und historische Wirklichkeit: Unters. zur Phase d. Übergangs von spätantiken zu mittelalterl. Denk- u. Lebensformen* (Stuttgart, 1976).

5. Jonathan Marks, *What It Means to Be 98% Chimpanzee: Apes, People, and Their Genes* (Berkeley, CA, 2003), 51–71.

6. See the discussion of *Kulturkreislehre* in Chapter 4.

7. Jones, "The Image of the Barbarian in Medieval Europe"; Hans-Werner Goetz, "*Gens*. Terminology and Perception of the 'Germanic' Peoples from Late Antiquity to the Early Middle Ages," in *The Construction of Communities in the Early Middle Ages: Texts, Resources, and Artefacts*, ed. R. Corrandini, M. Diesenberger, and H. Reimitz (Leiden, 2003).

8. Franz Boas, "New Evidence in Regard to the Instability of Human Types," *Proceedings of the National Academy of Sciences of the United States of America* 2 (1916).

9. Michael Moerman, "Ethnic Identification in a Complex Civilization: Who Are the Lue?," *American Anthropologist* 67 (1965).

10. Fredrik Barth, *Ethnic Groups and Boundaries. The Social Organization of Culture Difference. (Results of a Symposium Held at the University of Bergen, 23rd to 26th February 1967.)* (Bergen, 1969).

11. Thomas Hylland Eriksen, *Ethnicity and Nationalism: Anthropological Perspectives* (London, 2010); Marcus Banks, *Ethnicity: Anthropological Constructions* (New York, 1996); Richard Jenkins, *Social Identity* (New York, 2008).

12. Alexander Callander Murray, "Reinhard Wenskus on 'Ethnogenesis', Ethnicity, and the Origin of the Franks," in *On Barbarian Identity: Critical Approaches to Ethnicity in the Early Middle Ages*, ed. A. Gillett (Turnhout, Belguim, 2002).

13. Reinhard Wenskus, *Stammesbildung und Verfassung; das Werden der frühmittelalterlichen Gentes* (Cologne, 1961).

14. Walter Pohl, "Telling the Difference: Signs of Ethnic Identity," in *Strategies of Distinction: The Construction of the Ethnic Communities, 300–800*, ed. Walter Pohl and Helmut Reimitz (Leiden, 1998), 67; see also Walter Pohl, "Conceptions of Ethnicity in Early Medieval Studies," *Archaeologia Polona* 29 (1991); Herwig Wolfram, *History of the Goths* (Berkeley, 1988); Patrick J. Geary, "Ethnic Identity as a Situational Construct in the Early Middle Ages," *Mitteilungen der Anthropologischen Gesellschaft in Wien* 113 (1983).

15. Hans J. Hummer, "The Fluidity of Barbarian Identity: The Ethnogenesis of Alemanni and Suebi, AD 200–500," *Early Medieval Europe* 7 (1998); Peter Hoppenbrouwers, "Such Stuff as People Are Made On: Ethnogenesis and the Construction of Nationhood in Medieval Europe," *The Medieval History Journal* 9 (2006); Ildar H. Garipzanov, Patrick J. Geary, and P. Urbanczyk, eds, *Franks, Northmen, and Slavs: Identities and State Formation in Early Medieval Europe* (Turnhout, Belgium, 2008).

16. Goffart, *Barbarian Tides*; Patrick Amory, *People and Identity in Ostrogothic Italy, 489–554* (Cambridge, 1997).

17. Andrew Gillett, "Ethnogenesis: A Contested Model of Early Medieval Europe," *History Compass* 4 (2006).

18. Frank Siegmund, "Social Structure and Relations," in *Franks and Alamanni in the Merovingian Period: An Ethnographic Perspective*, ed. I. N. Wood (Rochester, NY, 1998), 186–87.

19. Michel Kazanski and Patrick Périn, "Foreign Objects in the Merovingian Cemeteries of Northern Gaul," in *Foreigners in Early Medieval Europe: Thirteen International Studies on Early Medieval Mobility*, ed. D. Quast (Mainz, 2009), 151.

20. For another defense of this approach, see Volker Bierbrauer, "Zur ethnischen Interpretation in der frühgeschichtlichen Archäologie," in *Die Suche nach den Ursprüngen. Von der Bedeutung des frühen Mittelalters*, ed. W. Pohl (Vienna, 2004).

21. Stephen Shennan, *Archaeological Approaches to Cultural Identity* (Boston, 1989); Sian Jones, *The Archaeology of Ethnicity: Constructing Identities in the Past and Present* (New York, 1997).

22. Bonnie Effros, "Dressing Conservatively: Women's Brooches as Markers of Ethnic Identity?" in *Gender in the Early Medieval World: East and West, 300–900*, ed. L. Brubaker and J. Smith (Cambridge, 2004); Guy Halsall, "Ethnicity and Early Medieval Cemeteries," *Arqueología y Territorio Medieval* 18 (2011).

23. Amory, *People and Identity in Ostrogothic Italy*, 13; Peter Heather, "Ethnicity, Group Identity, and Social Status in the Migration Period," in Garipzanov, Geary and Urbanczyk, *Franks, Northmen, and Slavs*, 37; Pohl, "Conceptions of Ethnicity in Early Medieval Studies"; Goetz, "*Gens*. Terminology and Perception."

24. Examples of this "interpretive" approach include Søren M. Sindbæk, "A Magyar Occurrence: Process, Practice and Ethnicity between Europe and the Steppes," *Acta Archaeologica* 70 (1999); Falko Daim, "Archaeology, Ethnicity and the Structures of Identification: The Example of the Avars, Carantanians and Moravians in the Eighth Century," in *Strategies of Distinction: The Construction of Ethnic Communities, 300–800*, ed. W. Pohl and H. Reimitz (Boston, 1998); Guy Halsall, "Burial, Ritual and Merovingan Society," in *The Community, the Family, and the Saint: Patterns of Power in Early Medieval Europe*, ed. J. Hall and M. Swan (Turnhout, 1998); John Moreland, *Archaeology, Theory, and the Middle Ages* (London, 2011); and I. Mirnik Prezelj, "Re-thinking Ethnicity in Archaeology," in *Slovenija in sosednje dezele med antiko in karolinsko dobo: zacetki slovenske etnogeneze = Slowenien und die Nachbarländer zwischen Antike und karolingischer Epoche: Anfänge der slowenischen Ethnogenese*, ed. R. Bratož (Ljubljana, 2000).

25. Florin Curta, "Some Remarks on Ethnicity in Medieval Archaeology," *Early Medieval Europe* 15 (2007): 179–80.

26. Daim, "Archaeology, Ethnicity and the Structures of Identification," 84, 73.

27. Dick Harrison, "Dark Age Migrations and Subjective Ethnicity: The Example of the Lombards," *Scandia: Tidskrift för historisk forskning* 57 (1991); Walter Pohl and Helmut Reimitz, eds. *Strategies of Distinction: The Construction of Ethnic Communities, 300–800* (Boston, 1998); Walter Pohl, "Archaeology of Identity: Introduction," in *Archaeology of Identity*, ed. W. Pohl and M. Mehofer (Vienna, 2010).

28. Sebastian Brather, "Ethnic Identities as Constructions of Archaeology: The Case of the *Alamanni*," in Gillett, *On Barbarian Identity*, 172 (emphasis in original).

29. See Barth, *Ethnic Groups and Boundaries*, 14; Polly Wiessner, "Style and Social Information in Kalahari San Projectile Points," *American Antiquity* 48 (1983): 270; Stephen Chrisomalis and Bruce Trigger, "Reconstructing Prehistoric Ethnicity: Problems and Possibilities," in *A Passion for the Past, Papers in Honour of James F. Pendergast*, ed. J.V. Wright and J.-L. Pilon (Gatineau, 2003).

30. Sebastian Brather, *Ethnische Interpretationen in der frühgeschichtlichen Archäologie: Geschichte, Grundlagen und Alternativen* (Berlin, 2004); Heather, "Ethnicity, Group Identity, and Social Status"; Halsall, "Ethnicity and Early Medieval Cemeteries."

31. Curta, "Some Remarks on Ethnicity"; Danijel Dzino, *Becoming Slav, Becoming Croat: Identity Transformations in Post-Roman and Early Medieval Dalmatia* (Boston, 2010).

32. It should be noted that the problem of a lack of an agreed-upon definition of ethnicity is not unique to archaeology; see Ronald Cohen, "Ethnicity: Problem and Focus in Anthropology," *Annual Review of Anthropology* 7 (1978); Banks, *Ethnicity*, 4.

33. Jones, *The Archaeology of Ethnicity*, xiii.

34. Christopher Hawkes, "Archaeological Theory and Method: Some Suggestions from the Old World," *American Anthropologist* 56 (1954).

35. Robin Boast, "A Small Company of Actors," *Journal of Material Culture* 2 (1997); Tim Ingold, "Making Culture and Weaving the World," in *Matter, Materiality, and Modern Culture*, ed. P. Graves-Brown (London, 2000); Chantal Conneller, *An Archaeology of Materials: Substantial Transformations in Early Prehistoric Europe* (New York, 2011).

36. Bruno Latour, "The Powers of Association," in *Power, Action, and Belief: A New Sociology of Knowledge?*, ed. J. Law (London, 1986).

37. Bruno Latour and S. C. Strum, "Human Social Origins: Oh Please, Tell Us Another Story," *Journal of Social and Biological Systems* 9 (1986).

38. Naofše Mac Sweeney, "Beyond Ethnicity: The Overlooked Diversity of Group Identities," *Journal of Mediterranean Archaeology* 22 (2009).

39. Heather, "Ethnicity, Group Identity, and Social Status," 43, 44.

40. Sauro Gelichi, "Ceramic Production and Distribution in the Early Medieval Mediterranean Basin Seventh to Tenth Centuries AD between Town and Countryside," in *Towns and Their Territories between Late Antiquity and the Early Middle Ages*, ed. G. P. Brogiolo, N. Gauthier, and N. Christie (Boston, 2000); Hajnalka Herold, "Die awarenzeitliche Keramik von Zillingtal im Burgenland (Österreich) – ein archäologische und naturwissenschaftliche Analyse," *Bodendenkmalpflege in Mecklenburg-Vorpommern* 50 (2002); Sabine Ladstätter, "Zur Charakterisierung des spätantiken Keramikspektrums im Ostalpenraum," in *Frühe Kirchen im östlichen Alpengebiet*, ed. H.R. Sennhauser (Munich, 2003); Zvezdana Modrijan, "Keramika," in *Poznoantična utrjena naselbina Tonovcov grad pri Kobaridu: najdbe*, ed. Z. Modrijan and T. Milavec (Ljubljana, 2011).

41. See especially Michael Dietler and Ingrid Herbich, "*Habitus*, Techniques, Style: An Integrated Approach to the Social Understanding of Material Culture and Boundaries," in *The Archaeology of Social Boundaries*, ed. M.T. Stark (Washington, DC, 1998); Miriam T. Stark, Ronald L. Bishop, and Elizabeth Miksa, "Ceramic Technology and Social Boundaries: Cultural Practices in Kalinga Clay Selection and Use," *Journal of Archaeological Method and Theory* 7 (2000); Bill Sillar, "Dung by Preference: The Choice of Fuel as an Example of How Andean Pottery Production is Embedded within Wider Technical, Social, and Economic Practices," *Archaeometry* 42 (2000); and A. Livingstone Smith, "Processing Clay for Pottery in Northern Cameroon: Social and Technical Requirements," *Archaeometry* 42 (2000).

42. The foundational text for this concept is Jean Lave and Etienne Wenger, *Situated Learning: Legitimate Peripheral Participation* (New York, 1991); see also Susan Squires and Michael L. Van De Vanter, "Communities of Practice," in *A Companion to Organizational Anthropology*, ed. D.D. Caulkins and A.T. Jordan (New York, 2012); Stephen Fox, "Communities of Practice, Foucault and Actor-Network Theory," *Journal of Management Studies* 37 (2000).

43. Ingold, "Making Culture and Weaving the World."

44. Curta, "Some Remarks on Ethnicity," 177; cf. P. Graves-Brown, "'All Things Bright and Beautiful?' Species, Ethnicity and Cultural Dynamics," in *Cultural Identity and Archaeology: The Construction of European Communities* (London; New York, 1996); Stephanie Wynne-Jones, "It's What You Do With It That Counts: Performed Identities in the East African Coastal Landscape," *Journal of Social Archaeology* 7 (2007).

45. Marcel Mauss, "Les techniques du corps," *Journal de Psychologie* 32 (1935); Jean-Pierre Warnier, "A Praxeological Approach to Subjectivation in a Material World," *Journal of Material Culture* 6 (2001).

46. Sandy Budden and Joanna Sofaer, "Non-discursive Knowledge and the Construction of Identity Potters, Potting and Performance at the Bronze Age Tell of Százhalombatta, Hungary," *Cambridge Archaeological Journal* 19 (2009): 216.

47. Lambros Malafouris, "The Brain–Artefact Interface (BAI): A Challenge for Archaeology and Cultural Neuroscience," *Social Cognitive and Affective Neuroscience* 5 (2010); Eran Dayan and Leonardo G. Cohen, "Neuroplasticity Subserving Motor Skill Learning," *Neuron* 72 (2011).

48. For example, Jill Minar has demonstrated how particular styles of textile production in the prehistoric southeast US (such as the "S" and "Z" twist direction) were better explained by these communities of practice than by ethnicity or other functional characteristics. C. Jill Minar, "Motor Skills and the Learning Process: The Conservation of Cordage Final Twist Direction in Communities of Practice," *Journal of Anthropological Research* 57 (2001); see also Kenneth Sassaman and Wictoria Rudolphi, "Communities of Practice in the Early Pottery Traditions of the American Southeast," *Journal of Anthropological Research* 57 (2001); Sarah Peelo, "Pottery-Making in Spanish California: Creating Multi-Scalar Social Identity through Daily Practice," *American Antiquity* 76 (2011).

49. Sander van der Leeuw, "Giving the Potter a Choice: Conceptual Aspects of Pottery Techniques," in *Technological Choices: Transformation in Material Cultures since the Neolithic*, ed. P. Lemmonier (London, 1993).

50. Marcia-Anne Dobres, "Technology's Links and Chaînes: The Processual Unfolding of Technique and Technician," in *The Social Dynamics of Technology: Practice, Politics, and World Views*, ed. M.A. Dobres and C.R. Hoffman (Washington, DC, 1999). It is also worth noting that a number of scholars have examined questions of technological choice in medieval contexts, including Louise Joyner, "Cooking Pots as Indicators of Cultural Change: A Petrographic Study of Byzantine and Frankish Cooking Wares from Corinth," *Hesperia* 76 (2007); Hajnalka Herold, "Materielle Kultur – technologische Traditionen – Identität: Untersuchungen zur Archäologie des Frühmittelalters in Niederösterreich," *Zeitschrift für Archäologie des Mittelalters* 37 (2009); Mats Roslund, *Guests in the House: Cultural Transmission between Slavs and Scandinavians 900 to 1300 AD* (Leiden; Boston, 2007); and Asbjørn Engevik, *Bucket-Shaped Pots: Style, Chronology and Regional Diversity in Norway in the Late Roman and Migration Periods* (Oxford, 2008).

51. The *chaîne opératoire* of pottery production is complex, and generally includes: (1) obtaining of raw materials (clays and other aplastic materials used as "temper"); (2) preparing these materials (removing coarse particles from the raw materials through sieving, levigation, winnowing, etc.); (3) preparing the body (mixing clays, adding water and/or temper); (4) forming the vessel (by hand coiling or slab building, turning on a slow or fast potter's wheel); (5) adding surface treatments (glazes, slips, decorations, etc.); (6) firing the vessel either in an open pit or a kiln. See Owen S. Rye, *Pottery Technology: Principles and Reconstruction* (Washington, DC, 1981).

52. Olivier Gosselain, "Materializing Identities: An African Perspective," *Journal of Archaeological Method and Theory* 7 (2000): 193.

53. Jenkins, *Social Identity*.

54. Curta, "The Early Slavs in the Northern and Eastern Adriatic Region," 322.

55. Allen Leeper, *A History of Medieval Austria* (London, 1941); Kos, *Izbrano delo*.

56. Tina Milavec, "A Review of Research into the Early Middle Ages in Slovenia," *Arheološki vestnik* 60 (2009).

57. Milan Sagadin, *Kranj–Križišče Iskra (nekropola iz časov preseljevanja ljudstev in staroslovanskega obdobja) = Kranj–Iskra Crossroads: A Cemetery from the Migration Period and the Early Slavic Period* (Ljubljana, 1987), 135.

58. Uroš Bavec, "Predhodno poročilo o poznoantičnem grobišču na Vrajku v Gorenjem Mokronogu (Preliminary Report on the Late Roman Cemetery at Vrajk in Gorenji

Mokronog)," *Arheološki vestnik* 54 (2003). Similar situations are also evident at the Eastern Alpine sites of Bled-Pristava, Komenda, and Ptuj.

59. Curta, "The Early Slavs in the Northern and Eastern Adriatic Region," 322.

60. It should be noted that while no early medieval phase has been confidently identified at Rifnik, it was included in the study as a useful comparison with nearby Tinje.

61. The first step was to create broad fabric groups of the coarse-ware assemblages at each site using macroscopic fabric analysis, a method that systematically characterizes ceramic fabrics with the aid of a 30x hand lens in terms of surface/core color, hardness, texture, and surface treatments. This also allows the fabric groups to be correlated with other stylistic variables such as form and decoration (in most cases, there were not strong correlations between particular fabric styles and either of these stylistic variables). Once broad fabric groups were established, representative samples from each were selected for petrographic analysis, which examines ceramic fabric under a polarizing light microscope. This requires the creation of a ceramic "thin section," in which a small sample (c. 2 x 3 cm) of a ceramic vessel is ground to 0.03 mm in thickness and mounted on a glass slide. Three major components of the ceramic fabric (the matrix, non-plastic inclusions, and voids) can then be assessed microscopically. The "matrix" (or groundmass) is the very fine-grained materials (<30 μm fraction) in which coarser particles are embedded. It can be characterized by fracture, color, and birefringence (i.e. anisotropic or optically active). The term "non-plastic inclusion" is used to describe all coarser rock, mineral, and organic materials present in the matrix, whether naturally present or artificially added (i.e. temper). Most mineral inclusions can be identified through a range of optical properties (e.g. shape, color, relief, cleavage, pleochroism, birefringence, extinction, opacity, etc.) under plane- and cross-polarized light. These non-plastic inclusions can also be described in terms of abundance, roundedness, size, orientation, sortedness, and other meaningful qualities. Finally, the term "void" refers to pores in the matrix that once held non-plastic inclusions prior to firing; these can also be described in terms of their abundance and shape. The methodology used here broadly follows the one outlined by Robert B. Mason, in *Shine Like the Sun: Lustre-Painted and Associated Pottery from the Medieval Middle East* (Costa Mesa, CA, 2004).

62. For full results of this study, see K. Patrick Fazioli, "Technology, Identity, and Time: Studies in the Archaeology and Historical Anthropology of the Eastern Alpine Region from Late Antiquity to the Early Middle Ages" (Graz, 2013); K. Patrick Fazioli, "Ceramic Technology in the Southeastern Alpine Region in Late Antiquity and the Early Middle Ages: Results of Macroscopic and Microscopic Analyses," *Arheološki vestnik* 63 (2012).

63. Radovan Cunja, *Poznorimski in zgodnjesrednjeveški Koper (Arheološko izkopavanje na bivšem Kapucinskem vrtu v letih 1986-1987 v luči drobnih najdb 5. do 9. stoletja). Capodistria Tardoromana e Altomedievale (Lo scavo archeologico nell'ex orto dei Cappuccini negli anni 1986-1987 alla luce dei reperti dal V al IX secolo)* (Koper, 1996).

64. These results broadly concur with a more comprehensive macroscopic analysis previously undertaken with similar material by Modrijan, "Keramika."

65. Slavko Ciglenečki, Zvezdana Modrijan, and Tina Milavec, eds, *Tonovcov grad. Naselbinski ostanki in interpretacija/Tonovcov grad. Settlement Remains and Interpretation* (Ljubljana, 2011).

66. Slavko Ciglenečki, *Tinje nad Loko pri Žusmu. Poznoantična in zgodnjesrednjeveška naselbina* (Ljubljana, 2000).

67. Pero Mioč, "Outline of the Geology of Slovenia," *Acta Geologica Hungarica* 46 (2003).

68. Bill Sillar and M.S. Tite, "The Challenge of 'Technological Choices' for Materials Science Approaches in Archaeology," *Archaeometry* 42 (2000).

CHAPTER 7

Christianization, Syncretism, and an Archaeology of Time

Even at the moment that it is evolving, society returns to its past. It enframes the new elements that it pushes to the forefront in a totality of remembrances, traditions, and familiar ideas.
—Maurice Halbwachs, *On Collective Memory*

Christianizing the Late Roman and Early Medieval Eastern Alps

The fourth century was a critical turning point in the history of Christianity. In less than one hundred years, this small, socially marginalized sect became the official—and only lawful—religion of the most powerful state in the Western world.[1] The key moment for the bourgeoning Christian movement came in 312 CE, when the Roman Emperor Constantine I credited their God with his victory over Maxentius at the Battle of Milvian Bridge. The following year Constantine and his eastern counterpart Licinius issued the Edict of Milan, ending the state persecution of Christianity and granting toleration to all religions in the empire. Even more significantly, Constantine's embrace of this new faith would be followed by all his successors, with the sole exception of the brief rule of Julian the Apostate.

By the late fourth century, Christian emperors like Theodosius I began to enact increasingly exclusivist religious policies meant to discourage the practice of traditional Roman polytheism. Pagan rituals and institutions were systematically outlawed, public temples allowed to fall into disrepair, and even the Altar of Victory was removed from the Senate.[2] Over the next half-century the rapid spread of Christianity radically transformed the religious topography of the Roman Empire.[3] In the Eastern Alpine region, changes in the sacred landscape are evident in the widespread abandonment of pagan temples and appearance of Christian architecture and artifacts.[4]

Yet just as Christianity was rising to social and political prominence, the Roman Empire was rapidly hurtling toward an existential crisis. Less than one hundred years after Christianity became the state religion, a combination of prolonged civil strife and external military pressures caused the western half of the empire to disintegrate into a patchwork of "barbarian" kingdoms. Like many of the former imperial provinces, the once prosperous and densely populated lowlands of the Eastern Alps were largely abandoned in the fifth and sixth centuries, with the remnants of "Romanized" Christian communities fleeing to more easily defensible locations in the uplands or along the Mediterranean coast.[5]

Greater stability returned to the region only in the late sixth century, when Slavic-speaking groups from the east began to settle the Alpine river valleys. During the seventh century, these new communities, who were not yet Christian, enjoyed a degree of political autonomy from the Germanic kingdoms in the west and the Avar and Byzantine empires to the east. Christianity only returned to the Eastern Alps in the middle of the eighth century, when the local Slavic nobility pledged their fealty to Bavarian dukes in exchange for military assistance against the Avars. This political submission was soon accompanied by missionary activity from the Archbishopric of Salzburg.[6] As part of this agreement, the Slavic Duke Borut of Carantania sent his son and nephew as hostages to the court of the Agilolfing Duke Odilo, where they converted to Christianity.

While early missionary activity was not well received by the local pagan communities in the Eastern Alps, their rebellion was brutally crushed by Duke Tassilo in 772 CE. Although the burning of St. Maximilian's Church in Bischofshofen (Austria) in 820 CE points to continued pockets of resistance, efforts at Christianization proved more effective in the ninth century, as the majority of Slavic peasants followed their nobility in embracing the new faith.[7] It is also during this period that Christian symbols became more widespread in burials throughout the region.[8] Although the Eastern Alps continued to be a site of contestation between the Archbishopric in Salzburg, the Patriarchate of Aquileia, and the Slavonic Byzantine Church, by the end of the early Middle Ages it had become fully absorbed into European Christendom.

Challenges to Studying Christianization

The above narrative of Christianization in the Eastern Alpine region during the first millennium CE is not unlike the story told about the rise of Christianity in other parts of Western Europe, with distinct waves of conversion in the late Roman period and early Middle Ages. Initial missionary efforts tended to focus on the local elites, who often faced powerful political, military, and/or social pressures to adopt this new faith. Once the nobility were converted, Christianity's subsequent spread among the broader population was essentially a *fait accompli* (notwithstanding a few stubborn pockets of resistance). Yet even if this narrative is accurate in broad scope, it proves disappointingly incomplete for understanding how and why Christianity proved so effective at replacing indigenous pre-Christian religions.

Part of the problem is the fragmented and one-sided nature of the evidence concerning ancient and medieval Christianization. Since most written sources defending or promoting traditional polytheism during the later Roman Empire were systematically destroyed by zealous Christians, the extant historical record from that period sheds little light on what was surely a lively and fascinating theological debate. The relative dearth of "pro-pagan" sources, so to speak, has subtly pushed many historians of Christianity to uncritically accept the polemics of the victors.[9] Turning to the early Middle Ages, reliable accounts of European paganism are even rarer, since our knowledge of these practices comes almost exclusively from church documents with little interest in providing objective accounts of them.[10] This makes it very difficult not only to reconstruct pre-Christian European religions in any detail, but also to truly understand how these pagan communities perceived this new ideology and what factors contributed to their eventual conversion.

Archaeological research can provide an important complement to the fragmented written sources in tracing the spread of Christianity during the first millennium CE, but the material record comes with its own set of ambiguities and limitations. Many elements of religious belief and ritual practice leave no lasting impression in the archaeological record, and even recoverable traces have proven notoriously difficult to interpret. Even a seemingly straightforward task like distinguishing pagan from Christian graves—through burial practices, cremation vs. inhumation, body orientation, artifacts, etc.—has been shown to be quite problematic.[11] Moreover, scholars remain divided over whether any early medieval "pagan" structures have been credibly identified in East Central Europe.[12]

Yet, even putting aside the inherent limitations of the historical and archaeological evidence, our understanding of the spread of early

Christianity has been hindered by the very concept of "Christianization." That is to say, insufficient theoretical attention has been paid to the actual mechanism by which Christianity was disseminated in late antiquity and the early Middle Ages, not just among the nobility, but also among the broader population. The question is a deceivingly simple one: how do we explain Christianity's remarkable success in the Roman, Germanic, Slavic, and Celtic worlds? Surprisingly, many studies of early Christianity do not explicitly address this question, and those hypotheses that are offered tend to be frustratingly vague. For example, many early church historians credited Christianity's rise on the intrinsic appeal of its message, the charisma of its early proselytizers, or the role of the caregiving institutions (hospitals, orphanages, leprosaria, etc.) that it admirably pioneered.[13] While such factors could indeed have played a role, to explain Christianity's success primarily by its self-evident "superiority" to other religions not only engages in facile *post hoc* reasoning, but is undermined by sociological research showing that most conversions are not a direct response to religious teachings, but instead tend to be "a matter of aligning their religiousness with that of their friends, relatives, and associates, who have preceded them into the faith."[14] Simply put, explaining the spread of Christianity as the sum total of innumerable individual spiritual epiphanies is analytically insufficient.

But if conversion is not just a matter of personal spirituality, what else is going on? More recently, scholars have focused on the role of political, economic, military, and other sociocultural factors in the rise of Christianity. For example, conversion of the political elite may have reflected a strategically savvy decision—perhaps cementing a key alliance or consolidating political support—or even been a *quid pro quo* in return for perceived supernatural intervention in an important military victory (like Constantine after Milvian Bridge or Clovis after Tolbiac). In a similar way, the subsequent conversion of the "masses" could be framed as the most logical choice for anyone seeking social advancement or avoiding marginalization. But while there is no question that, in some cases, such *realpolitik* factors indeed facilitated the spread of Christianity, this "rational choice" explanatory framework tends to downplay the role that genuine theological or spiritual issues played in this process. As the British archaeologist William Kilbride has pointed out:

> If Christianity was only ever a veneer, then the lack of mechanisms for its replication and dissemination present us with little real problem. If, however unfashionably, we think that at some point at least someone in Europe might have been Christian, or that someone might have made that claim, then we are supposed to believe that the mechanisms that performed this stunt existed entirely outwith the religious frame.[15]

Syncretism and Christianity as a "Full Service" Religion

Both of these standard explanations for Christianity's incredible success are theoretically problematic: traditional church histories have often ignored the role of social or political factors in the spread of Christianity, while those more recent historians who reduce religious conversion to other factors too readily dismiss the possibility that spirituality could actually have mattered in such decisions. Despite coming from opposite perspectives, what these two positions have in common is that neither takes seriously enough the psychological and emotional commitment that European "pagans" would have had to their own beliefs and practices.

Therefore, in order to develop a framework that can account for the significance of religious belief in the lives of pre-Christian peoples, while also positing a plausible mechanism for the rapid spread of Christianity, we must reimagine the process of Christianization from the wholesale replacement of one cosmology by another to the *syncretic blending* of pagan and Christian beliefs and practices into something new and distinct. The French sociologist Maurice Halbwachs's groundbreaking work, penned over a century ago, offers a useful starting point for this alternative approach. Halbwachs argued that socio-religious changes must always be framed within a group's perceptions of its past—what he famously termed the "collective memory"—writing:

> Above all when a society transforms its religion, it advances somewhat into unknown territory … Society is aware that the new religion is not an absolute beginning. The society wishes to adopt these larger and deeper beliefs without entirely rupturing the framework of notions in which it has matured up until this point. That is why at the same time that society projects into its past conceptions that were recently elaborated, it is also intent on incorporating into the new religion elements of old cults that are assimilable into a new framework. Society must persuade its members that they already carry these beliefs within themselves at least partially, or even that they will recover beliefs which had been rejected some time ago.[16]

While the context of this passage is how early Christianity portrayed itself as a continuation of the Hebraic traditions, it applies equally well to its later encounter with Roman, Germanic, Celtic, and Slavic polytheism. In order to understand how Christianity was able to so effectively take hold within a diverse range of pagan societies in late antiquity and the early Middle Ages, we must consider the ways in which it was able to root itself in a community's day-to-day routines and experiences.

As Christianity rapidly spread across the Roman Empire in the fourth century, appropriation became an increasingly necessary strategy for conversion. The writings of early bishops reveal that many newly baptized Christians during this period were skeptical that an omnipotent and omnipresent God could possibly be concerned with the minutiae of their everyday lives. So while pagans could call upon a range of supernatural intercessors to help with daily challenges, Christians had not yet developed their own "special language of gestures and symbols in which to express their feelings or their wishes to, or regarding, the divine."[17] Simply put, who could Christians call upon if a family member fell ill, or to ask for a bountiful harvest, or to petition during personal crises? Similar concerns would be expressed as Christianity encountered the indigenous polytheistic religions of the Celtic, Germanic, and Slavic worlds.[18] Christianity's success was heavily dependent on its ability to become what historian Ramsay MacMullen has termed a "full service religion" that could effectively attend to the psychological and emotional needs of its adherents.[19]

This goal was most effectively accomplished by absorbing, borrowing, and transforming elements of pagan and polytheistic beliefs and rituals into its own cosmological framework. For example, the psychological need for divine intermediaries was eventually satisfied by the Christian cults that developed around saints and angels, where, in many cases, the shift from pagan to Christian patrons entailed little more than a change in name.[20] As French medievalist Philippe Walter has argued, "medieval hagiography was the machine used for Christianizing the old European myths ... hagiographic legends or the passions of the martyrs are often nothing but potpourris of features borrowed from folk tradition."[21] In the Eastern Alps, many scholars have claimed that the qualities and characteristics of Slavic pagan deities were Christianized beginning in the early Middle Ages. For example, it has been argued that mythological elements surrounding Perun, the Slavic god of lightning and thunder, and Veles, the Slavic god of the underworld, were transferred onto traditions and legends of St. George or Elijah (the Old Testament prophet who brought fire down from the sky), while worship of the goddess Mokoš was replaced by veneration of the Virgin Mary.[22]

Finally, alongside the cult of the dead, Christianity also appropriated the pagan calendar, placing liturgical holidays (e.g. Christmas, Carnival, and Easter) on the dates of pagan festivals.[23] Valerie Flint's seminal study of magic in early medieval Europe similarly reveals how astrological rituals, belief in angels and demons, and the mystical "power of the cross" must be understood as an extension of magical thinking already prevalent in the worldview of the non-Christian population.[24]

Documents from early church councils show that the ecclesiastical leadership was aware of (and quite concerned with) Christian adaptations of pagan beliefs, practices, and mythology.[25] Nevertheless, bishops and priests were forced to walk a fine line between the strict enforcement of Christian orthodoxy and making their religion comprehensible and appealing to the local populace. This made doctrinal flexibility a necessary, if not ideal strategy. So while church leadership rhetorically projected a struggle between two incompatible worldviews, in practice, the divisions between Christianity and paganism remained blurry well into the Middle Ages, particularly outside of the educated elite.[26] Walter has argued that the spread of Christianity into the Celtic world required a deliberate obscuring of the inherent ideological disparities between Christian and pagan worldviews in order to expedite the spread of the faith, noting that "Christianity would have had no chance of imposing itself in the West if, on certain points of dogma and rites, it had not responded to the religious needs of the converted pagans."[27] While church authorities often justified this accommodation by assuming that more rigorous ethical and dogmatic training would follow the initial wave of conversion, this rarely occurred.[28]

However, to conclude that early medieval Europeans were never "authentically" Christian—as is sometimes asserted[29]—draws a common but mistaken equivalence between "authenticity" and "purity." Anthropologists Rosalind Shaw and Charles Stewart have observed that this antipathy toward syncretism is widespread in religious scholarship, but argue that "'authenticity' or 'originality' do not necessarily depend on purity. They are claimable as 'uniqueness,' and both pure and mixed traditions can be unique. What makes them 'authentic' and valuable is a separate issue, a discursive matter involving power, rhetoric and persuasion."[30] Indeed, there was never a single "authentic" or "pure" Christianity, but always multiple, fluid, and heterogeneous Christianities.[31] The process by which Roman Christianity became the "orthodox" and "authentic" interpretation entailed several centuries of such "power, rhetoric, and persuasion."[32]

Appropriating Sacred Objects, Places, and Landscapes in the Late Antique and Early Medieval Eastern Alps

Without completely discounting the role that sociopolitical factors played in the process of Christianization, approaching this issue from a syncretic perspective provides the most plausible mechanism for its rapid dissemination among Roman, Germanic, Celtic, and Slavic pagan communities. It is not difficult to see how convincing people that the new system was, at least in part, a continuation of the old would have greatly facilitated the process of Christianization, even if it required appropriating elements of non-Christian ritual and belief. The following section considers the complex and multifaceted ways in which Christianity appropriated aspects of paganism, with a particular focus on three "scales" at which this occurred in the Eastern Alpine region: through sacred objects, sacred places, and sacred landscapes.

This will help us to better appreciate what an archaeological perspective can provide in examining this important issue.

Sacred Pagan Objects

Sociologists of religion have long maintained that social networks are crucial to spreading a new faith. Most scholarship in this vein has focused on how interpersonal relationships (i.e. friends, family, and colleagues) influence an individual's decision to convert, while the role of material objects in this process remains relatively unexplored. The relational social ontology sketched in Chapter 6 demands that one take seriously the agency not only of humans, but also of non-human actors. So what role did "object agency" play in the process of Christianization?

One aspect to consider is the sensuous, embodied element to religious ritual that Christianity adopted from Roman paganism. For example, the use of altars, bell-ringing, offerings of incense and candlelight, as well as the apotropaic power of placing crosses in doorways and the singing of psalms were all borrowed from extant pagan traditions.[33] Secondly, there is evidence that Christians incorporated actual pagan objects into the physical structures of their own sacred buildings. The re-use of old materials in new architectural constructions (usually referred to as spolia) was a widespread practice in late antiquity and the early Middle Ages, particularly as a tool of political propaganda.[34] Constantine, Theodoric, and Charlemagne all sought out spolia for their monumental construction projects because—as seen throughout this book—emphasizing continuity with the past is an effective way to legitimize one's political authority.[35]

On the other hand, the purposes behind using pagan sacred spolia in Christian buildings are less clear. Nevertheless, stone blocks featuring inscriptions or images of pagan gods have been found in early Christian churches across the European continent. Examples from the Eastern Alps include the Hemmaberg in southern Austria—the largest and most important Christian ecclesiastical complex in the region—where the name of the pagan god *Iovenat* is preserved on an altar discovered in the late antique church.[36] Similarly, at the late antique site of Rifnik in eastern Slovenia, two stone pillars with inscriptions to the local water divinity Aquo were re-used in the construction of an early fifth-century church.[37] A third example in this region comes from the late antique ecclesiastical complex at Kučar in southeastern Slovenia, where excavations have uncovered a smashed altar dedicated to Jupiter, which had been re-used for one of the smaller podiums in the lower church.[38] This latter case has intriguing parallels with a notable example from Fontaine-Valmont in Hainault (Belgium), where a "Jupiter-Giant" column was found supporting a chapel dedicated to St. Wido.[39] To be clear, the re-use of spolia in churches does not necessarily indicate that

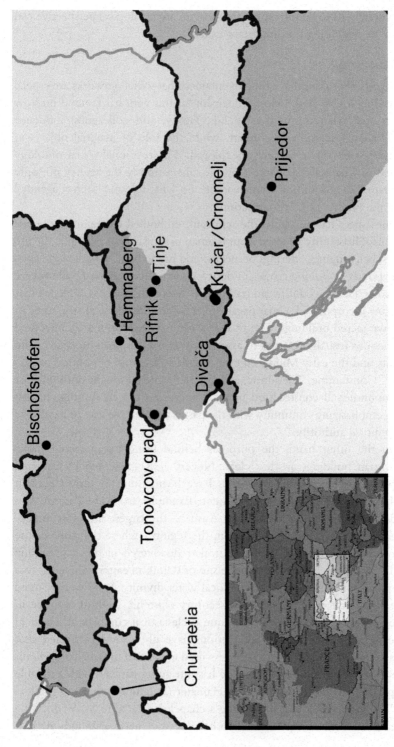

Map 7.1. Location of sites discussed in chapter.

such churches were built directly over pagan sanctuaries. The Aquo pillars at Rifnik, for example, were likely taken from a shrine that originally stood along a nearby stream.[40]

Why would Christians have deliberately incorporated pagan imagery and inscriptions into their houses of worship? Although one cannot discount the possibility that these objects were simply sought out as high-quality building materials, it seems likely that this practice also carried more ideologically infused purposes. Placing pagan objects into newly constructed churches may have been an attempt to assign them a new meaning, thereby neutralizing their dangerous magical powers,[41] or perhaps it represented a "symbolic conquest" over paganism and a "conscious statement of the victory of the new religion."[42] However, keeping in mind the syncretic nature of Christianity outlined above, spolia may have been less a symbolic statement about the absolute victory of the new faith, but rather an acknowledgment of the continuing power of the old ways, as well as a reminder of the continuity between past and present. Along these lines, there is some evidence that such objects were thought to possess the ability to ward off evil spirits.[43] Even more interesting is that nearly identical practices were carried out during the European colonization of the New World, such as when Spanish missionaries incorporated the broken remains of pre-Hispanic god idols into Catholic churches across Mesoamerica under the direct instructions of Holy Roman Emperor Carlos V.[44]

Appropriating Sacred Pagan Places

Another key strategy for implanting Christianity within the established cosmological framework of European paganism entailed the appropriation of sacred spaces. The religious topography of pre-Christian Europe was filled with numinous places; mountains, caves, streams, lakes, trees, and stones were often seen as potential conduits for contact with the preternatural world.[45] This sacred geography was deeply embedded in people's cognitive maps and daily routines, thereby constituting an indispensable component of their spiritual *habitus*. While early church leadership surely believed in the intrinsic appeal of their message and the charisma of their missionaries, they also recognized that this would not be enough to convert most of the non-Christian population. But if these sacred traditions and customs would not be easily forgotten or abandoned, perhaps they could be subtly redirected.[46]

Although some church leaders advocated the complete abandonment of pagan spaces, which they viewed as demonic or ritually polluted, many others adopted a more pragmatic approach, perhaps understanding that religion was not merely a matter of belief, but also of embodied practice that was deeply shaped by the way individuals perceived and inhabited their world.[47] One of the most famous examples comes from a letter sent in AD

601 from Pope Gregory I to the Abbot Milletus of London, in which the pope encouraged the conversion of pagan temples into Christian sanctuaries with the hope that: "When this people [*sic*] see that their shrines are not destroyed they will be able to banish error from their hearts and be more ready to come to the places they are familiar with, but now recognizing and worshipping the one true God."[48]

Although direct transformation of pagan temples into Christian churches was relatively rare for both practical and ideological reasons,[49] more common was a Christian "rebranding" of pagan sacred places, particularly those associated with nature.[50] For instance, in his *In Gloria Confessorum*, the sixth-century bishop Gregory of Tours provides an account of a sacred lake on Mount Helarius (France) that the local population would frequently visit to give offerings or animal sacrifices. After his preaching against such practices proved ineffective, the local bishop decided to build a chapel to St. Hilarius next to the lake, encouraging the local people to use the saint, rather than water god, as their protector and intercessor.[51] A similar story is found in the village of Divača (Slovenia), where local women having difficulty conceiving would pray for help to the god Triglav at a nearby rock shelter. In response, the church built at this location a chapel to St. Francis of Paula, a saint who also assisted with such troubles.[52] The fact that over one-third of all active Christian pilgrimage sites in contemporary Europe are associated with natural places (trees, grottos, streams, stones, etc.) hints at the widespread nature of this practice.[53]

Archaeology provides further evidence for the Christian appropriation of pagan sacred spaces in late antiquity in the early Middle Ages. At the site of Gradina Zecovi near Prijedor (Bosnia), evidence of a *taurobolium* ritual—a widespread cultic practice in the ancient Mediterranean that involved the bloody sacrifice of a bull to the "Great Mother Goddess"—was uncovered only a few meters away from the site of a fifth century Christian church.[54] Similarly, recent excavations at the hilltop settlement of Tonovcov grad in western Slovenia have uncovered traces of a late Iron Age cult site situated directly beneath a large late antique ecclesiastical complex. The presence of fibula fragments, bronze rings, glass beads, military artifacts, and an offering plate—along with an absence of domestic ceramics—is diagnostic of ritual sites in this region.[55] While no structural remains of a sanctuary have yet been uncovered, they may have been destroyed in the construction of the late antique churches, or may simply have left a faint archaeological footprint.

A third example of the Christian appropriation of sacred places comes from the aforementioned site of the Hemmaberg (southern Austria), where the discovery of a *Weihinschrift* (dedicatory inscription) in one of the churches, combined with local toponymical evidence, strongly suggests that a sanctuary to the Celtic god *Iovenat* was previously located at this hilltop site.[56] A local grotto with natural springs below the site, today dedicated to St. Rosalia, provides another example of the transformation of an old pagan sacred place into a Christian shrine.[57]

Appropriating Sacred Pagan Landscapes

Finally, and most controversially, some scholars have claimed that Christian appropriation of pagan sacred geography in late antiquity and the early Middle Ages even occurred across entire landscapes. Many recent archaeological studies have explored the impact of Christianity on early medieval landscapes in Scandinavia, England, and Spain, but perhaps the most dramatic example comes from the Alpine region of Churraetia, today in eastern Switzerland.[58] As Randon Jerris has argued, not only were Christian churches placed on top of pagan ritual sites, but they were also built on astronomically significant places in the landscape. By examining the location of early medieval churches on "sun-terraces" across the region, Jerris demonstrated their alignment with important solar events, such as the precise location of the sunrise on the summer (N55°E) and winter (S56°E) solstices.[59] He further hypothesized that these churches were all built on top of prehistoric astronomical markers, such as menhirs or megaliths, which organized the pre-Christian agricultural and ritual calendar.

At the other end of the Alps, a similar line of interdisciplinary research has been undertaken by Andrej Pleterski, who has provocatively argued that the early medieval landscape of Slovenia was organized around the pre-Christian concept of *tročan*, which connects the three forces of nature with symbolic points in the landscape: (1) fire, oriented toward the "high place" of the thunder god Perun; (2) earth, represented by Veles, god of the underworld; and (3) water, embodied by the goddess Mokoš.[60] Pleterski contends that important sacred places in the landscape (graveyards, shrines, churches, place-names, etc.) associated with these forces are each aligned along a 23° angle, which reflects the angle of the sun from due east and west at the solstices (at midwinter solstice, it is 23° south of east/west, and at midsummer solstice it is 23° north of east/west). While the names of these places were often switched from pagan gods to saints after Christianization, the basic pattern and structure of the landscape remained largely intact.[61]

Despite the promise of this line of research, we should not overlook some of the possible complications with using folkloric and philological data for reconstructing early medieval religious landscapes.[62] While the synthesis of historical, archaeological, and ethnographic datasets has the potential to provide a powerful interdisciplinary model for investigating past landscapes, one cannot afford to ignore the distinct nature of these categories of evidence. As Aleks Pluskowski and Philippa Patrick have warned, projecting folklore back onto the distant past "is dangerous because it may reflect potential re-inventions within the framework of the Christian paradigm."[63]

Archaeology and Non-Spatial Time

This final section brings us back full-circle to the first chapter by considering what the case study of Christianization reveals about the conceptual limitations of current formulations of temporality and historicity. There we highlighted some of the underlying assumptions of the "standard" view of time in Western social science: its linearity, uniformity, and spatial nature. It is not difficult to see how implicit theoretical presuppositions have informed traditional approaches to Christianization, in which the "old" paganism is superseded and supplanted by a "new" Christianity. The notion of a complete annihilation of pagan ritual and belief seems, at first glance, to have support in written sources, because they tend to reiterate the polemics of the victor, as well as the archaeological record, where the rapid spread of Christian objects and architecture seem to erase any traces of the old religion. However, as we have seen, closer investigation reveals a far more subtle and complex picture.

In contrast, the alternative theoretical framework advanced above—with its focus on syncretism, landscape, and materiality—points toward a very different approach to time. Rather than being replaced by the present, elements of the past persist in a powerful, albeit transformed manner. Landscape reveals time to be a palimpsest, where the present is continually layered on, altering the past but not fully erasing it. Therefore, past and present coexist, intermingle, and unfold in a dialectic relationship. Conventional historical time imagines sequential "events" strung along on a single "timeline," but this *heterogeneous* temporality envisions a single present comprised of objects from different times, yet all from the same time, constantly undergoing change, being (re)formed, (re)utilized, deposited, forgotten, remembered, and ultimately annihilated. The relationship between the objects in this time is nonlinear, chaotic, and unpredictable.[64] Due to the nature of its evidence, archaeology is in a unique position to account for and investigate this temporal complexity. Even "closed finds" in archaeology are not from a single "moment" of time, but are composed of materials from different times, often operating on different temporal scales, from the geological to the eventful.[65]

However, developing a more sophisticated approach to temporality requires us to discard one of the most deeply held and ubiquitous assumptions about time: that it is a kind of fourth dimension of space, in which events occurring in the recent past are literally nearer to the present than those occurring earlier. A generation ago, British archaeologists Christopher

Tilley and Michael Shanks argued that such a spatialized understanding of time was central to what they called "the problematic past": "Although the past is completed and gone, it is nevertheless physically present with us in its material traces. But the attribution of the traces to a 'perfect' past, distant from the present, brings ambiguity, the problem."[66]

In other words, the spatial way we conceptualize temporality—which assumes an ontological distinction between the past and present—is belied by the *continued* persistence of the past into the present through material things. But meaningful discussion or even conceptualization of non-spatial time is severely hindered by the limitations of language, since, as noted in Chapter 1, our very way of speaking about time is suffused with spatial metaphors.[67] Moreover, ethnographic research has shown that "spatialized time" is not unique to Western modernity, but is pervasive throughout most (if not all[68]) human societies, probably because our brains have evolved to process casual relationships in a spatial manner. Nevertheless, some ambitious thinkers have attempted to develop non-spatial models of time, of which the most influential has been French philosopher Henri Bergson's concept of *la durée* (duration). Understanding Bergson's non-spatial time requires first making a distinction between quantitative and qualitative multiplicities. The former are spatial, homogeneous, and numerical; consider, for example, a bowl of jellybeans that are spatially discrete, countable, and whose multiplicities (3, 30, 300, etc.) are one of degree rather than kind. On the other hand, qualitative multiplicities are non-spatial, heterogeneous, and continuous rather than discrete. Their difference is one of kind (not degree) like musical notes melting seamlessly into one another, which Bergson describes as "a mutual penetration, an interconnection and organization of elements, each one of which represents the whole, and cannot be distinguished or isolated from it except by abstract thought."[69]

This seemingly abstract distinction is crucial for Bergson because he argues that our everyday notion of time as infinitely divisible into ever-smaller units (hours, minutes, seconds etc.), assumes that it is a quantitative multiplicity, while *la durée* is a qualitative one. For *la durée*, time is not a succession of many moments, but only one moment: the moment of motion. Yet this "moment" is not synonymous with the present (which is already passing), but is what Bergson calls the moment of the *actual*, which includes past, present, and future. This brings us to another one of Bergson's key distinctions: "mathematical" time versus "lived" time. The former entails not only our commonsense notion of time in daily life, but also the way that scientists describe the universe (e.g. Einstein's space-time). While Bergson did not dismiss the utility of this conception of time for physicists' mathematical models of space, he saw it as fundamentally different from "lived time," which was indivisible, heterogeneous, and continuous. As Michel

Serres would argue many years later, "*People usually confuse time and the mea-surement of time*, which is a metrical reading on a straight line."[70]

But if time as *la durée* is compressed into a single moment of movement, then how do we account for the motion of time? Furthermore, what exactly is the relationship of past, present, and future? These critical questions were taken up a half-century later by another seminal French philosopher, Gilles Deleuze, who formulated three "syntheses" of time that further developed Bergson's concept of *la durée*.[71] His first synthesis dealt with the importance of the present as the time in which action occurs, where life is constituted through need, habit, and contemplation. In a non-spatial time, the present cannot become the past, so the "living present" of the first synthesis cannot be coextensive with time itself. There has to be another dimension of time in which the present occurs, which Deleuze calls the a priori past, of which he writes:

> The past would never be constituted if it did not coexist with the present whose past it is. The past and the present do not denote two successive moments, but two elements which coexist: One is present which does not cease to pass, and the other is the past, which does not cease to be but through which all presents pass.[72]

Therefore, the past must be coexistent with the present. Although Deleuze uses the term "past," its meaning is not the same as the "datable past" of spatialized conceptions of time. His past is not a former present, but rather "a general region in which particular presents preserve themselves so that it is possible to focus on and represent them in the present present."[73] For Deleuze, this is not a specific past, but rather "it is *all* our past which coexists with each present."[74] This past must therefore pre-exist the passing present: "The past does not follow the present, but on the contrary, is presupposed by it as the pure condition without which it would not pass. In other words, each present goes back to itself as past."[75] The a priori past "is the synthesis of the whole of time rather than part of a series of times; it is the whole of time in itself, outside the living present, the whole of the past coexisting with each present."[76] This past is not dependent on the present for its existence, but "preserves itself in itself."[77] This is critical because it explains the apparent movement of time: the present can "become" the past precisely because it is always/already the past.

The implications of Bergson and Deleuze's non-spatial notion of tem-porality for studying the medieval past are profound. Rejecting the onto-logical division between past and present allows medieval historians and archaeologists not only to be more cognizant of the appropriation of the Middle Ages by modern political agendas, but also to recognize the poly-temporal nature of the sites, settlements, and societies that we study. This was evident in the above case study, in which pagan "past" and Christian "present" were enmeshed in the religious *habitus* and *doxa* of late antique and early medieval peoples of the Eastern Alps. The chapter closes with another example of blending of "past" and "present" in this region, focused not on religion but culture. Specifically, there are number of fascinating examples of "anachronistic" artifacts appearing at late antique and early medieval sites, which suggest an attempt to maintain a sense of Roman-ness decades and centuries after the western half of the empire collapsed. For example, at the upland fortified site of Tonovcov grad (see Chapter 6), a female grave dated to the end of the sixth century at latest contained a Keller 1a fibula, which was a style popular two hundred years earlier![78]

Similarly, at the late antique cemetery of Črnomelj in southeastern Slovenia, graves stratigraphically dated to the sixth century are furnished with bronze jewelry (arm rings, fibulae, and pins) more typical of the third or fourth century.[79] What is particularly fascinating about this situation is that ceramic evidence at the settlement reveals that these people were still connected to Mediterranean trade routes, so they would surely have been aware of the more fashionable styles of these bronze artifacts. In fact, bronze casting waste uncovered during excavation suggests that local craftsmen were actively producing these seemingly antiquated styles.[80] Not only do these sites reveal an intriguing possibility of social memory expressed by members of the Romanized communities of the post-Roman Eastern Alps, but they are excellent illustrations of the polytemporal nature of the material that archaeologists interpret. It offers a fitting point with which to close this chapter: the use of the past for political, social, or ideological purposes is not unique to the modern era, but appears to have been, in many cases, an equally significant dynamic of medieval, ancient, and even prehistoric societies.[81]

Notes

1. Portions of this chapter previously appeared in K. Patrick Fazioli, "The Transformation of Sacred Landscapes: Approaching the Archaeology of Christianization in the Late Antique and Early Medieval Eastern Alpine-Adriatic Region," in *Landscape and Identity: Archaeology and Human Geography*, ed. Kurt Springs (Oxford, 2015).

2. R. A. Fletcher, *The Barbarian Conversion: From Paganism to Christianity* (New York, 1997), 38.

3. Béatrice Caseau, "Sacred Landscapes," in *Late Antiquity: A Guide to the Postclassical World*, ed. G.W. Bowersock, P. Brown, and O. Grabar (Cambridge, MA, 1999).

4. R. Bratož, "The Development of the Early Christian Research in Slovenia and Istria between 1976 and 1986," in *Actes du XIe Congrès international d'archéologie chrétienne*, ed. N. Duval, F. Baritel, and P. Pergola (Lyon; Vienne; Grenoble; Genève; Aoste, 1989); Sabine Ladstätter, *Die materielle Kultur des Spätantike in den Ostalpen. Eine Fallstudie am Beispiel der westlichen Doppelkirchenanlage auf dem Hemmaberg* (Vienna, 2000).

5. Slavko Ciglenečki, "Results and Problems in the Archaeology of the Late Antiquity in Slovenia," *Arheološki vestnik* 50 (1999).

6. Herwig Wolfram, *Conversio Bagoariorum et Carantanorum: das Weissbuch der Salzburger Kirche über die erfolgreiche Mission in Karantanien und Pannonien* (Vienna, 1979); Aloysius L. Kuhar, *The Conversion of the Slovenes, and the German-Slav Ethnic Boundary in the Eastern Alps* (New York, 1959).

7. Fritz Posch, "Die Anfänge der Steiermark," in *Österreich im Hochmittelalter (907 bis 1246),* ed. A.-M. Drabek and G. Sommer (Vienna, 1991); Kurt Karpf, "Die Karantanen und das Christentum," in *Karantanien: Mutter von Kärnten und Steiermark,* ed. W. Baier and D. Kramer (Klagenfurt, 2003).

8. Jochen Giesler, "Zur Archäologie des Ostalpenraumes vom 8. bis 11. Jahrhundert," *Archäologisches Korrespondenzblatt* 10 (1980); Volker Bierbrauer, "The Cross Goes North: From Late Antiquity to Merovingian Times South and North of the Alps," in *The Cross Goes North: Processes of Conversion in Northern Europe, AD 300–1300,* ed. M. Carver (York, 2004).

9. Ramsay MacMullen, *Christianity and Paganism in the Fourth to Eighth Centuries* (New Haven, CT, 1997), 2.

10. Ken Dowden, *European Paganism: The Realities of Cult from Antiquity to the Middle Ages* (New York, 2000).

11. Bailey K. Young, "The Myth of the Pagan Cemetery," in *Spaces of the Living and the Dead: An Archaeological Dialogue,* ed. C. Karkov, K. Wickham-Crowley, and B. Young (Oxford, 1999).

12. Jiří Macháček and Andrej Pleterski, "Altslawische Kultstrukturen in Pohansko bei Břeclav (Tschechische Republik)," *Studia Mythologica Slavica* 3 (2000); cf. Florin Curta, "The Making of the Slavs between Ethnogenesis, Invention, and Migration," *Studia Slavica et Balcanica Petropolitana* 2 (2008): 162.

13. John Van Engen, "The Christian Middle Ages as an Historiographical Problem," *The American Historical Review* 91 (1986): 522; Will Durant, *Caesar and Christ: The Story of Civilization* (New York, 2011).

14. Rodney Stark, "Efforts to Christianize Europe, 400–2000," *Journal of Contemporary Religion* 16 (2001): 106.

15. William G. Kilbride, "Why I Feel Cheated by the Term 'Christianisation'," *Archaeological Review from Cambridge* 17 (2000): 12.

16. Maurice Halbwachs, *On Collective Memory* (Chicago, 1992), 86.

17. MacMullen, *Christianity and Paganism,* 150.

18. James C. Russell, *The Germanization of Early Medieval Christianity: A Sociohistorical Approach to Religious Transformation* (New York, 1994); Philippe Walter, *Christianity: The Origins of a Pagan Religion* (Rochester, VT, 2006).

19. MacMullen, *Christianity and Paganism,* 154.

20. Peter Brown, *The Cult of the Saints: Its Rise and Function in Latin Christianity* (Chicago, 1981).

21. Walter, *Christianity,* 183; see also Boštjan Kravanja, "Sacred Meaning: The Significance of Extraordinary Places in Ordinary Settings," in *Ethnography of Protected Areas: Endangered Habitats—Endangered Cultures,* ed. P. Simonič (Ljubljana, 2006), 54.

22. For investigations into the syncretic blending of Old Slavic paganism and Christianity in the Eastern Alpine region, see B. Štular and I.M. Hrovatin, "Slovene Pagan Sacred Landscape Study Case: The Bistrica Plain," *Studia Mythologica Slavica* 5 (2002); Andrej Pleterski, "Strukture tridelne ideologije v prostoru pri Slovanih," *Zgodovinski Časopis* 50 (1996); Monika Kropej, *Supernatural Beings from Slovenian Myth and Folktales* (Ljubljana, 2012); Mirjam Mencej, "Wolf Holidays among Southern Slavs in the Balkans," *Acta Ethnographica Hungarica* 54 (2009); Vladimir P. Goss, "Two St. Georges and the Earliest Slavic Cultural Landscape between the Sava and the Drava Rivers," *Peristil* 51 (2008); and Boštjan Kravanja, "Rekonstrukcija svetega

prostora na primeru lokacije sv. Hilarija in Tacijana pri Robiču," *Studia Mythologica Slavica* 10 (2007). It should be noted that many of these (often speculative) arguments rely on an integration of ethnographic, toponymical, textual, and archaeological lines of evidence that is not universally accepted by scholars. As noted above, the historical and artifactual evidence for pre-Christian religions in Europe is highly fragmented and problematic. Since there are no known written sources on this subject from the Eastern Alps, scholars must use a comparative approach drawing on our limited knowledge of "Old Slavic" beliefs and rituals from other regions like the Kievan Rus (Russia) and Polabia (northeastern Germany). Although the extent to which the pre-Christian religion of the Alpine Slavs was similar to these other Slavic-speaking communities is highly debated, the existence of shared themes and motifs in local folklore and place-names suggests the possibility of broad parallels. For a summary of the current state of knowledge on Slavic religion, see Leszek Słupecki, "Slavic Religion," in *The Handbook of Religions in Ancient Europe*, ed. L.B. Christensen, O. Hammer, and D. Warburton (New York, 2014).

23. Walter, *Christianity*.

24. Valerie I. Flint, *The Rise of Magic in Early Medieval Europe* (Princeton, NJ, 1991).

25. Ibid.; Leslie Grinsell, "The Christianisation of Prehistoric and Other Pagan Sites," *Landscape History* 8 (1986).

26. Jean Delumeau, *Le catholicisme entre Luther et Voltaire* (Paris, 1971); Schmitt, *The Holy Greyhound*; Ludovicus Milis, ed., *The Pagan Middle Ages* (Suffolk, UK, 1998).

27. Walter, *Christianity*, 184.

28. Russell, *The Germanization of Early Medieval Christianity*, 211.

29. Stark, "Efforts to Christianize Europe."

30. Rosalind Shaw and Charles Stewart, *Syncretism/Anti-syncretism: The Politics of Religious Synthesis* (London, 1994), 6.

31. Aleksander Pluskowski and Philippa Patrick, "'How Do You Pray to God?' Fragmentation and Variety in Early Medieval Christianity," in Carver, *The Cross Goes North*.

32. Cf. John Phillip Jenkins, *Jesus Wars: How Four Patriarchs, Three Queens, and Two Emperors Decided What Christians Would Believe for the Next 1,500 Years* (New York, 2010).

33. MacMullen, *Christianity and Paganism*, 103–49.

34. Arnold Esch, "On the Reuse of Antiquity: The Perspectives of the Archaeologist and of the Historian," in *Reuse Value: Spolia and Appropriation in Art and Architecture from Constantine to Sherrie Lavine*, ed. R. Brilliant and D. Kinney (Burlington, VT, 2011).

35. Beat Brenk, "Spolia from Constantine to Charlemagne: Aesthetics versus Ideology," *Dumbarton Oaks Papers* 41 (1987).

36. Marjeta Šašel Kos, *Pre-Roman Divinities of the Eastern Alps and Adriatic* (Ljubljana, 1999), 41.

37. Lojze Bolta, *Rifnik pri Šentjurju. Poznoantična naselbina in grobišče* (Ljubljana, 1981); Marjeta Šašel Kos, "Celtic Divinities from Celeia and Its Territories: Who Were the Dedicators?" in *Dedicanti e Cultores nelle Religioni Celtiche*, ed. A. Sartori (Milan, 2008).

38. Janez Dular, Slavko Ciglenečki, and Anja Dular, *Kučar. Železnodobno naselje in zgodnjekrščanski stavbni kompleks na Kučarju pri Podzemlju (Eisenzeitliche Siedlung und frühchristlicher Gebäudekomplex auf dem Kučar bei Podzemelj)* (Ljubljana, 1995), 137.

39. Alain Dierkins, "The Evidence of Archaeology," in Milis, *The Pagan Middle Ages*, 42; Germaine Faider-Feytmans, "Les aspects religieux du site des Castellains à Fontaine-Valmont (Hainaut, Belgique)," *Bulletin de la Société Nationale des Antiquaires de France Paris* 5 (1978).

40. Šašel Kos, "Celtic Divinities from Celeia and Its Territories," 282.

41. Esch, "On the Reuse of Antiquity," 26; Michael Camille, *The Gothic Idol: Ideology and Image-Making in Medieval Art* (Cambridge, 1989), 74.

42. Alain Schnapp, *The Discovery of the Past* (New York, 1997), 88; see also Dierkins, "The Evidence of Archaeology," 42.

43. Michael Camille, *Image on the Edge: The Margins of Medieval Art* (Cambridge, MA, 1992).

44. Byron Ellsworth Hamann, "Chronological Pollution," *Current Anthropology* 49 (2008): 813.

45. Dowden, *European Paganism*.

46. Grinsell, "The Christianisation of Prehistoric and Other Pagan Sites," 27.

47. This approach bears an uncanny resemblance to the recent "material turn" in religious studies, which seeks to "take seriously the native actor's lived world and to explore the biological, social, and historical conditions that make religious experience possible as well as the effects these experiences have on self, culture, and nature." Manuel A. Vásquez, *More Than Belief: A Materialist Theory of Religion* (Oxford; New York, 2011), 5; see also Sonia Hazard, "The Material Turn in the Study of Religion," *Religion and Society: Advances in Research* 4 (2013).

48. As quoted in John Howe, "The Conversion of the Physical World: The Creation of a Christian Landscape," in *Varieties of Religious Conversion in the Middle Ages*, ed. J. Muldoon (Gainesville, FL, 1997), 67.

49. Bryan Ward-Perkins, "Reconfiguring Sacred Space: From Pagan Shrines to Christian Churches," in *Die spätantike Stadt und ihre Christianisierung*, ed. B. Gunnar and H.-G. Severin (Wiesbaden, 2003); Richard Bayliss, *Provincial Cilicia and the Archaeology of Temple Conversion* (Oxford, 2004).

50. Grinsell. "The Christianisation of Prehistoric and Other Pagan Sites"; Paul Davies and John G. Robb, "The Appropriation of the Material of Places in the Landscape: The Case of Tufa and Springs," *Landscape Research* 27 (2002).

51. Flint, *The Rise of Magic*, 255.

52. Čok, *V siju mesečine*, 174.

53. Mary Lee Nolan, "Pilgrimage Traditions and the Nature Mystique in Western European Culture," *Journal of Cultural Geography* 7 (1986).

54. Slavko Ciglenečki, "Late Traces of the Cults of Cybele and Attis. The Origins of the Kurenti and of the Pinewood Marriage ('Borovo Gostüvanje')," *Studia Mythologica Slavica* 2 (1999): 25; for an overview of the *taurobolium* ritual, see Robert Duthoy, *The Taurobolium. Its Evolution and Terminology* (Leiden, 1969).

55. Dragan Božič, "Prazgodovinske najdbe s Tonovcovega gradu in železnodobna kultna mesta v Posočju (Prehistoric Finds from Tonovcov Grad and Iron Age Cult Places in the Posočje Area)," in *Poznoantična utrjena naselbina Tonovcov grad pri Kobaridu: najdbe*, ed. Z. Modrijan and T. Milavec (Ljubljana, 2011), 267–69; Tina Milavec, "Sacred Places? Eighth Century Graves Near Sixth Century Churches at Tonovcov Grad (Slovenia)," in *Rome, Constantinople and Newly-Converted Europe*, ed. M. Salamon, M. Woloszyn, A. Musin, and P. Špehar (Krakow, 2012), 478.

56. Franz Glaser, *Die römische Siedlung Iuenna und die frühchristlichen Kirchen am Hemmaberg: ein Führer durch die Ausgrabungen und durch das Museum in der Gemeinde Globasnitz mit einem Anhang zu den antiken Denkmälern des Jauntales* (Klagenfurt, 1982), 12.

57. Sabine Ladstätter, "Kontinuität trotz Katastrophe: Zur Spätantike im südlichen Noricum," in *Epochenwandel? Kunst und Kultur zwischen Antike und Mittelalter*, ed. F. Bauer and N. Zimmermann (Mainz am Rhein, 2001).

58. For Scandinavia, see Charlotte Fabech, "Centrality in Sites and Landscapes," in *Settlement and Landscape: Proceedings of a Conference in Arhus, Denmark, May 4–7 1998*, ed. C. Fabech and J. Ringtved (Moesgard, Hojbjerg, 1999); and Anders Andrén, "The Significance of Places: The Christianization of Scandinavia from a Spatial Point of View," *World Archaeology* 45 (2013); for England, see Sam Turner, *Making a Christian Landscape: The Countryside in Early Medieval Cornwall, Devon and Wessex* (Exeter, 2006); and Sarah Foster, "Religion and the Landscape—How the Conversion Affected the Anglo-Saxon Landscape and Its Role in

Anglo-Saxon Ideology," *The School of Historical Studies Postgraduate Forum E-Journal Edition* 6 (2008); for Spain, see César Parcero Oubiña, Felipe Criado Boado, and Manuel Santos Estévez, "Rewriting Landscape: Incorporating Sacred Landscapes into Cultural Traditions," *World Archaeology* 30 (1998).

59. Randon Jerris, "Cult Lines and Hellish Mountains: The Development of Sacred Landscape in the Early Medieval Alps," *Journal of Medieval and Early Modern Studies* 32 (2002): 94.

60. Pleterski, *The Invisible Slavs*; Čok, *V siju mesečine*.

61. See also Kravanja, "Sacred Meaning," 54.

62. Curta, "The Making of the Slavs."

63. Pluskowski and Patrick, "'How Do You Pray to God?'," 43. It is worth making a distinction here between two different kinds of ethnographic analogy. We must be skeptical of the *direct historical approach* in which an unbroken connection is posited between contemporary and ancient peoples in a particular area. So, for example, the notion that the specific traditions or practices of the early medieval Alpine Slavs have been preserved in contemporary rural communities in Slovenia must be approached with great caution. On the other hand, ethnographic analogies applied in a more general (nomothetic) sense are based on a well-supported assumption that similar kinds of social, political, or economic conditions will often produce similar kinds of human behaviors or social relationships. It is this latter kind of inferential analogy that was employed in the previous chapter in terms of pottery technology and social identity.

64. Olivier, *The Dark Abyss of Time*, 63.

65. Laurent Olivier, "The Hochdorf 'Princely' Grave and the Question of the Nature of Archaeological Funerary Assemblages," in *Time and Archaeology*, ed. T. Murray (London, 1999); Geoff Bailey, "Time Perspectives, Palimpsests and the Archaeology of Time," *Journal of Anthropological Archaeology* 26 (2007); Douglas J. Bolender, ed., *Eventful Archaeologies: New Approaches to Social Transformation in the Archaeological Record* (Albany, 2010).

66. Michael Shanks and Christopher Y. Tilley, *Re-constructing Archaeology: Theory and Practice* (New York, 1992), 9.

67. See Chapter 1, note 37.

68. Sinha et al., "When Time Is Not Space."

69. Henri Bergson, *Time and Free Will, an Essay on the Immediate Data of Consciousness* (London, 1910), 101.

70. Michel Serres and Bruno Latour, *Conversations on Science, Culture, and Time* (Ann Arbor, 1995), 60–61, emphasis in original.

71. The two key works here are Gilles Deleuze, *Bergsonism* (New York, 1988); and Gilles Deleuze, *Difference and Repetition* (London, 1994).

72. Deleuze, *Bergsonism*, 58–59.

73. Philip Turetzky, *Time* (New York, 1998), 214.

74. Deleuze, *Bergsonism*, 59, emphasis in original.

75. Ibid., 59.

76. Turetzky, *Time*, 215.

77. Deleuze, *Bergsonism*, 59.

78. A *terminus post quem* is evident in that this burial is cut into the ashy destruction layer in one of the churches, which has been confidently dated to the mid sixth century. The other grave goods suggest an even later (eighth century) date for the burial; see Zvezdana Modrijan, "Continuity in Late Antiquity Slovenian Fortified Hilltop Settlements," in *Keszthely-Fenékpuszta im Kontext spätantiker Kontinuitätsforschung zwischen Noricum und Moesia*, ed. O. Heinrich-Tamaska (Budapest, 2011).

79. Philip Mason, "Late Roman Črnomelj and Bela Krajina," *Arheološki vestnik* 49 (1998): 292. The graves cut into (and therefore must postdate) a cobbled surface which has been securely dated to phase 3 (late fifth or early sixth century).

80. Ibid., 294.

81. Richard Bradley, *The Past in Prehistoric Societies* (London, 2002); Howard Williams, "Material Culture as Memory: Combs and Cremation in Early Medieval Britain," *Early Medieval Europe* 12 (2003); Yitzhak Hen and Matthew Innes, eds, *The Uses of the Past in the Early Middle Ages* (New York, 2000).

Conclusion

Mourning Modernity and the Myth of the Middle Ages

We all need mirrors to remind ourselves who we are.
—Leonard Shelby, in *Memento* [Motion Picture]

This book has sought to expose the role of history in the ideology of modernity by revealing how the mytho-historical category of "the Middle Ages" has been appropriated by an array of political and intellectual agendas over the past five hundred years. This brief conclusion revisits some of the central arguments woven through the preceding seven chapters while also proposing another way to unpack the complex, contradictory, and ambiguous place of the medieval in the Western historical imagination.

The myth of the Middle Ages has far deeper historical origins than most realize. As noted in Chapter 2, this concept was first articulated by four-teenth-century Renaissance humanists seeking to define the era preceding their own as one of "darkness" and was subsequently enshrined in Western historiography as part of the tripartite periodization of ancient, medieval, and modern. Once framed in this manner, the "Middle" of this three-age taxonomy came to embody everything antithetical to the modern world, thereby allowing it to be repurposed by any political project in need of a historical straw man. Over the past five centuries, Renaissance humanists, Protestant theologians, Enlightenment *philosophes*, Romantic artists, colonial administrators, and nationalist historians—as well as scholars, politicians, and journalists of all ideological persuasions—have flattened the Middle Ages into a two-dimensional caricature that reveals less about past lifeways than contemporary ideologies and agendas.

But why do the European Middle Ages—arguably more than any other era of Western history—haunt our modern historical consciousness? From

---

where does this era derive its unique power to simultaneously allure and repulse? The answer lies in the project of modernity itself, which has been founded upon an assumption of a radical break with its past and its own historical exceptionalism. These core ideological elements of *rupture* and *difference*, which underlie all theories of modernity, necessitated the creation of a historical Other against which the modern West could define and understand itself.[1] The Middle Ages therefore represent nothing less than the foundational historical myth of the modern world, and continue to be "a prior presence and an ongoing horror in the mirror of modernity," as Saurabh Dube has so vividly described.[2]

The significance of the mirror metaphor should be by now quite obvious; one of this book's recurrent themes is that the myth of the medieval has always been as much about the present as the past. Modernity gazes into the mirror of the medieval and sees (some distorted image of) itself. Yet we cannot overlook the emotional reaction—"ongoing horror"—evoked by this reflection. Without question, the medieval has a visceral and primal quality unlike other historical periods. Why else would Quentin Tarantino have Marsellus Wallace, the gangster from his neo-noir classic *Pulp Fiction*, threaten to "get *medieval* on your ass"? Similarly, it is no coincidence that groups expressing violent opposition to Western modernity, such as Al-Qaeda and ISIS, are regularly described as "medieval" in their worldview and tactics. The Middle Ages are not part of a distant, forgotten past, but continue to lurk ominously in the shadows of modernity.

The immanence of the medieval past in the modern world challenges our commonsense notions of history and time. If the Middle Ages have truly been superseded, as the ideology of modernity would have it, then why should they be frightening at all? If the medieval is truly "dead and gone," why is it constantly resurrected only to be (symbolically) killed again? As noted above, answers to these questions cannot be found in the medieval past, but rather in our present sociohistorical conditions. Here we might benefit from the insights of modernity's greatest critics—from Marx, Nietzsche, and Weber to Freud, Baudelaire, and Dostoyevsky—who warned us about the consequences of the pervasive social disorientation, rootlessness, alienation, and *anomie* generated by the forces of capitalism and colonialism, globalization and mass migration, ideological fragmentation and rapid technological change. As Marshall Berman has more recently asserted, the modern mind struggles to reconcile a set of contradictory desires about its relationship with the past: "we want to be rooted in a stable and coherent past, but also have a need for limitless growth that destroys our emotional links with those worlds."[3] In other words, as a number of political theorists have argued, the experience of modernity is ultimately characterized by profound *loss*, and the inability to properly mourn what has been lost.[4] Since the tools of psychoanalysis are particularly well suited to investigating individual and group responses to loss and trauma, this framework offers a potentially useful way to think about the meaning of the medieval past in contemporary socio-political discourse that complements some of the key findings of this book.

Medieval as Defense: Some Insights from Object Relations Theory

If we accept the thesis that loss has been fundamental to the experience of modernity, then the myth of the Middle Ages could be understood as a collective psychological defense or resistance to properly mourning that loss. Although this may seem like a strange way to approach historical thinking, the myriad connections between trauma, temporality, and the writing of history have been explored by a growing number of scholars in recent years, including several prominent medievalists.[5] While recognizing the potential dangers in applying too literally psychoanalytical interpretations to a social category as heterogeneous as Western modernity, the goal here is simply to sketch out another explanation for the ambiguous and paradoxical place of the medieval in the Western historical imagination.

We have seen throughout this book that the medieval past has been alternately imagined in two contradictory ways: as a "dark age" of violence, ignorance, backwardness, and filth, and a "golden age" of stability, authenticity, and chivalry. This paradoxical historical fantasy bears striking resemblance to the condition of "splitting" in Object Relations Theory. Splitting occurs when children react to the disconcerting discovery that their parents are not perfect by splitting them into two "parents": one all-good (through a process called idealization) and the other all-bad (through devaluation). Although normal psychological development would entail a move from this "paranoid/schizoid" state to a healthier "depressive" state, many adults also employed "splitting" as a means of coping with extreme stress, loss, or trauma.[6]

How might "splitting" help us to understand the "dark age" and "golden age" motifs of the medieval past? Let us begin with the former trope, primarily examined in Chapters 2 and 3. Despite overwhelming evidence that the "dark age" portrayal of the Middle Ages is wildly distorted (at best), such stereotypes remain prevalent not only among the general public, but also in the minds of many academics (as detailed in histories of anthropology in Chapter 3). This disconnect between historical perceptions and past realities makes sense if we think of it as a psychological defense to mourning the loss of modernity. That is to say, if we pretend that the shift from the medieval to the modern world was an unambiguously positive cultural/historical development, then there was no loss at all. A collective insistence of the depravity and incivility of the Middle Ages is designed to turn our attention to the achievements and successes of modernity.

I would argue that this "dark age" motif further serves to resolve the cognitive dissonance between Western modernity's ideological aspirations (liberty, rationality, and equality) and the practices that allowed it to dominate and exploit the rest of the world (slavery, rationalization, and hierarchy). For example, Chapter 2 examined Kathleen Davis's assertion that the historical concept of "feudalism" arose in the seventeenth and eighteenth centuries as a way of transferring a narrative of servitude onto the medieval past, expunging it from modernity just as the colonial slave trade was growing exponentially. Similarly, Tison Pugh and Angela Weisl have pointed out the irony of terms like "neo-feudalism," which some political scientists use to describe oppressive and authoritarian politico-economic systems, despite the fact that "the defining characteristic of medieval feudalism was not so much control at the top but the interdependence that a political system emerging from an agrarian economy required."[7] Curiously, there is a long tradition of associating political absolutism with the Middle Ages, even though this type of government did not become prevalent in Europe until the late seventeenth century. The power of medieval monarchs, in contrast, tended to be circumscribed by the church, feudal lords, consultative bodies (like the Anglo-Saxon *Witan*), and medieval political traditions more generally.[8]

What is particularly fascinating about these examples is that they not only distort and mischaracterize the Middle Ages, but also redefine some of modernity's most shameful elements *as* medieval.[9] As John Dagenais has observed, the medieval "comprises the very things that modernism cannot shake, the things it cannot keep but cannot give up."[10] Carol Symes highlights another striking example in a popular series of French histories, *Trente journées qui ont fait la France* ("Thirty days that made France"), launched in 1959. In these works, which "can be read as a barometer and an arbiter of French historical consciousness in the postwar era," all episodes of colonial expansion were limited to the Middle Ages (as part of a narrative of national unification) and were attributed to medieval institutions such as the monarchy and church.[11] In contrast, important colonial events from the modern era—from the invasion of Algeria and creation of French Indochina to the Dreyfus affair—shockingly received no attention in this series.

In addition to splitting described above, these examples are also reminiscent of the psychological defense of projective identification, which rids the self of any internal parts perceived as bad by locating them in other people.[12] In this fantasy "[a]n individual unconsciously projects a part of the self into another human being as a means of converting an inner struggle over badness and unacceptability into an external one. The hope is that the forces of goodness will prevail and the individual will feel better about himself as a human being."[13] This accurately describes the ideological function of the medieval myth in the modern historical imagination: there is no need to confront the evils of chattel slavery, political absolutism, or colonial exploitation in the modern world if they are safely consigned to a distant medieval past.

In contrast, Chapters 4 and 5 presented a very different conception of the medieval past in the modern historical imagination: not a backwards, horrific era to be left behind, but rather an idealized "golden age" to be revived. In particular, we saw that many European nationalist movements have summoned a romantic, prelapsarian Middle Ages to give their "imagined communities" a sense of identity, pride, and common purpose. This is why Germans looked to the cultural and political achievements of their early medieval ancestors as proof of their inherent rights to dominate East-Central Europe, especially after their collective experience of humiliation at the end of World War I. Similarly, Slovenian nationalists regularly romanticized the early Middle Ages as an era of political autonomy and cultural flourishing during a time when they not only lacked their own independent state, but were regularly disparaged by German imperialists as lacking true history or culture.

Like the "dark age" motif described above, the medieval as "golden age" could also be interpreted as an immature psychological reaction to the experience of modernity as loss. For groups that perceive themselves as oppressed (or repulsed) by modern institutions and principles—including ethnic minorities, certain strains of Islamic or Roman Catholic fundamentalism, and reactionary political movements like the Ku Klux Klan—imagining a whitewashed Middle Ages offers the promise of a return to stability, hierarchy, and/or cultural authenticity.[14] The past is kept alive in order to deflect the painful experience of the present. In a way, such groups refuse to believe that such an idealized, romanticized medieval past is lost, and hold on to the fantasy that this past can be revived in the present.

From Melancholia to Mourning: "Working Through" the Medieval Past

For Freud, an inability to properly mourn the loss of a love object can result in melancholia, a state of severe depression where we cannot let go of what has been lost, but also hate it for leaving us.[15] The love object is kept "alive" in our minds, but does not provide the comfort we desire. We may employ various defenses, like splitting, projection, or rationalization, as a means of coping with the psychological pain produced by the loss. If Chapters 2 through 5 described how the modern historical consciousness has dealt with this melancholic state, then Chapters 6 and 7 seek to develop a novel framework for conceptualizing and reconstructing the medieval past that does not so easily fall into the dark or golden age tropes, which have proven dangerously susceptible to political manipulation.

Some historians who conceptualize the past as a collective trauma have argued that the writing of history can provide an effective means of "working through," a therapeutic process in which the patient recognizes their resistances to mourning and figures out a way to overcome them.[16] The shift from melancholia to mourning requires us to come to terms with the new reality of the world without the love object that we have lost. For medieval historians and archaeologists, I would argue that it is not sufficient to rhetorically reject the "dark age" and "golden age" tropes that underlie colonialist and nationalist discourses. Even though most contemporary academics have disavowed the crass politicization of their work, their narratives of the past nevertheless continue to be appropriated by such agendas. What we need to develop is a different way of approaching and writing the past, and this begins with a rethinking of two key concepts: identity and temporality.

As Chapter 6 argues, a preoccupation with the concept of ethnicity has discouraged scholars from investigating other manifestations of social identity in the post-Roman world and also played into the hands of ethno-nationalists who seek to posit an unbroken line of continuity from early medieval *gentes* to modern ethnic groups. In particular, archaeologists should consider how other dimensions of group identity can be recovered from the material record, even when their names are not recorded in the written sources. We have seen how the "community of practice" might constitute one such localized expression of identity among early medieval potters in the Eastern Alps. A reconceptualization of temporality is also essential for developing a more sophisticated approach to the medieval past. As noted in Chapter 7, the separation of the past from the present is at the heart of the problematic past.[17] When we close off the past from the present, we make it an Other that then has no meaning except as a mirror for the now.

Patrick Geary has shown how medieval histories tend to fall into one of two camps that parallel the dark and golden age tropes: were the Middle Ages an unknowable alterity, an exotic Other that we cannot possibly understand, or were they a site of origins, a place where we can search for the embryonic stages of modernity?[18] Historians and archaeologists must reject this narcissistic approach that always frames the medieval in terms of modernity. They must be able to write a medieval past that does not lapse into either one of these meta-narratives, but rather approaches the medieval on its own terms. This requires us to adopt a position of empathy that Dominick LaCapra has described as moving "out of oneself toward the other without eliminating or assimilating the difference or alterity of the other."[19] Only by coming to terms with the myth of the Middle Ages will we be able to properly mourn what was lost—as well as acknowledge all that has been gained—in the project of modernity.

Notes

1. Bhambra, *Rethinking Modernity*, 2; Osborne, "Modernity Is a Qualitative, Not a Chronological, Category."

2. See opening quote of Chapter 2.

3. Marshall Berman, *All That Is Solid Melts into Air: The Experience of Modernity* (New York, 1982), 35.

4. Charles Taylor, *The Malaise of Modernity* (Toronto, 2003); Peter Marris, *Loss and Change* (New York, 1974); Isaac D. Balbus, *Mourning and Modernity: Essays in the Psychoanalysis of Contemporary Society* (New York, 2005); Peter Homans, ed., *Symbolic Loss: The Ambiguity of Mourning and Memory at Century's End* (Charlottesville, 2000); Matthew H. Bowker, *Ideologies of Experience: Trauma, Failure, Deprivation, and the Abandonment of the Self* (New York, 2016).

5. Recent examples include Ankersmit, *Sublime Historical Experience*; Michael S. Roth, *Memory, Trauma, and History: Essays on Living with the Past* (New York, 2012); Dominick LaCapra, *History in Transit: Experience, Identity, Critical Theory* (Ithaca, NY, 2004). Psychoanalytically informed approaches to medievalism and the Middle Ages include: Biddick, *The Shock of Medievalism*; L.O. Aranye Fradenburg, *Sacrifice Your Love: Psychoanalysis, Historicism, Chaucer* (Minneapolis, 2002); Michael Uebel, "Opening Time: Psychoanalysis and Medieval Culture," in *Cultural Studies of the Modern Middle Ages*, ed. E. Joy, M. Seaman, K. Bell, and M. Ramsey (New York, 2007).

6. See W. Ronald D. Fairbairn, *An Object-Relations Theory of the Personality* (New York, 1954).

7. Tison Pugh and Angela Jane Weisl, *Medievalisms: Making the Past in the Present* (New York, 2012), 150.

8. Robinson, "Medieval, the Middle Ages," 754.

9. Symes, "When We Talk about Modernity," 721.

10. Dagenais, "The Postcolonial Laura," 374.

11 Symes, "The Middle Ages between Nationalism and Colonialism," 40.

12. Melanie Klein, "Some Notes on Schizoid Mechanisms," *International Journal of Psychoanalysis* 27 (1946).

13. Sheldon Cashdan, *Object Relations Therapy: Using the Relationship* (New York, 1988), 56–57.

14. Pugh and Weisl, *Medievalisms*; John Aberth, *A Knight at the Movies: Medieval History on Film* (New York, 2003); Ute Berns and Andrew James Johnston, "Medievalism: A Very Short Introduction," *European Journal of English Studies* 15 (2011).

15. Sigmund Freud, "Mourning and Melancholia," *The Journal of Nervous and Mental Disease* 56 (1922).

16. LaCapra, *History in Transit*; Saul Friedlander, "Trauma, Transference and 'Working Through' in Writing the History of the 'Shoah'," *History and Memory* 4 (1992).

17. Shanks and Tilley, *Re-constructing Archaeology*, 9.

18. Patrick J. Geary, *Writing History: Identity, Conflict, and Memory in the Middle Ages* (Bucharest, 2012).

19. LaCapra, *History in Transit*, 77.

References

Aberth, John. *A Knight at the Movies: Medieval History on Film*. New York: Routledge, 2003.

Ackerman, Robert. "Anthropology and the Classics." In *A New History of Anthropology*, edited by Henrietta Kulick, 143–58. Malden, MA: Blackwell, 2008.

Adorno, Theodor W. *Negative Dialectics*. New York: Seabury Press, 1973.

Amory, Patrick. *People and Identity in Ostrogothic Italy, 489–554*. Cambridge: Cambridge University Press, 1997.

Anderson, Benedict. *Imagined Communities: Reflections on the Origin and Spread of Nationalism*. London: Verso, 1983.

Andrén, Anders. "The Significance of Places: The Christianization of Scandinavia from a Spatial Point of View." *World Archaeology* 45, no. 1 (2013): 27–45.

Ankersmit, Frank R. *Sublime Historical Experience*. Stanford, CA: Stanford University Press, 2005.

Appadurai, Arjun. "The Past as a Scarce Resource." *Man* 16, no. 2 (1981): 201–19.

Arnold, Bettina. "The Past as Propaganda: Totalitarian Archaeology in Nazi Germany." *Antiquity* 64 (1990): 464–78.

Arnold, John. *Belief and Unbelief in Medieval Europe*. London: Hodder Arnold, 2005.

Asad, Talal. *Anthropology & the Colonial Encounter*. New York: Humanities Press, 1973.

———. "Medieval Heresy: An Anthropological View." *Social History* 11 (1986): 345–62.

———. "Notes on Body Pain and Truth in Medieval Christian Ritual." *Economy and Society* 12, no. 3 (1983): 287–327.

Aubin, Hermann. *Von Raum und Grenzen des deutschen Volkes; Studien zur Volksgeschichte*. Breslau: Priebatsch, 1938.

Austin, David. "The 'Proper Study' of Medieval Archaeology." In *From the Baltic to the Black Sea: Studies in Medieval Archaeology*, edited by David Austin and Leslie Alcock, 9–42. London: Routledge, 1990.

Axel, Brian Keith. "Introduction: Historical Anthropology and Its Vicissitudes." In *From the Margins: Historical Anthropology and Its Futures*, edited by Brian Keith Axel, 1–45. Durham, NC: Duke University Press, 2002.

Bacon, Francis. *Novum Organum*. Translated by Thomas Fowler. Oxford: Clarendon Press, 1878.

Bailey, Geoff. "Time Perspectives, Palimpsests and the Archaeology of Time." *Journal of Anthropological Archaeology* 26, no. 2 (2007): 198–223.

Bajt, Veronika. "Myths of Nationhood: Slovenians, Caranthania and the Venetic Theory." *Annals for Istrian and Mediterranean Studies. Series historia et sociologia* 21, no. 2 (2011): 249–60.

———. "Slovenian Nationalism." *Sprawy Narodowościowe* 24/25 (2004): 9–32.

Baker, Peter. "'Millennia' of Marriage Being between Man and Woman Weigh on Court." *The New York Times*, 29 April 2015.

Bakič-Hayden, Milica. "Nesting Orientalisms: The Case of Former Yugoslavia." *Slavic Review* 54 (1995): 917–31.

Balbus, Isaac D. *Mourning and Modernity: Essays in the Psychoanalysis of Contemporary Society.* New York: Other Press, 2005.

Banks, Marcus. *Ethnicity: Anthropological Constructions.* New York: Routledge, 1996.

Barford, P.M. *The Early Slavs: Culture and Society in Early Medieval Eastern Europe.* London: British Museum Press, 2001.

Barkun, Michael. *A Culture of Conspiracy: Apocalyptic Visions in Contemporary America.* Vol. 15, Berkeley: University of California Press, 2013.

Barth, Fredrik. *Ethnic Groups and Boundaries. The Social Organization of Culture Difference. (Results of a Symposium Held at the University of Bergen, 23rd to 26th February 1967.).* Bergen: Universitetsforlaget; Allen & Unwin, 1969.

Bartlett, Robert. *Gerald of Wales, 1146–1223.* Oxford: Oxford University Press, 1982.

———. "Medieval and Modern Concepts of Race and Ethnicity." *Journal of Medieval and Early Modern Studies* 31, no. 1 (2001): 41–56.

Bartsch, Rudolf Hans. *Zwölf aus der Steiermark.* Leipzig: Verlag von L. Staadmann, 1908.

Bassin, Mark. "Race Contra Space: The Conflict between German Geopolitik and National Socialism." *Political Geography Quarterly* 6, no. 2 (1987): 115–34.

Bavec, Uroš. "Predhodno poročilo o poznoantičnem grobišču na Vrajku v Gorenjem Mokronogu (Preliminary Report on the Late Roman Cemetery at Vrajk in Gorenji Mokronog)." *Arheološki vestnik* 54 (2003): 325–30.

Bayliss, Richard. *Provincial Cilicia and the Archaeology of Temple Conversion.* Oxford: Archaeopress, 2004.

Beasley-Murray, Timothy. "German-Language Culture and the Slav Stranger Within." *Central Europe* 4, no. 2 (2006): 131–45.

Beiser, Frederick C. *The German Historicist Tradition.* Oxford: Oxford University Press, 2011.

Bejczy, I. "Tolerantia: A Medieval Concept." *Journal of the History of Ideas* 58, no. 3 (1997): 365–84.

Benjamin, Walter. *Illuminations.* Translated by Harry Zohn. 1st ed. New York: Harcourt, 1968.

Bennett, John W. "Comments on 'the Renaissance Foundations of Anthropology'." *American Anthropologist* 68, no. 1 (1966): 215–20.

Berger, Stefan. *Writing the Nation: A Global Perspective.* New York: Palgrave Macmillan, 2007.

Berger, Stefan, Mark Donovan, and Kevin Passmore, eds. *Writing National Histories: Western Europe since 1800.* London; New York: Routledge, 1999.

Bergson, Henri. *Time and Free Will, an Essay on the Immediate Data of Consciousness.* Translated by Frank Lubecki Pogson. London: S. Sonnenschein & Co., 1910.

Berman, Marshall. *All That Is Solid Melts into Air: The Experience of Modernity.* New York: Simon and Schuster, 1982.

Berns, Ute, and Andrew James Johnston. "Medievalism: A Very Short Introduction." *European Journal of English Studies* 15, no. 2 (2011): 97–100.

Bhambra, Gurminder K. *Rethinking Modernity: Postcolonialism and the Sociological Imagination.* New York: Palgrave, 2007.

Biddick, Kathleen. "Coming out of Exile: Dante on the Orient(alism) Express." *The American Historical Review* 105 (2000): 1234–49.

_____. *The Shock of Medievalism*. Durham, NC: Duke University Press, 1998.

Bierbrauer, Volker. "The Cross Goes North: From Late Antiquity to Merovingian Times South and North of the Alps." In *The Cross Goes North: Processes of Conversion in Northern Europe, AD 300–1300*, edited by Martin Carver, 429–42. York: York Medieval Press, 2004.

_____. "Zur ethnischen Interpretation in der frühgeschichtlichen Archäologie." In *Die Suche nach den Ursprüngen. Von der Bedeutung des frühen Mittelalters*, edited by Walter Pohl, 45–84. Vienna: Österreichischen Akademie der Wissenschaften, 2004.

Birth, Kevin. "The Creation of Coevalness and the Danger of Homochronism." *Journal of the Royal Anthropological Institute* 14, no. 1 (2008): 3–20.

Blanckaert, Claude. *Naissance de l'ethnologie? Anthropologie et missions en Amérique XVIe–XVIIIe siècle*. Paris: Editions du Cerf, 1985.

Bloor, David. *Knowledge and Social Imagery*. London: Routledge & K. Paul, 1976.

Boas, Franz. "The Aims of Anthropological Research." *Science* 76 (1932): 605–13.

_____. "New Evidence in Regard to the Instability of Human Types." *Proceedings of the National Academy of Sciences of the United States of America* 2, no. 12 (1916): 713.

Boast, Robin. "A Small Company of Actors." *Journal of Material Culture* 2, no. 2 (1997): 173–98.

Bolender, Douglas J., ed. *Eventful Archaeologies: New Approaches to Social Transformation in the Archaeological Record*. Albany: State University of New York Press, 2010.

Bollmus, R. *Das Amt Rosenberg und seine Gegner: Studien zum Machtkampf im nationalsozialistischen Herrschaftssystem*. Munich: R. Oldenbourg, 1970.

Bolta, Lojze. *Rifnik pri Šentjurju. Poznoantična naselbina in grobišče* [in summary in German]. Ljubljana: Narodni muzej v Ljubljani, 1981.

Boon, James A. "Comparative De-enlightenment: Paradox and Limits in the History of Ethnology." *Daedalus* 109, no. 2 (1980): 73–91.

Bosl, Karl. *Die Reichsministerialität als Träger staufischer Staatspolitik in Ostfranken und auf dem bayerischen Nordgau*. Ansbach: Brügel, 1941.

Bouchard, Michel. "A Critical Reappraisal of the Concept of the 'Imagined Community' and the Presumed Sacred Languages of the Medieval Period." *National Identities* 6, no. 1 (2004): 3–24.

Bowker, Matthew H. *Ideologies of Experience: Trauma, Failure, Deprivation, and the Abandonment of the Self*. New York: Routledge, 2016.

Božič, Dragan. "Prazgodovinske najdbe s Tonovcovega gradu in železnodobna kultna mesta v Posočju (Prehistoric Finds from Tonovcov Grad and Iron Age Cult Places in the Posočje Area)." In *Poznoantična utrjena naselbina Tonovcov grad pri Kobaridu: najdbe*, edited by Z. Modrijan and T. Milavec, 239–78. Ljubljana: Inštitut za arheologijo ZRC SAZU: Založba ZRC, 2011.

Brackmann, Albert. "Die Ostpolitik Ottos des Grossen." *Historische Zeitschrift* 134 (1926): 242–56.

Bradley, Richard. *The Past in Prehistoric Societies*. London: Routledge, 2002.

Brather, Sebastian. "Ethnic Identities as Constructions of Archaeology: The Case of the Alamanni." In *On Barbarian Identity*, edited by Andrew Gillett, 149–75. Turnhout, Belgium: Brepols, 2002.

_____. *Ethnische Interpretationen in der frühgeschichtlichen Archäologie: Geschichte, Grundlagen und Alternativen*. Berlin: W. De Gruyter, 2004.

Bratož, R. "The Development of the Early Christian Research in Slovenia and Istria between 1976 and 1986." In *Actes du XIe Congrès international d'archéologie chrétienne*, edited by N. Duval, F. Baritel, and P. Pergola, 2345–88. Lyon; Vienne; Grenoble; Genève; Aoste: Ecole française de Rome, 1989.

Bratož, Rajko, and H.-D. Kahl, eds. *Slovenija in sosednje dezele med antiko in karolinsko dobo: zacetki slovenske etnogeneze = Slowenien und die Nachbarländer zwischen Antike und karolingischer Epoche: Anfänge der slowenischen ethnogeneseslovenske Etnogeneze.* 2 vols. Ljubljana: Narodni muzej Slovenije, 2000.

Brenk, Beat. "Spolia from Constantine to Charlemagne: Aesthetics Versus Ideology." *Dumbarton Oaks Papers* 41 (1987): 103–9.

Brown, Catherine. "In the Middle." *Journal of Medieval and Early Modern Studies* 30, no. 3 (2000): 547–74.

Brown, Peter. *The Cult of the Saints: Its Rise and Function in Latin Christianity.* Chicago: University of Chicago Press, 1981.

Brunner, Otto. *Land und Herrschaft: Grundfragen der territorialen Verfassungsgeschichte Südostdeutschlands im Mittelalter.* Baden bei Wien: Rohrer, 1939.

Buc, Philippe. *The Dangers of Ritual: Between Early Medieval Texts and Social Scientific Theory.* Princeton, NJ: Princeton University Press, 2001.

Buchowski, Michal. "The Specter of Orientalism in Europe: From Exotic Other to Stigmatized Brother." *Anthropological Quarterly* 79, no. 3 (2006): 463–82.

Buck-Morss, Susan. *Hegel, Haiti and Universal History.* Pittsburgh, PA: University of Pittsburgh Press, 2009.

Budden, Sandy, and Joanna Sofaer. "Non-Discursive Knowledge and the Construction of Identity Potters, Potting and Performance at the Bronze Age Tell of Százhalombatta, Hungary." *Cambridge Archaeological Journal* 19, no. 2 (2009): 203–20.

Burleigh, Michael. *Germany Turns Eastwards: A Study of Ostforschung in the Third Reich.* New York: Cambridge University Press, 1988.

Camille, Michael. *The Gothic Idol: Ideology and Image-Making in Medieval Art.* Cambridge: Cambridge University Press, 1989.

———. *Image on the Edge: The Margins of Medieval Art.* Cambridge, MA: Harvard University Press, 1992.

Carey, Daniel. "Anthropology's Inheritance: Renaissance Travel, Romanticism and the Discourse of Identity." *History and Anthropology* 14, no. 2 (2003): 107–26.

Carmichael, Catherine. "Ethnic Stereotypes in Early European Ethnographies: A Case Study of the Habsburg Adriatic c. 1770–1815." *Narodna umjetnost—Hrvatski časopis za etnologiju i folkloristiku* 33, no. 2 (1996): 197–209.

Carretero, Mario. *Constructing Patriotism: Teaching History and Memories in Global Worlds.* Charlotte, NC: Information Age Pub., 2011.

Carvalho, Susana, and François Gemenne. *Nations and Their Histories: Constructions and Representations.* Houndmills; New York: Palgrave Macmillan, 2009.

Caseau, Béatrice. "Sacred Landscapes." In *Late Antiquity: A Guide to the Postclassical World*, edited by G. W. Bowersock, Peter Brown, and Oleg Grabar, 21–59. Cambridge, MA: Harvard University Press, 1999.

Cashdan, Sheldon. *Object Relations Therapy: Using the Relationship.* 1st ed. New York: Norton, 1988.

Chakrabarty, Dipesh. *Provincializing Europe: Postcolonial Thought and Historical Difference.* Princeton, NJ: Princeton University Press, 2000.

Champion, Timothy. "Medieval Archaeology and the Tyranny of the Historical Record." In *From the Baltic to the Black Sea: Studies in Medieval Archaeology*, edited by David Austin and Leslie Alcock, 79–95. London: Routledge, 1990.

Chiantera-Stutte, Patricia. "Space, Grössraum and Mitteleuropa in Some Debates of the Early Twentieth Century." *European Journal of Social Theory* 11, no. 2 (2008): 185–201.

Chrisomalis, Stephen, and Bruce Trigger. "Reconstructing Prehistoric Ethnicity: Problems and Possibilities." In *A Passion for the Past, Papers in Honour of James F. Pendergast*, edited by

James V. Wright and Jean-Luc Pilon, 1–21. Gatineau: Canadian Museum of Civilization, 2003.

Cicero, Marcus Tullius. *De Oratore*. 2 vols. Cambridge: W. Heinemann Ltd., 1942.

Ciglenečki, Slavko. "Late Traces of the Cults of Cybele and Attis. The Origins of the Kurenti and of the Pinewood Marriage ('Borovo Gostüvanje')." *Studia Mythologica Slavica* 2 (1999): 21–31.

———. "Results and Problems in the Archaeology of the Late Antiquity in Slovenia." *Arheološki vestnik* 50 (1999): 287–309.

———. *Tinje nad Loko pri Žusmu. Poznoantična in zgodnjesrednjeveška naselbina*. Ljubljana: Inštitut za arheologijo ZRC ZAZU, 2000.

Ciglenečki, Slavko, Zvezdana Modrijan, and Tina Milavec, eds. *Tonovcov grad. Naselbinski ostanki in interpretacija / Tonovcov grad. Settlement Remains and Interpretation*. Ljubljana: Inštitut za arheologijo ZRC ZAZU, 2011.

Classen, Albrecht. "Die Heidin: A Late-Medieval Experiment in Cultural Rapprochement between Christians and Saracens." *Medieval Encounters* 11, no. 1–2 (2005): 50–70.

———, ed. *Meeting the Foreign in the Middle Ages*. New York: Routledge, 2002.

———. "Multiculturalism in the German Middle Ages? The Rediscovery of a Modern Concept in the Past: The Case of *Herzog Ernst*." In *Multiculturalism and Representation*, edited by J. Rieder and Larry Smith, 198–219. Honolulu: College of Languages, Linguistics, and Literature, University of Hawaii, 1996.

Clifford, James. "Rearticulating Anthropology." In *Unwrapping the Sacred Bundle: Reflections on the Disciplining of Anthropology*, edited by D. Segal and S. Yanagisako, 24–48. Durham, NC: Duke University Press, 2005.

Coakley, John. "Mobilizing the Past: Nationalist Images of History." *Nationalism and Ethnic Politics* 10, no. 4 (2004): 531–60.

———. *Nationalism, Ethnicity and the State: Making and Breaking Nations*. London: SAGE, 2012.

Cobb, Charles R. "Archaeology and the 'Savage Slot': Displacement and Emplacement in the Premodern World." *American Anthropologist* 107, no. 4 (2005): 563–74.

Cohen, Jeffrey Jerome. *Medieval Identity Machines*. Minneapolis: University of Minnesota Press, 2003.

Cohen, Ronald. "Ethnicity: Problem and Focus in Anthropology." *Annual Review of Anthropology* 7 (1978): 379–403.

Cohn, Bernard S. "History and Anthropology: The State of Play." *Comparative Studies in Society and History* 22, no. 2 (1980): 198–221.

Čok, Boris. *V siju mesečine: ustno izročilo Lokve, Prelož in bližnje okolice (Outlines of Mythic Characters in the Villages of Lokev and Pre015e in the Context of Slavic Mythology)* [in summary in English]. Ljubljana: Inštitut za arheologijo ZRC SAZU, 2012.

Colish, Marcia L. *Medieval Foundations of the Western Intellectual Tradition, 400–1400*. New Haven, CT: Yale University Press, 1997.

Comaroff, John L., and Jean Comaroff. *Ethnography and the Historical Imagination*. Boulder, CO: Westview Press, 1992.

Conneller, Chantal. *An Archaeology of Materials: Substantial Transformations in Early Prehistoric Europe*. New York: Routledge, 2011.

Cottinger, Henry Marcus. *Elements of Universal History for Higher Institutes in Republics and for Self-Instruction*. Boston: C. H. Whiting, 1884.

Cunja, Radovan. *Poznorimski in zgodnjesrednjeveški Koper (Arheološko izkopavanje na bivšem Kapucinskem vrtu v letih 1986–1987 v luči drobnih najdb 5. do 9. stoletja). Capodistria Tardoromana e Altomedievale (Lo scavo archeologico nell'ex orto dei Cappuccini negli anni 1986–1987 alla luce dei reperti dal V al IX secolo)* [in Slovenian and Italian, with summary in

English]. Koper: Zgodovinsko društvo za južno Primorsko, Znanstveno raziskovalno središče Republike Slovenije, Koper, Pokrajinski muzej Koper, 1996.

Curta, Florin. "The Early Slavs in the Northern and Eastern Adriatic Region: A Critical Approach." *Archaeologia Medievale* 37 (2010): 307–29.

———. "The Making of the Slavs between Ethnogenesis, Invention, and Migration." *Studia Slavica et Balcanica Petropolitana* 2, no. 4 (2008): 155–72.

———. *The Making of the Slavs: History and Archaeology of the Lower Danube Region, ca. 500–700.* Cambridge; New York: Cambridge University Press, 2001.

———. "Some Remarks on Ethnicity in Medieval Archaeology." *Early Medieval Europe* 15, no. 2 (2007): 159–85.

Cvirn, Janez. "The Slovenes from the German Perspective (1848–1918)." *Slovene Studies Journal* 15 (1993): 51–62.

Dagenais, John. "The Postcolonial Laura." *MLQ: Modern Language Quarterly* 65, no. 3 (2004): 365–89.

Dagenais, John, and Margaret Greer. "Decolonizing the Middle Ages: Introduction." *Journal of Medieval and Early Modern Studies* 30, no. 3 (2000): 431–48.

Daim, Falko. "Archaeology, Ethnicity and the Structures of Identification: The Example of the Avars, Carantanians and Moravians in the Eighth Century." In *Strategies of Distinction: The Construction of Ethnic Communities, 300–800*, edited by Walter Pohl and Helmut Reimitz, 71–93. Boston: Brill, 1998.

Darbellay, Frédéric. "Rethinking Inter- and Transdisciplinarity: Undisciplined Knowledge and the Emergence of a New Thought Style." *Futures* 65 (2015): 163–174.

Darnell, Regna. "History of Anthropology in Historical Perspective." *Annual Review of Anthropology* 6 (1977): 399–417.

Davies, Martin L. *Imprisoned by History: Aspects of Historicized Life.* New York: Routledge, 2010.

———. "The Redundancy of History in a Historicized World." *Rethinking History* 15, no. 3 (2011): 335–53.

Davies, Paul, and John G. Robb. "The Appropriation of the Material of Places in the Landscape: The Case of Tufa and Springs." *Landscape Research* 27, no. 2 (2002): 181–85.

Davies, R. R. *The Age of Conquest: Wales, 1063–1415.* Oxford: Oxford University Press, 2000.

Davis, Kathleen. *Periodization and Sovereignty: How Ideas of Feudalism and Secularization Govern the Politics of Time.* Philadelphia: University of Pennsylvania Press, 2008.

———. "Time behind the Veil: The Media, the Middle Ages, and Orientalism." In *The Postcolonial Middle Ages*, edited by J.J. Cohen, 105–21. New York: Palgrave, 2000.

Dawdy, Shannon Lee. "Clockpunk Anthropology and the Ruins of Modernity." *Current Anthropology* 51, no. 6 (2010): 761–93.

Dayan, Eran, and Leonardo G. Cohen. "Neuroplasticity Subserving Motor Skill Learning." *Neuron* 72, no. 3 (2011): 443–54.

de Certeau, Michel. *Heterologies: Discourse on the Other.* Minneapolis: University of Minnesota Press, 1986.

———. *The Writing of History.* New York: Columbia University Press, 1988.

de Grazia, Margreta. "The Modern Divide: From Either Side." *Journal of Medieval and Early Modern Studies* 37, no. 3 (2007): 453–67.

de Jong, Mayke. "The Foreign Past. Medieval Historians and Cultural Anthropology." *Tijdschrift voor Geschiedenis* 109 (1996): 326–42.

De-Juan, Oscar, and Fabio Monsalve. "Morally Ruled Behaviour: The Neglected Contribution of Scholasticism." *The European Journal of the History of Economic Thought* 13, no. 1 (2006): 99–112.

Deleuze, Gilles. *Bergsonism.* New York: Zone Books, 1988.

————. *Difference and Repetition*. London: Athlone Press, 1994.

Deloria, Vine. *Custer Died for Your Sins; an Indian Manifesto*. New York: Macmillan, 1969.

Delumeau, Jean. *Le catholicisme entre Luther et Voltaire*. 1st ed. Paris: Presses universitaires de France, 1971.

Den Hollander, Jaap, Herman Paul, and Rik Peters. "Introduction: The Metaphor of Historical Distance." *History and Theory* 50, no. 4 (2011): 1–10.

Denby, David. "Herder: Culture, Anthropology and the Enlightenment." *History of the Human Sciences* 18, no. 1 (2005): 55–76.

Denk, S. "Neue Funde der köttlacher Kultur im Erlauf-Gebiet 1953–1956." *Unsere Heimat, Monatsblatt des Vereines für Landeskunde von Niederösterreich und Wien* 28 (1957): 152–254.

Díaz-Andreu García, Margarita. *A World History of Nineteenth-Century Archaeology: Nationalism, Colonialism, and the Past*. Oxford: Oxford University Press, 2007.

Dierkins, Alain. "The Evidence of Archaeology." In *The Pagan Middle Ages*, edited by L. Milis, 39–64. Rochester, NY: Boydell Press, 1998.

Dietler, Michael. "Celticism, Celtitude, and Celticity: The Consumption of the Past in the Age of Globalization." In *Celtes et Gaulois dans l'histoire, l'historiographie et l'ideologie modern*, edited by S. Rieckhoff, 237–48. Glux-en-Glenne: Centre Archaeologique Europeen, 2006.

————. "'Our Ancestors the Gauls': Archaeology, Ethnic Nationalism, and the Manipulation of Celtic Identity in Modern Europe." *American Anthropologist* 96 (1994): 584–605.

Dietler, Michael, and Ingrid Herbich. "*Habitus*, Techniques, Style: An Integrated Approach to the Social Understanding of Material Culture and Boundaries." In *The Archaeology of Social Boundaries*, edited by Miriam T. Stark, 232–63. Washington, DC: Smithsonian Press, 1998.

Dinklage, Karl. "Frühdeutsche Volkskultur der Ostmark im Spiegel der Bodenfunde von Untersteiermark und Krain." *Mitteilungen der Anthropologischen Gesellschaft in Wien* 71 (1941): 235–54.

Ditt, Karl. "The Idea of German Cultural Regions in the Third Reich: The Work of Franz Petri." *Journal of Historical Geography* 27, no. 2 (2001): 241–58.

Dobres, Marcia-Anne. "Technology's Links and Chaînes: The Processual Unfolding of Technique and Technician." In *The Social Dynamics of Technology: Practice, Politics, and World Views*, edited by Marcia Ann Dobres and Christopher R. Hoffman, 124–46. Washington, DC: Smithsonian Institution Press, 1999.

Dow, James R., and Hannjost Lixfeld. *The Nazification of an Academic Discipline: Folklore in the Third Reich*. Bloomington: Indiana University Press, 1994.

Dowden, Ken. *European Paganism: The Realities of Cult from Antiquity to the Middle Ages*. New York: Routledge, 2000.

Dube, Saurabh. "Introduction: Enchantments of Modernity." *South Atlantic Quarterly* 101, no. 4 (2002): 729–55.

Dular, Janez, Slavko Ciglenečki, and Anja Dular. *Kučar. Železnodobno naselje in zgodnjekrščanski stavbni kompleks na Kučarju pri Podzemlju (Eisenzeitliche Siedlung und frühchristlicher Gebäudekomplex auf dem Kučar bei Podzemelj)* [in Slovenian and German]. Ljubljana: Znanstvenoraziskovalni center SAZU, 1995.

Durant, Will. *Caesar and Christ: The Story of Civilization*. Vol. 3. New York: Simon and Schuster, 2011.

Duthoy, Robert. *The Taurobolium. Its Evolution and Terminology*. Leiden: E. J. Brill, 1969.

Dzino, Danijel. *Becoming Slav, Becoming Croat: Identity Transformations in Post-Roman and Early Medieval Dalmatia*. Boston: Brill, 2010.

Effros, Bonnie. "Dressing Conservatively: Women's Brooches as Markers of Ethnic Identity?" In *Gender in the Early Medieval World: East and West, 300–900*, edited by L. Brubaker and Julia Smith, 165–84. Cambridge: Cambridge University Press, 2004.

Eichert, Stefan. "Karantanische Slawen—slawische Karantanen. Überlegungen zu ethnischen und sozialen Strukturen im Ostalpenraum des frühen Mittelalters." In *Der Wandel um 1000: Beiträge der Sektion zur slawischen Frühgeschichte der 18. Jahrestagung des Mittel- und Ostdeutschen Verbandes für Altertumsforschung in Greifswald, 23. bis 27. März 2009*, edited by F. Biermann, T. Kersting, and A. Klammt, 433–40. Langenweißbach: Beier & Beran, 2011.

Engevik, Asbjørn. *Bucket-Shaped Pots: Style, Chronology and Regional Diversity in Norway in the Late Roman and Migration Periods*. Oxford: Archaeopress, 2008.

Erickson, Paul A., and Liam D. Murphy. *A History of Anthropological Theory*. 3rd ed. Peterborough, ON: Broadview Press, 2008.

Eriksen, Thomas Hylland. *Ethnicity and Nationalism: Anthropological Perspectives*. 3rd ed. London: Pluto Press, 2010.

Erjavec, Karmen. "Discourse on the Admission of Slovenia to the European Union: Internal Colonialism." *Journal of Multicultural Discourses* 3, no. 1 (2008): 36–52.

Esch, Arnold. "On the Reuse of Antiquity: The Perspectives of the Archaeologist and of the Historian." In *Reuse Value: Spolia and Appropriation in Art and Architecture from Constantine to Sherrie Lavine*, edited by R. Brilliant and D. Kinney, 13–32. Burlington, VT: Ashgate, 2011.

Etherington, Norman. "Barbarians Ancient and Modern." *The American Historical Review* 116 (2011): 31–57.

Evans-Pritchard, E.E. *Anthropology and History*. Manchester: University Press, 1961.

Evans-Pritchard, E.E., and André Singer. *A History of Anthropological Thought*. New York: Basic Books, 1981.

Fabech, Charlotte. "Centrality in Sites and Landscapes." In *Settlement and Landscape: Proceedings of a Conference in Arhus, Denmark, May 4–7 1998*, edited by C. Fabech and J. Ringtved, 455–73. Moesqard, Hojbjerg: Jutland Archaeological Society, 1999.

Fabian, Johannes. *Time and the Other: How Anthropology Makes Its Object*. New York: Columbia University Press, 1983.

Faider-Feytmans, Germaine. «Les Aspects Religieux Du Site Des Castellains À Fontaine-Valmont (Hainaut, Belgique).» *Bulletin de la Société Nationale des Antiquaires de France Paris* 5 (1978): 207–14.

Fairbairn, W. Ronald D. *An Object-Relations Theory of the Personality*. New York: Basic Books, 1954.

Fasolt, Constantin. *The Limits of History*. Chicago: University of Chicago Press, 2004.

Faubion, James D. "History in Anthropology." *Annual Review of Anthropology* 22 (1993): 35–54.

Fazioli, K. Patrick. "Ceramic Technology in the Southeastern Alpine Region in Late Antiquity and the Early Middle Ages: Results of Macroscopic and Microscopic Analyses." *Arheološki vestnik* 63 (2012): 199–234.

———. "The Erasure of the Middle Ages from Anthropology's Intellectual Genealogy." *History and Anthropology* 25, no. 3 (2014): 336–55.

———. "From First Reich to Third Reich: German Imperialism and Early Medieval Scholarship in the Southeastern Alpine Region (c. 1919–1945)." *Archaeologies* 8, no. 2 (2012): 116–44.

———. "Rethinking Ethnicity in Early Medieval Archaeology: Social Identity, Technological Choice, and Communities of Practice." In *From West to East: Current Approaches to Medieval Archaeology*, edited by Scott Stull, 21–41. Newcastle upon Tyne, UK: Cambridge Scholars Publishing, 2014.

———. *Technology, Identity, and Time: Studies in the Archaeology and Historical Anthropology of the Eastern Alpine Region from Late Antiquity to the Early Middle Ages*. Graz: Historischen Landeskommission für Steiermark, 2013.

————. "The Transformation of Sacred Landscapes: Approaching the Archaeology of Christianization in the Late Antique and Early Medieval Eastern Alpine-Adriatic Region." In *Landscape and Identity: Archaeology and Human Geography*, edited by Kurt Springs, 71–81. Oxford: Archaeopress, 2015.

Feder, Kenneth L. *Frauds, Myths, and Mysteries: Science and Pseudoscience in Archaeology*. 7th ed. New York: McGraw-Hill, 2011.

Fehr, Hubert. "Prehistoric Archaeology and German Ostforschung: The Case of the Excavations at Zantoch." *Archaeologia Polona* 42 (2004): 197–228.

Fernandez-Armesto, Felipe. "Medieval Ethnography." *Journal of the Anthropological Society of Oxford* 13 (1982): 275–86.

Fetten, Frank. "Archaeology and Anthropology in Germany before 1945." In *Archaeology, Ideology, and Society: The German Experience*, edited by Heinrich Harke, 140–79. Frankfurt am Main: Peter Lang, 2000.

Feyerabend, Paul. "How to Defend Society against Science." *Radical Philosophy* 11 (1975): 54–65.

Flasch, Kurt, and Udo Reinhold Jeck, eds. *Das Licht der Vernunft: Die Anfänge der Aufklärung im Mittelalter*. Orig. ed. Munich: Verlag C.H. Beck, 1997.

Fletcher, R.A. *The Barbarian Conversion: From Paganism to Christianity*. 1st American ed. New York: H. Holt and Co., 1997.

Flint, Valerie I. "Monsters and the Antipodes in the Early Middle Ages and Enlightenment." *Viator* 15 (1984): 65–80.

————. *The Rise of Magic in Early Medieval Europe*. Princeton, NJ: Princeton University Press, 1991.

Foster, Sarah. "Religion and the Landscape—How the Conversion Affected the Anglo-Saxon Landscape and Its Role in Anglo-Saxon Ideology." *The School of Historical Studies Postgraduate Forum E-Journal Edition* 6 (2008): 1–19.

Foucault, Michel. *Les mots et les choses; une archéologie des sciences humaines*. Paris: Gallimard, 1966.

Fox, Stephen. "Communities of Practice, Foucault and Actor-Network Theory." *Journal of Management Studies* 37, no. 6 (2000): 853–68.

Fradenburg, L.O. Aranye. *Sacrifice Your Love: Psychoanalysis, Historicism, Chaucer*. Minneapolis: University of Minnesota Press, 2002.

Freud, Sigmund. "Mourning and Melancholia." *The Journal of Nervous and Mental Disease* 56, no. 5 (1922): 543–45.

Friedlander, Saul. "Trauma, Transference and 'Working Through' in Writing the History of the 'Shoah'." *History and Memory* 4, no. 1 (1992): 39–59.

Friedman, Jonathan. "The Past in the Future: History and the Politics of Identity." *American Anthropologist* 94, no. 4 (1992): 837–59.

————. "Review of Islands of History by Marshall Sahlins." *History and Theory* 26 (1987): 72–99.

Friedman, John Block. *The Monstrous Races in Medieval Art and Thought*. Syracuse, NY: Syracuse University Press, 2000.

Fuentes, Agustin. *Race, Monogamy, and Other Lies They Told You: Busting Myths about Human Nature*. Berkeley: University of California Press, 2012.

Gabrijelčič, Luka. *The Dissolution of the Slavic Identity of the Slovenes in the 1980s. The Case of the Venetic Theory*. Budapest: Central European University, 2008.

Ganim, John M. *Medievalism and Orientalism: Three Essays on Literature, Architecture, and Cultural Identity*. 1st ed. New York: Palgrave Macmillan, 2005.

Ganshof, François Louis. *Feudalism*. Toronto: University of Toronto Press, 1964.

Garipzanov, Ildar H., Patrick J. Geary, and P. Urbanczyk, eds. *Franks, Northmen, and Slavs: Identities and State Formation in Early Medieval Europe*. Turnhout, Belgium: Brepols, 2008.

Geary, Patrick J. "Ethnic Identity as a Situational Construct in the Early Middle Ages." *Mitteilungen der Anthropologischen Gesellschaft in Wien* 113 (1983): 15–26.

———. *Living with the Dead in the Middle Ages*. Ithaca, NY: Cornell University Press, 1994.

———. *Medieval Germany in America*. Washington, DC: German Historical Institute, 1996.

———. *The Myth of Nations: The Medieval Origins of Europe*. Princeton, NJ: Princeton University Press, 2002.

———. "Slovenian Gentile Identity: From Samo to the Fürstenstein." In *Franks, Northmen, and Slavs: Identities and State Formation in Early Medieval Europe*, edited by Ildar H. Garipzanov, Patrick J. Geary, and P. Urbańczyk, 243–57. Turnhout, Belgium: Brill, 2008.

———. *Writing History: Identity, Conflict, and Memory in the Middle Ages*. Bucharest: Editura Academiei Române, 2012.

Geary, Patrick J., and Gábor Klaniczay, eds. *Manufacturing Middle Ages: Entangled History of Medievalism in Nineteenth-Century Europe*. Leiden: Brill, 2013.

Geertz, Clifford. "Anti Anti-Relativism." *American Anthropologist* 86 (1984): 263–78.

———. *The Interpretation of Cultures: Selected Essays*. New York: Basic Books, 1973.

Gelichi, Sauro. "Ceramic Production and Distribution in the Early Medieval Mediterranean Basin Seventh to Tenth Centuries AD between Town and Countryside." In *Towns and Their Territories between Late Antiquity and the Early Middle Ages*, edited by Gian Pietro Brogiolo, Nancy Gauthier, and Neil Christie, 115–39. Boston: Brill, 2000.

Gentner, Dedre, Mutsumi Imai, and Lera Boroditsky. "As Time Goes By: Evidence for Two Systems in Processing Space → Time Metaphors." *Language and Cognitive Processes* 17, no. 5 (2002): 537–65.

Giesler, Jochen. "Köttlachkultur." In *Reallexikon der Germanischen Altertumskunde. 17: Kleinere Götter— Landschaftsarchäologie*, edited by J. Hoops, 155–61. Berlin: Walter de Gruyter, 2001.

———. "Zur Archäologie des Ostalpenraumes vom 8. bis 11. Jahrhundert." *Archäologisches Korrespondenzblatt* 10 (1980): 85–98.

Gillett, Andrew. "Ethnogenesis: A Contested Model of Early Medieval Europe." *History Compass* 4, no. 2 (2006): 241–60.

Giordano, Christian. "Actualizing History in Eastern and Western Europe. The History of the Historian and That of the Anthropologist." *Ethnologia Balkanica* 2 (1998): 19–29.

Glaser, Franz. *Die römische Siedlung Iuenna und die frühchristlichen Kirchen am Hemmaberg: ein Führer durch die Ausgrabungen und durch das Museum in der Gemeinde Globasnitz mit einem Anhang zu den antiken Denkmälern des Jauntales*. Klagenfurt: Verlag des Geschichtsvereines für Kärnten, 1982.

Gliozzi, G. *Adamo et il nuovo mondo. La nascita dell'antropologia come ideologia coloniale: dalle genealogie bibliche alle teorie razziali (1500–1700)*. Florence: Franco Angeli, 1977.

Goetz, Hans-Werner. "*Gens*. Terminology and Perception of the 'Germanic' Peoples from Late Antiquity to the Early Middle Ages." In *The Construction of Communities in the Early Middle Ages: Texts, Resources, and Artefacts*, edited by R. Corrandini, M. Diesenberger, and Helmut Reimitz, 39–64. Leiden: Brill, 2003.

Goffart, Walter. *Barbarian Tides: The Migration Age and the Later Roman Empire*. Philadelphia: University of Pennsylvania Press, 2006.

Goh, Daniel P.S. "Imperialism and 'Medieval' Natives." *International Journal of Cultural Studies* 10, no. 3 (2007): 323–41.

Goody, Jack. *The Development of the Family and Marriage in Europe*. Cambridge: Cambridge University Press, 1983.

———. *The Theft of History*. Cambridge: Cambridge University Press, 2006.

Goss, Vladimir P. "Two St. Georges and the Earliest Slavic Cultural Landscape between the Sava and the Drava Rivers." *Peristil* 51 (2008): 7–28.

Gosselain, Olivier. "Materializing Identities: An African Perspective." *Journal of Archaeological Method and Theory* 7, no. 3 (2000): 187–217.

Graeber, David. "The Anthropology of Globalization (with Notes on Neomedievalism, and the End of the Chinese Model of the Nation-State)." *American Anthropologist* 104, no. 4 (2002): 1222–27.

———. *Debt: The First 5,000 Years.* Brooklyn, NY: Melville House, 2011.

Grafenauer, Bogo. *Ustoličevanje koroških vojvod in država karantanskih Slovencev* [summary in German]. Ljubljana Slovenska akademija, 1952.

———. *Zgodovina Slovenskega Naroda.* Vol. 1. Ljubljana: Kmečka knjiga, 1954.

Graves-Brown, P. "'All Things Bright and Beautiful?' Species, Ethnicity and Cultural Dynamics." In *Cultural Identity and Archaeology: The Construction of European Communities,* ed. P. Graves-Brown, S. Jones, and C. Gamble, 81–95. London; New York: Routledge, 1996.

Graves-Brown, P., S. Jones, and Clive Gamble. *Cultural Identity and Archaeology: The Construction of European Communities.* London; New York: Routledge, 1996.

Gray, John. *Al Qaeda and What It Means to Be Modern.* London: Faber & Faber, 2015.

Grinsell, Leslie. "The Christianisation of Prehistoric and Other Pagan Sites." *Landscape History* 8, no. 1 (1986): 27–37.

Gunn, John Alexander. *Bergson and His Philosophy.* London: Methuen & Co., 1920.

Gurevich, Aron I. Akovlevich, and Jana Howlett. *Historical Anthropology of the Middle Ages.* Chicago: University of Chicago Press, 1992.

Guštin, M., ed. *Zgodnji Slovani: zgodnjesrednjeveška lončenina na obrobju vzhodnih Alp (Die frühen Slawen: frühmittlalterliche Keramik am Rand der Ostalpen).* Ljubljana: Narodni muzej slovenije, 2002.

Gyug, Richard. *Medieval Cultures in Contact.* New York: Fordham University Press, 2003.

Hagen, Joshua. "The Most German of Towns: Creating an Ideal Nazi Community in Rothenburg Ob Der Tauber." *Annals of the Association of American Geographers* 94 (2004): 207–27.

Halbwachs, Maurice. *On Collective Memory* [Translated from *Les cadres sociaux de la mémoire* and from *La topographie légendaire des évangiles en terre sainte*]. Translated by Lewis A. Coser. Chicago: University of Chicago Press, 1992.

Halsall, Guy. "Burial, Ritual and Merovingan Society." In *The Community, the Family, and the Saint: Patterns of Power in Early Medieval Europe,* edited by Joyce Hall and Mary Swan, 325–38. Turnhout, Belgium: Brepols, 1998.

———. "Ethnicity and Early Medieval Cemeteries." *Arqueología y Territorio Medieval* 18 (2011): 15–28.

Hamann, Byron Ellsworth. "Chronological Pollution." *Current Anthropology* 49 (2008): 803–36.

Hampl, F. "Funde der Köttlacherkultur aus Kaiserbrunn, Krumbachgraben, Nö." *Nachrichtenblatt für die Österreichische Ur- und Frühgeschichtsforschung* 2 (1953): 29.

Harbsmeier, M. "Towards a Prehistory of Ethnography: Early Modern German Travel Writing as Traditions of Knowledge." In *Fieldwork and Footnotes: Studies in the History of European Anthropology,* edited by H.F. Vermeulen and A.A. Roldan, 39–58. London: Routledge, 1995.

Härke, Heinrich, ed. *Archaeology, Ideology, and Society: The German Experience.* Frankfurt am Main: Peter Lang, 2000.

Harkin, Michael E. "Ethnohistory's Ethnohistory Creating a Discipline from the Ground Up." *Social Science History* 34, no. 2 (2010): 113–28.

Harris, Marvin. *The Rise of Anthropological Theory; a History of Theories of Culture.* New York: Crowell, 1968.

Harris, Stephen J., and Bryon Lee Grigsby, eds. *Misconceptions about the Middle Ages*. New York: Routledge, 2008.

Harrison, Dick. "Dark Age Migrations and Subjective Ethnicity: The Example of the Lombards." *Scandia: Tidskrift för historisk forskning* 57 (1991): 19–36.

Hastrup, Kirsten. *Culture and History in Medieval Iceland: An Anthropological Analysis of Structure and Change*. Oxford: Oxford University Press, 1985.

Hauptmann, Gerhart. *Winckelmann, das Verhängnis, Roman*. Gütersloh: C. Bertelsmann, 1954.

Haushofer, Karl. *Grenzen in ihrer geographischen und politischen Bedeutung*. Berlin: K. Vowinckel, 1927.

Hawkes, Christopher. "Archaeological Theory and Method: Some Suggestions from the Old World." *American Anthropologist* 56 (1954): 155–68.

Hazard, Sonia. "The Material Turn in the Study of Religion." *Religion and Society: Advances in Research* 4, no. 1 (2013): 58–78.

Heather, Peter. "Ethnicity, Group Identity, and Social Status in the Migration Period." In *Franks, Northmen, and Slavs: Identities and State Formation in Early Medieval Europe*, edited by Ildar H. Garipzanov, Patrick J. Geary, and P. Urbanczyk, 17–49. Turnhout, Belgium: Brepols, 2008.

Heider, Karl G. "The Rashomon Effect: When Ethnographers Disagree." *American Anthropologist* 90, no. 1 (1988): 73–81.

Heimpel, Hermann. *Deutschlands Mittelalter Deutschlands Schicksal*. Freiburg im Breisgau: F. Wagner, 1933.

Heizer, Robert F. "The Background of Thomsen's Three-Age System." *Technology and Culture* 3, no. 3 (1962): 259–66.

Hen, Yitzhak, and Matthew Innes, eds. *The Uses of the Past in the Early Middle Ages*. Cambridge; New York: Cambridge University Press, 2000.

Heng, Geraldine. *Empire of Magic: Medieval Romance and the Politics of Cultural Fantasy*. New York: Columbia University Press, 2003.

Herold, Hajnalka. "Die Awarenzeitliche Keramik von Zillingtal im Burgenland (Österreich)— ein archäologische und naturwissenschaftliche Analyse." *Bodendenkmalpflege in Mecklenburg-Vorpommern* 50 (2002): 281–92.

———. "Materielle Kultur—technologische Traditionen—Identität: Untersuchungen zur Archäologie des Frühmittelalters in Niederösterreich." *Zeitschrift für Archäologie des Mittelalters* 37 (2009): 111–34.

Herzfeld, Michael. *Anthropology through the Looking-Glass: Critical Ethnography in the Margins of Europe*. Cambridge; New York: Cambridge University Press, 1987.

———. "Purity and Power: Anthropology from Colonialism to the Global Hierarchy of Value." *Reviews in Anthropology* 39, no. 4 (2010): 288–312.

Hindess, Barry. "'Been There, Done That…'." *Postcolonial Studies* 11, no. 2 (2008): 201–13.

———. "The Past Is Another Culture★." *International Political Sociology* 1, no. 4 (2007): 325–38.

Hippo, Augustine of, and Marcus Dods. *The City of God*. Edited by Hendrickson Publishers. Peabody, MA: Hendrickson Publishers, 2009.

Hirsch, Eric. "Valleys of Historicity and Ways of Power among the Fuyuge." *Oceania* (2007): 158–71.

Hirsch, Eric, and Charles Stewart. "Introduction: Ethnographies of Historicity." *History and Anthropology* 16, no. 3 (2005): 261–74.

Hoare, Richard Colt, and Geraldus Cambrensis. *The Description of Wales*. Edited by E. Rhys. London: J. M. Dent, 1912.

Hobsbawm, E. J. *Nations and Nationalism since 1780: Programme, Myth, Reality*. New York: Cambridge University Press, 1990.

Hobsbawm, E.J., and T.O. Ranger, eds. *The Invention of Tradition*. Cambridge; New York: Cambridge University Press, 1983.

Hodgen, Margaret T. *Early Anthropology in the Sixteenth and Seventeenth Centuries*. Philadelphia: University of Pennsylvania Press, 1964.

Hodges, Matt. "The Time of the Interval: Historicity, Modernity, and Epoch in Rural France." *American Ethnologist* 37, no. 1 (2010): 115–31.

Hoffman, Michael A. "The History of Anthropology Revisited—a Byzantine Viewpoint." *American Anthropologist* 75, no. 5 (1973): 1347–57.

Holsinger, Bruce W. *Neomedievalism, Neoconservatism, and the War on Terror*. 1st ed. Chicago: Prickly Paradigm Press, 2007.

———. *The Premodern Condition: Medievalism and the Making of Theory* [text in English; Appendix I and II translated from French]. Chicago: University of Chicago Press, 2005.

Homans, Peter, ed. *Symbolic Loss: The Ambiguity of Mourning and Memory at Century's End*. Charlottesville: University Press of Virginia, 2000.

Honigmann, John Joseph. *The Development of Anthropological Ideas*. Homewood, IL: Dorsey Press, 1976.

Hoppenbrouwers, Peter. "Such Stuff as People Are Made On: Ethnogenesis and the Construction of Nationhood in Medieval Europe." *The Medieval History Journal* 9 (2006): 195–242.

Horkheimer, Max. *Eclipse of Reason*. New York: Oxford University Press, 1947.

Horkheimer, Max, Theodor W. Adorno, and Gunzelin Schmid Noerr. *Dialectic of Enlightenment: Philosophical Fragments*. Stanford, CA: Stanford University Press, 2002.

Howe, John. "The Conversion of the Physical World: The Creation of a Christian Landscape." In *Varieties of Religious Conversion in the Middle Ages*, edited by James Muldoon, 63–80. Gainesville: University Press of Florida, 1997.

Hoyland, Robert G. *In God's Path: The Arab Conquests and the Creation of an Islamic Empire*. New York: Oxford University Press, 2014.

Hudabiunigg, Ingrid. "The Otherness of Eastern Europe." *Journal of Multilingual and Multicultural Development* 25, no. 5–6 (2004): 369–88.

Hummer, Hans J. "The Fluidity of Barbarian Identity: The Ethnogenesis of Alemanni and Suebi, AD 200–500." *Early Medieval Europe* 7 (1998): 1–27.

Hyde, J.K. "Ethnographers in Search of an Audience." In *Literacy and Its Uses. Studies on Late Medieval Italy*, edited by D. Waley, 162–216. Manchester: Manchester University Press, 1991.

Hymes, Dell H. *Reinventing Anthropology*. 1st ed. New York: Pantheon Books, 1972.

Iggers, Georg G. *Historiography in the Twentieth Century: From Scientific Objectivity to the Postmodern Challenge*. Hanover, NH: Wesleyan University Press, 1997.

Ingold, Tim. "Making Culture and Weaving the World." In *Matter, Materiality, and Modern Culture*, edited by P. Graves-Brown, 50–70. London: Routledge, 2000.

Jackson, Peter. "William of Rubruck in the Mongol Empire: Perception and Prejudices." In *Travel Fact and Travel Fiction. Studies on Fiction, Literary Tradition, Scholarly Discovery and Observation in Travel Writing*, edited by Z. von Martels, 54–71. Leiden: Brill, 1994.

Jacobs, Jerry A. and Scott Frickel. "Interdisciplinarity: A Critical Assessment." *Annual Review of Sociology* 35 (2009): 43–65.

Jacques, T. Carlos. "From Savages and Barbarians to Primitives: Africa, Social Typologies, and History in Eighteenth-Century French Philosophy." *History and Theory* 36, no. 2 (1997): 190–215.

Janson, H.W. *Apes and Ape Lore in the Middle Ages and the Renaissance*. London: Warburg Institute University of London, 1952.

Jenkins, John Phillip. *Jesus Wars: How Four Patriarchs, Three Queens, and Two Emperors Decided What Christians Would Believe for the Next 1,500 Years*. New York: Harper One, 2010.

Jenkins, Richard. *Social Identity*. 3rd ed. New York: Routledge, 2008.

Jerris, Randon. "Cult Lines and Hellish Mountains: The Development of Sacred Landscape in the Early Medieval Alps." *Journal of Medieval and Early Modern Studies* 32, no. 1 (2002): 85–108.

Jones, Sian. *The Archaeology of Ethnicity: Constructing Identities in the Past and Present*. New York: Routledge, 1997.

Jones, W.R. "The Image of the Barbarian in Medieval Europe." *Comparative Studies in Society and History* 13, no. 4 (1971): 376–407.

Joyner, Louise. "Cooking Pots as Indicators of Cultural Change: A Petrographic Study of Byzantine and Frankish Cooking Wares from Corinth." *Hesperia* 76 (2007): 183–227.

Judson, Pieter. *Guardians of the Nation: Activists on the Language Frontiers of Imperial Austria*. Cambridge, MA: Harvard University Press, 2006.

———. "Inventing Germanness: Class, Ethnicity, and Colonial Fantasy at the Margins of the Habsburg Monarchy." *Social Analysis* 33 (1993): 47–67.

———. "'Whether Race or Conviction Should Be the Standard': National Identity and Liberal Politics in Nineteenth-Century Austria." *Austrian History Yearbook* 22 (1991): 76–95.

Kabir, Ananya Jahanara. "An Enchanted Mirror for the Capitalist Self: The Germania in British India." In *Medievalisms in the Postcolonial World: The Idea of "the Middle Ages" Outside Europe*, edited by Kathleen Davis and Nadia Altschul, 51–79. Baltimore, MD: John Hopkins University Press, 2009.

Kahl, Hans Dietrich. *Der Staat Der Karantanen. Fakten, Thesen Und Fragen Zu Einer Frühen Slawischen Machtbildung Im Ostalpenraum (7.-9. Jh.)*. Ljubljana: Slovenian Academy of Sciences and Arts, 2002.

———. "Slovenci in Karantanci. Evropski Problem Identitete / Slowenen und Karantanen. Ein europäisches Identitätsproblem." In *Slovenija in sosednje dežele med antiko in karolinško dobo*, edited by R. Bratož and H.-D. Kahl, 978–92. Ljubljana: Narodni muzej Slovenije, 2000.

Kapferer, Bruce. "Anthropology and the Dialectic of Enlightenment: A Discourse on the Definition and Ideals of a Threatened Discipline." *The Australian Journal of Anthropology* 18, no. 1 (2007): 72–94.

Karpf, Kurt. "Die Karantanen und das Christentum." In *Karantanien: Mutter von Kärnten und Steiermark*, edited by W.R. Baier and D. Kramer, 101–09. Klagenfurt: Verlag Hermagoras, 2003.

———. "Slawische Fürsten und Bairischer Adel: Das Frühmittelalterliche Karantanien Am Schnittpunkt Zweier Kulturen." *Hortus artium medievalium: Journal of the International Research Center for Late Antiquity and the Middle Ages* 8 (2002): 209–22.

Kazanski, Michel, and Patrick Périn. "Foreign Objects in the Merovingian Cemeteries of Northern Gaul." In *Foreigners in Early Medieval Europe: Thirteen International Studies on Early Medieval Mobility*, edited by D. Quast, 149–67. Mainz: Romisch-Germanisches Zentralmuseum, 2009.

Khanmohamadi, Shirin. *In Light of Another's Word: European Ethnography in the Middle Ages*. 1st ed. Philadelphia: University of Pennsylvania Press, 2014.

———. "The Look of Medieval Ethnography: William of Rubruck's Mission to Mongolia." *New Medieval Literatures* 10, no. 1 (2008): 87–114.

———. *Proximate Others and Distant Selves: Writing Culture in Late Medieval Europe*. New York: Columbia University, 2005.

Kilbride, William G. "Why I Feel Cheated by the Term 'Christianisation'." *Archaeological Review from Cambridge* 17, no. 2 (2000): 1–17.

Klein, Melanie. "Some Notes on Schizoid Mechanisms." *International Journal of Psychoanalysis* 27 (1946): 99–110.

Klejn, Leo S. "Soviet Archaeology and the Role of the 'Vikings in the Early History of the Slavs." *Norwegian Archaeological Review* 6, no. 1 (1973): 1–4.

Kluckhohn, Clyde. *Anthropology and the Classics*. Providence, RI: Brown University Press, 1961.

———. "Some Reflections on the Method and Theory of the Kulturkreislehre." *American Anthropologist* 38, no. 2 (1936): 157–96.

Kohn, Richard H. "History and the Culture Wars: The Case of the Smithsonian Institution's Enola Gay Exhibition." *The Journal of American History* (1995): 1036–63.

Korošec, Paola. *Zgodnjesrednjeveška arheološka slika karantanskih Slovanov = Archäologisches Bild der karantanischen Slawen im frühen Mittelalter*. 2 vols. Ljubljana: Slovenska akademija znanosti in umetnosti, 1979.

Kos, Franc. *Izbrano Delo*. Ljubljana: Slovenska matica, 1982.

Kramer, Fritz W. "Empathy—Reflections on the History of Ethnology in Pre-Fascist Germany: Herder, Creuzer, Bastian, Bachofen, and Frobenius." *Dialectical Anthropology* 9, no. 1 (1985): 337–47.

Kranzmayer, Eberhard. "Reste Germanischen Lebens in Kärntner Ortsnamen." *Carinthia I* 132, no. 1 (1942): 105–11.

Kravanja, Boštjan. "Rekonstrukcija svetega prostora na primeru lokacije sv. Hilarija in Tacijana pri Robiču." *Studia Mythologica Slavica* 10 (2007): 277–95.

———. "Sacred Meaning: The Significance of Extraordinary Places in Ordinary Settings." In *Ethnography of Protected Areas: Endangered Habitats—Endangered Cultures*, edited by P. Simonič, 49–70. Ljubljana: Filozofska fakulteta, Oddelek za etnologijo in kulturno antropologijo, 2006.

Krech III, Shepard. "The State of Ethnohistory." *Annual Review of Anthropology* (1991): 345–75.

Kroeber, A. L. *An Anthropologist Looks at History*. Berkeley: University of California Press, 1963.

———. "History and Science in Anthropology." *American Anthropologist* 37 (1935): 539–69.

———. "On the Principle of Order in Civilization as Exemplified by Changes of Fashion." *American Anthropologist* 21 (1919): 235–63.

Kroeber, A.L., and Clyde Kluckhohn. *Culture; a Critical Review of Concepts and Definitions*. Cambridge, MA: The Museum, 1952.

Kropej, Monika. *Supernatural Beings from Slovenian Myth and Folktales*. Ljubljana: Založba ZRC, 2012.

Kuhar, Aloysius L. *The Conversion of the Slovenes, and the German-Slav Ethnic Boundary in the Eastern Alps*. New York: League of C. S. A., 1959.

Kuper, Adam. *The Invention of Primitive Society: Transformations of an Illusion*. New York: Psychology Press, 1988.

Kuus, Merje. "Europe's Eastern Expansion and the Reinscription of Otherness in East-Central Europe." *Progress in Human Geography* 28, no. 4 (2004): 472–89.

Labuda, Gerard. "A Historiographic Analysis of the German Drang Nach Osten." *Polish Western Affairs* 5 (1964): 221–65.

———. "The Slavs in Nineteenth Century German Historiography." *Polish Western Affairs* 10 (1969): 177–234.

LaCapra, Dominick. *History in Transit: Experience, Identity, Critical Theory*. Ithaca, NY: Cornell University Press, 2004.

Ladstätter, Sabine. *Die materielle Kultur des Spätantike in den Ostalpen. Eine Fallstudie am Beispiel der westlichen Doppelkirchenanlage auf dem Hemmaberg*. Vienna: Österreichische Akademie der Wissenschaften, 2000.

———. "Kontinuität trotz Katastrophe: zur Spätantike im südlichen Noricum." In *Epochenwandel? Kunst und Kultur zwischen Antike und Mittelalter*, edited by F. Bauer and N. Zimmermann, 57–66. Mainz am Rhein: Ph. von Zabern, 2001.

————. "Zur Charakterisierung des spätantiken Keramikspektrums im Ostalpenraum." In *Frühe Kirchen im ostlichen Alpengebiet*, edited by H. R. Sennhauser, 831–57. Munich: Bayerischen Akademie der Wissenschaften, 2003.

Lambek, Michael. "The Sakalava Poiesis of History: Realizing the Past through Spirit Possession in Madagascar." *American Ethnologist* 25, no. 2 (1998): 106–27.

Latour, Bruno. *Pandora's Hope: Essays on the Reality of Science Studies*. Cambridge, MA: Harvard University Press, 1999.

————. "The Powers of Association." In *Power, Action, and Belief: A New Sociology of Knowledge?* edited by John Law, 264–80. London: Routledge, 1986.

————. *We Have Never Been Modern*. Cambridge, MA: Harvard University Press, 1993.

————. "Why Has Critique Run out of Steam? From Matters of Fact to Matters of Concern." *Critical Inquiry* 30, no. 2 (2004): 225–48.

Latour, Bruno, and S.C. Strum. "Human Social Origins: Oh Please, Tell Us Another Story." *Journal of Social and Biological Systems* 9, no. 2 (1986): 169–87.

Laursen, John Christian, and Cary J. Nederman. *Beyond the Persecuting Society: Religious Toleration before the Enlightenment*. Philadelphia: University of Pennsylvania Press, 1998.

Lave, Jean, and Etienne Wenger. *Situated Learning: Legitimate Peripheral Participation*. New York: Cambridge University Press, 1991.

Leaf, Murray J. *Man, Mind, and Science: A History of Anthropology*. New York: Columbia University Press, 1979.

Leeper, Allen. *A History of Medieval Austria*. London: Oxford University Press, 1941.

Lencek, Rado L. "Carantania." *Slovene Studies Journal* 15, no. 1 (1993): 191–96.

Lepore, Jill. *The Whites of Their Eyes: The Tea Party's Revolution and the Battle over American History*. Princeton, NJ: Princeton University Press, 2010.

Levinger, Matthew, and Paula Franklin Lytle. "Myth and Mobilisation: The Triadic Structure of Nationalist Rhetoric." *Nations and Nationalism* 7, no. 2 (2001): 175–94.

Lévi-Strauss, Claude. *The Savage Mind*. Chicago: University of Chicago Press, 1966.

Li, Victor. *The Neo-Primitivist Turn: Critical Reflections on Alterity, Culture, and Modernity*. Toronto: University of Toronto Press, 2006.

Liebersohn, Harry. "Anthropology before Anthropology." In *A New History of Anthropology*, edited by H. Kulick, 17–32. Malden, MA: Blackwell, 2008.

Lilley, Keith D. "Geography's Medieval History." *Dialogues in Human Geography* 1, no. 2 (2011): 147–62.

Lindstrom, Nicole. "Between Europe and the Balkans: Mapping Slovenia and Croatia's 'Return to Europe' in the 1990s." *Dialectical Anthropology* 27, no. 3–4 (2003): 313–29.

Little, Daniel. "Philosophy of History." In *Stanford Encyclopedia of Philosophy*. Winter 2012 Edition, edited by E.N. Zalta. Stanford, CA: Stanford University. Retrieved 11 Nov. 2013 from http://plato.stanford.edu/archives/win2012/entries/history/, 2012.

Locke, John. *Second Treatise of Government: An Essay Concerning the True Original, Extent and End of Civil Government*. Hoboken, NJ: John Wiley & Sons, 2014.

Loewen, James W. *Lies My Teacher Told Me: Everything Your American History Textbook Got Wrong*. New York: New Press, 1995.

Lotter, Friedrich. *Severinus von Noricum, Legende und historische Wirklichkeit: Unters. zur Phase d. Übergangs von spätantiken zu mittelalterl. Denk- u. Lebensformen*. Stuttgart: Hiersemann, 1976.

Lowie, Robert H. *The History of Ethnological Theory*. New York: Farrar & Rinehart, 1937.

————. "Oral Tradition and History." *American Anthropologist* 17, no. 3 (1915): 579–99.

Lubbock, John. *Pre-Historic Times, as Illustrated by Ancient Remains, and the Manners and Customs of Modern Savages*. New York: D. Appleton and Company, 1872.

Mac Sweeney, Naofse. "Beyond Ethnicity: The Overlooked Diversity of Group Identities." *Journal of Mediterranean Archaeology* 22 (2009): 101–26.

Macfarlane, Alan. "The Origins of English Individualism: Some Surprises." *Theory and Society* 6, no. 2 (1978): 255–77.

Macháček, Jiří. "Disputes over Great Moravia: Chiefdom or State? The Morava or the Tisza River?" *Early Medieval Europe* 17, no. 3 (2009): 248–67.

Macháček, Jiří, and Andrej Pleterski. "Altslawische Kultstrukturen in Pohansko bei Břeclav (Tschechische Republik)." *Studia Mythologica Slavica* 3 (2000): 9–22.

MacMullen, Ramsay. *Christianity and Paganism in the Fourth to Eighth Centuries.* New Haven, CT: Yale University Press, 1997.

Malafouris, Lambros. "The Brain–Artefact Interface (BAI): A Challenge for Archaeology and Cultural Neuroscience." *Social Cognitive and Affective Neuroscience* 5, no. 2–3 (June/September 2010): 264–73.

Malefijt, Annemarie de Waal. *Images of Man; a History of Anthropological Thought.* 1st ed. New York: Knopf, 1974.

Mali, Joseph. *Mythistory: The Making of a Modern Historiography.* Chicago: The University of Chicago Press, 2003.

Mannheim, Karl. *Essays on the Sociology of Knowledge.* New York: Oxford University Press, 1952.

Mansoor, Peter R. *Surge: My Journey with General David Petraeus and the Remaking of the Iraq War.* New Haven: Yale University Press, 2013.

Marett, R. R., ed. *Anthropology and the Classics.* Oxford: The Clarendon Press, 1908.

Marks, Jonathan. *What It Means to Be 98% Chimpanzee: Apes, People, and Their Genes.* Berkeley, CA: University of California Press, 2003.

Marris, Peter. *Loss and Change.* 1st American ed. New York: Pantheon Books, 1974.

Marx, Karl. *The Eighteenth Brumaire of Louis Bonaparte.* London: G. Allen & Unwin, 1926.

––––––. *Grundrisse.* New York: Penguin, 1993.

Mason, Philip. "Late Roman Črnomelj and Bela Krajina." *Arheološki vestnik* 49 (1998): 285–313.

Mason, Robert B. *Shine Like the Sun: Lustre-Painted and Associated Pottery from the Medieval Middle East.* Costa Mesa, CA: Mazda Publishers in association with Royal Ontario Museum, 2004.

Mauss, Marcel. "Les techniques du corps." *Journal de Psychologie* 32 (1935): 271–93.

McGrane, Bernard. *Beyond Anthropology: Society and the Other.* New York: Columbia University Press, 1989.

McNeill, William H. "Mythistory, or Truth, Myth, History, and Historians." *The American Historical Review* 91 (1986): 1–10.

McNiven, Ian J., and Lynette Russell. *Appropriated Pasts: Indigenous Peoples and the Colonial Culture of Archaeology.* Lanham, MD: AltaMira Press, 2005.

Mees, Bernard. *The Science of the Swastika.* New York: Central European University Press, 2008.

Meiners, Christoph. *Geschichte der Ungleichheit der Stände unter den vornehmsten europäischen Völkern.* Vol. 2. Hanover: Helwing, 1792.

Melegh, Attila. *On the East-West Slope: Globalization, Nationalism, Racism and Discourses on Eastern Europe.* 1st ed. New York: Central European University Press, 2006.

Melik, Anton. *Planine v Julijskih Alpah.* Ljubljana: Dela Inštituta za Geografijo v Slovenski Akademiji Znanosti in Umetnosti, 1950.

Mencej, Mirjam. "Wolf Holidays among Southern Slavs in the Balkans." *Acta Ethnographica Hungarica* 54, no. 2 (2009): 337–58.

Mihelj, Sabina. "To Be or Not to Be a Part of Europe: Appropriations of the Symbolic Borders of Europe in Slovenia." *Journal of Borderlands Studies* 20, no. 2 (2005): 109–28.

Milavec, Tina. "A Review of Research into the Early Middle Ages in Slovenia." *Arheološki vestnik* 60 (2009): 249–70.

_____. "Sacred Places? Eighth Century Graves near Sixth Century Churches at Tonovcov Grad (Slovenia)." In *Rome, Constantinople and Newly-Converted Europe*, edited by M. Salamon, M. Woloszyn, A. Musin, and P. Špehar, 475–88. Krakow: Instytut Archeologii Uniwersytetu Rzeszowskiego, 2012.

Milis, Ludovicus, ed. *The Pagan Middle Ages*. Suffolk, UK: Boydell & Brewer Ltd, 1998.

Mill, John Stuart. *Representative Government*. Kitchener, ON: Batoche Books, 2001.

Miller, William Ian. *Bloodtaking and Peacemaking: Feud, Law, and Society in Saga Iceland*. Chicago: University of Chicago Press, 1990.

Minar, C. Jill. "Motor Skills and the Learning Process: The Conservation of Cordage Final Twist Direction in Communities of Practice." *Journal of Anthropological Research* 57 (2001): 381–405.

Mintz, Sidney Wilfred. *Sweetness and Power: The Place of Sugar in Modern History*. New York: Viking, 1985.

Mioč, Pero. "Outline of the Geology of Slovenia." *Acta Geologica Hungarica* 46, no. 1 (2003): 3–27.

Mitchell, Stephen. *A History of the Later Roman Empire, AD 284–641: The Transformation of the Ancient World*. Malden, MA: Blackwell Pub., 2007.

Modrijan, Walter. "Der Forschungstand zum Karantanisch-Köttlacher Kulturkreis." *Archäologisches Korrespondenzblatt* 7 (1977): 291–94.

Modrijan, Zvezdana. "Continuity in Late Antiquity Slovenian Fortified Hilltop Settlements." In *Keszthely-Fenékpuszta im Kontext spätantiker Kontinuitätsforschung zwischen Noricum und Moesia*, edited by O. Heinrich-Tamaska, 157–71. Budapest: Verlag Marie Leidorf, 2011.

_____. "Keramika." In *Poznoantična utrjena naselbina Tonovcov grad pri Kobaridu: najdbe*, edited by Zvezdana Modrijan and Tina Milavec, 121–220. Ljubljana: Inštitut za arheologijo ZRC SAZU: Založba ZRC, 2011.

Moerman, Michael. "Ethnic Identification in a Complex Civilization: Who Are the Lue?" *American Anthropologist* 67 (1965): 1215–30.

Moll, Martin. "The German-Slovene Language Border in Southern Austria: From Nationalist Quarrels to Friendly Co-existence (19th to 21st Centuries)." In *Imagining Frontiers, Contesting Identities*, edited by Steven Ellis and Lud'a Klusakova, 205–27. Pisa: Pisa University Press, 2007.

Mommsen, T.E. "Petrarch's Conception of the 'Dark Ages'." *Speculum* 17, no. 2 (1942): 226–42.

Moore, Michael E. Hoenicke. "Euro-Medievalism: Modern Europe and the Medieval Past." *Collegium: News from the College of Europe= nouvelles du Collège d'Europe* 24 (2002): 67–80.

Moreland, John. "Archaeology and Texts: Subservience or Enlightenment." *Annual Review of Anthropology* 35, no. 1 (2006): 135–51.

_____. *Archaeology, Theory, and the Middle Ages*. London: Duckworth, 2011.

Morgan, Lewis Henry. *Ancient Society; or, Researches in the Lines of Human Progress from Savagery through Barbarism to Civilization*. London: MacMillan and Co., 1877.

Mühle, Eduard. "The European East on the Mental Map of German Ostforchung." In *Germany and the European East in the Twentieth Century*, edited by E. Mühle, 107–30. Oxford: Berg, 2003.

Muldoon, James. "The Nature of the Infidel: The Anthropology of the Cannon Lawyers." In *Discovering New Worlds: Essays on Medieval Exploration and Imagination*, edited by S. Westrem, 115–24. London: Garland Publishing, 1991.

_____. *Popes, Lawyers, and Infidels: The Church and the Non-Christian World, 1250–1550*. Philadelphia: University of Pennsylvania Press, 1979.

_____, ed. *Travellers, Intellectuals, and the World beyond Medieval Europe*. Burlington, VT: Ashgate, 2010.

Murray, Alexander Callander. "Reinhard Wenskus on 'Ethnogenesis,' Ethnicity, and the Origin of the Franks." In *On Barbarian Identity: Critical Approaches to Ethnicity in the Early Middle Ages*, edited by A. Gillett, 39–68. Turnhout, Belguim: Brepols, 2002.

Necak, Dusan. "The 'Yugoslav Question': Past and Future." In *State and Nation in Multi-Ethnic Societies: The Breakup of Multinational States*, edited by Uri Ra'anan, Maria Mesner, Keith Armes, and Kate Martin, 125–34. Manchester: Manchester University Press, 1991.

Nederman, Cary J. "Introduction: Discourses and Contexts of Tolerance in Medieval Europe." In *Beyond the Persecuting Society: Religious Toleration before the Enlightenment*, edited by John Christian Laursen and Cary J. Nederman, 13–24. Philadelphia: University of Pennsylvania Press, 1998.

———. *Worlds of Difference: European Discourses of Toleration, c. 1100–c. 1550*. University Park: Pennsylvania State University Press, 2000.

Nietzsche, Friedrich Wilhelm, and R. J. Hollingdale. *Untimely Meditations*. New York: Cambridge University Press, 1997.

Nikočević, Lidija. "State Culture and the Laboratory of Peoples: Istrian Ethnography during the Austro-Hungarian Monarchy." *Narodna umjetnost—Hrvatski časopis za etnologiju i folkloristiku* 43, no. 2 (2006): 41–57.

Nippel, Wilfried. "Facts and Fiction: Greek Ethnography and Its Legacy." *History and Anthropology* 9, no. 2–3 (1996): 125–38.

Nolan, Christopher. "Memento" [Motion Picture]. United States: Newmarket Films, 2000.

Nolan, Mary Lee. "Pilgrimage Traditions and the Nature Mystique in Western European Culture." *Journal of Cultural Geography* 7, no. 1 (1986): 5–20.

Novaković, Predrag. "Archaeology in Five States—a Peculiarity of Just Another Story at the Crossroads of 'Mitteleuropa' and the Balkans: A Case Study of Slovene Archaeology." In *Archaeologies of Europe: History, Methods, and Theories*, edited by P. Biehl, A. Gramsch, and A. Marciniak, 323–52. New York: Waxmann, 2002.

Oberkrome, Willi. *Volksgeschichte: methodische Innovation und völkische Ideologisierung in der deutschen Geschichtswissenschaft 1918–1945*. Göttingen: Vandenhoeck & Ruprecht, 1993.

Olivier, Laurent. *The Dark Abyss of Time: Archaeology and Memory*. Lanham, MD: AltaMira Press, 2012.

———. "The Hochdorf 'Princely' Grave and the Question of the Nature of Archaeological Funerary Assemblages." In *Time and Archaeology*, edited by Tim Murray, 109–37. London: Routledge, 1999.

Olsen, Glenn. "The Middle Ages in the History of Toleration: A Prolegomena." *Mediterranean Studies* 16 (2007): 1–20.

Ortenberg, Veronica. *In Search of the Holy Grail: The Quest for the Middle Ages*. New York: Hambledon Continuum, 2006.

Osborne, Peter. "Modernity Is a Qualitative, Not a Chronological, Category." *New Left Review* 192, no. 1 (1992): 65–84.

O'Sullivan, Jerry. "17. Nationalists, Archaeologists and the Myth of the Golden Age." In *Early Medieval Munster: Archaeology, History and Society*, edited by Michael Monk and John Sheehan, 178–189. Cork: Cork University Press, 1998.

Oubiña, César Parcero, Felipe Criado Boado, and Manuel Santos Estévez. "Rewriting Landscape: Incorporating Sacred Landscapes into Cultural Traditions." *World Archaeology* 30, no. 1 (1998): 159–76.

Pagden, Anthony. *The Fall of Natural Man: The American Indian and the Origins of Comparative Ethnology*. New York: Cambridge University Press, 1982.

Palmié, Stephan. "Historicist Knowledge and the Conditions of Its Impossibility." In *The Social Life of Spirits*, edited by Ruy Blanes and Diana Espirito Santo, 218–39. Chicago: University of Chicago Press, 2013.

Palmié, Stephan and Charles Stewart. "Introduction: For an Anthropology of History." *HAU: Journal of Ethnographic Theory* 6, no. 1 (2016): 207–36.

Pasnau, Robert. *Thomas Aquinas on Human Nature: A Philosophical Study of Summa Theologiae, 1a 75–89*. Cambridge: Cambridge University Press, 2002.

Peelo, Sarah. "Pottery-Making in Spanish California: Creating Multi-Scalar Social Identity through Daily Practice." *American Antiquity* 76, no. 4 (2011): 642–66.

Pemberton, Jo-Anne Claire. "The So-Called Right of Civilization in European Colonial Ideology, 16th to 20th Centuries." *Journal of the History of International Law* 15 (2013): 25–52.

Penny, H. Glenn, and Matti Bunzl, eds. *Worldly Provincialism: German Anthropology in the Age of Empire*. Ann Arbor: University of Michigan Press, 2003.

Pernoud, Régine. *Pour en finir avec le Moyen Age*. Paris: Éditions du Seuil, 1977.

Phillips, Seymour. "The Outer World in the European Middle Ages." In *Implicit Understandings: Observing, Reporting and Reflecting on the Encounters between Europeans and Other Peoples in the Early Modern Era*, edited by S. B. Schwartz, 23–63. Cambridge: Cambridge University Press, 1994.

Piskorski, Jan M. "After Occidentalism: The Third Europe Writes Its Own History. (Instead of Introduction)." In *Historiographical Approaches to Medieval Colonization of East Central Europe: A Comparative Analysis against the Background of Other European Inter-Ethnic Colonization Processes in the Middle Ages*, edited by Jan M. Piskorski, 7–23. Boulder, CO: Columbia University Press, 2002.

———. "The Medieval Colonization of Central Europe as a Problem of World History and Historiography." *German History* 22, no. 3 (2004): 323–43.

Pleterski, Andrej. *The Invisible Slavs: Župa Bled in the "Prehistoric" Middle Ages*. Ljubljana: Research Centre of the Slovenian Academy of Sciences and Arts, 2013.

———. "Strukture tridelne ideologije v prostoru pri Slovanih." *Zgodovinski Časopis* 50 (1996): 163–85.

Pluciennik, Mark. "Archaeology, Archaeologists and 'Europe'." *Antiquity* 72, no. 278 (1998): 816–24.

Pluskowski, Aleksander, and Philippa Patrick. "'How Do You Pray to God?' Fragmentation and Variety in Early Medieval Christianity." In *The Cross Goes North: Processes of Conversion in Northern Europe, AD 300–1300*, edited by Martin Carver, 29–57. York: York Medieval Press, 2003.

Pohl, Walter. "Archaeology of Identity: Introduction." In *Archaeology of Identity*, edited by Walter Pohl and M. Mehofer, 9–23. Vienna: OAW, 2010.

———. "Conceptions of Ethnicity in Early Medieval Studies." *Archaeologia Polona* 29 (1991): 39–49.

———. "National Origin Narratives in the Austro-Hungarian Monarchy." In *Manufacturing Middle Ages: Entangled History of Medievalism in Nineteenth Century Europe*, edited by Patrick J. Geary and Gábor Klaniczay, 13–50. Leiden: Brill, 2013.

———. "Ostarrîchi Revisited: The 1946 Anniversary, the Millennium, and the Medieval Roots of Austrian Identity." *Austrian History Yearbook* 27 (1996): 21–39.

———. "Telling the Difference: Signs of Ethnic Identity." In *Strategies of Distinction: The Construction of the Ethnic Communities, 300-800*, edited by Walter Pohl and Helmut Reimitz, 17-70. Leiden: Brill, 1998.

Pohl, Walter, and Helmut Reimitz, eds. *Strategies of Distinction: The Construction of Ethnic Communities, 300–800*. Boston: Brill, 1998.

Posch, Fritz. "Die Anfänge der Steiermark." In *Österreich im Hochmittelalter (907 bis 1246)*, edited by A.-M. Drabek and G. Sommer, 103–28. Vienna: Verlag der Österreichischen Akademie der Wissenschaften, 1991.

Prešeren, France, Miha Maleš, and Niko Grafenauer. *Sonetni Venec* [in Slovenian; also in Chinese, Czech, English, French, German, Italian, Russian, and Serbo-Croatian (roman) translation]. Ljubljana: Nova revija, 1995.

Prezelj, I. Mirnik. "Re-thinking Ethnicity in Archaeology." In *Slovenija in sosednje dezele med antiko in karolinsko dobo: zacetki slovenske etnogeneze = Slowenien und die Nachbarländer zwischen Antike und karolingischer Epoche: Anfänge der slowenischen Ethnogenese*, edited by Rajko Bratož, 581–605. Ljubljana: Narodni muzej Slovenije, 2000.

Priestly, Tom. "Vandals, Veneti, Windischer: The Pitfalls of Amateur Historical Linguistics." *Slovene Studies Journal* 19, no. 1 (2002): 3–41.

Promitzer, Christian. "The South Slavs in the Austrian Imagination: Serbs and Slovenes in the Changing View from German Nationalism to National Socialism." In *Creating the Other: Ethnic Conflict and Nationalism in Habsburg Central Europe*, edited by Nancy Wingfield, 183–215. New York: Berghahn Books, 2003.

Pugh, Tison, and Angela Jane Weisl. *Medievalisms: Making the Past in the Present*. New York: Routledge, 2012.

Purdy, Daniel. "Immanuel Kant and Anthropological Enlightenment." *Eighteenth-Century Studies* 38, no. 2 (2005): 329–32.

Rebay-Salisbury, Katharina C. "Thoughts in Circles: Kulturkreislehre as a Hidden Paradigm in Past and Present Archaeological Interpretations." In *Investigating Archaeological Cultures: Material Culture, Variability, and Transmission*, edited by Benjamin W. Roberts and Marc Vander Linden, 41–59: New York: Springer, 2011.

Reber, Ursula. "Concerns of the Periphery / Peripheral Concerns: Tempting Territories of the Balkans." *spacesofidentity.net* 2, no. 3 (2002). Retrieved 5 May 2010 from http://soi.journals.yorku.ca/index.php/soi/article/view/8029/7197.

Reinecke, Paul. "Slavish oder Karolingisch?" *Prähistorische Zeitschrift* 19 (1928): 268–79.

Restrepo, Eduardo, and Arturo Escobar. "'Other Anthropologies and Anthropology Otherwise'." *Critique of Anthropology* 25, no. 2 (2005): 99–129.

Riasanovsky, N. "The Norman Theory of the Origin of the Russian State." *Russian Review* 7, no. 1 (1947): 96–110.

Ribeiro, Gustavo Lins. "World Anthropologies." *Critique of Anthropology* 26, no. 4 (2006): 363–86.

Ricœur, Paul. *Time and Narrative*. 3 vols. Chicago: University of Chicago Press, 1984.

Riley-Smith, Jonathan. *The Crusades, Christianity, and Islam*. New York: Columbia University Press, 2008.

Robinson, F.C. "Medieval, the Middle Ages." *Speculum* 59, no. 4 (1984): 745–56.

Rogel, Carole. *The Slovenes and Yugoslavism, 1890–1914*. New York: Columbia University Press, 1977.

Rohrer, Wiebke. "Politics, Propaganda and Polemics: Prehistoric Archaeology in Upper Silesia 1918 to 1933." *Archaeologia Polona* 42 (2004): 155–96.

Roosevelt, Theodore. *The Winning of the West: An Account of the Exploration and Settlement of Our Country from the Alleghanies to the Pacific*. Vol. 2. New York: Putnam and Sons, 1917.

Rosaldo, Renato. *Ilongot Headhunting, 1883–1974: A Study in Society and History*. Stanford, CA: Stanford University Press, 1980.

Roslund, Mats. *Guests in the House: Cultural Transmission between Slavs and Scandinavians 900 to 1300 AD*. Leiden; Boston: Brill, 2007.

Roth, Michael S. *Memory, Trauma, and History: Essays on Living with the Past*. New York: Columbia University Press, 2012.

Routon, Kenneth. "Conjuring the Past: Slavery and the Historical Imagination in Cuba." *American Ethnologist* 35, no. 4 (2008): 632–49.

Rowe, John Howland. "The Renaissance Foundations of Anthropology." *American Anthropologist* 67, no. 1 (1965): 1–20.

Rubiés, Joan Pau. "The Emergence of a Naturalistic and Ethnographic Paradigm in Late Medieval Travel Writing." In *Voyages and Visions: Towards a Cultural History of Travel*, edited by Jaś Elsner and Joan Pau Rubiés, 29–46. London: Reaktion Books, 1999.

———, ed. *Medieval Ethnographies: European Perceptions of the World Beyond*. Burlington, VT: Ashgate, 2009.

Rupp-Eisenreich, Britta. *Histoires de l'anthropologie: XVIe-XIXe siècles: Colloque la Pratique de l'anthropologie aujourd'hui, 19–21 Novembre 1981, Sèvres*. Paris: Klincksieck, 1984.

Rüsen, Jörn, ed. *Time and History: The Variety of Cultures*. New York: Berghahn Books, 2007.

Russell, James C. *The Germanization of Early Medieval Christianity: A Sociohistorical Approach to Religious Transformation*. New York: Oxford University Press, 1994.

Rye, Owen S. *Pottery Technology: Principles and Reconstruction*. Washington, DC: Taraxacum, 1981.

Sagadin, Milan. *Kranj–Križišče Iskra (nekropola iz časov preseljevanja ljudstev in staroslovanskega obdobja) = Kranj–Iskra Crossroads: A Cemetery from the Migration Period and the Early Slavic Period*. Ljubljana: Narodni muzej, 1987.

Sahlins, Marshall. *Historical Metaphors and Mythical Realities: Structure in the Early History of the Sandwich Islands Kingdom*. Ann Arbor: University of Michigan Press, 1981.

———. "Other Times, Other Customs: The Anthropology of History." *American Anthropologist* 85, no. 3 (1983): 517–44.

Said, Edward W. *Orientalism*. 1st ed. New York: Pantheon Books, 1978.

Samarrai, A. "Beyond Belief and Reverence: Medieval Mythological Ethnography in the Near East and Europe." *Journal of Medieval and Early Modern Studies* 23, no. 1 (1993): 19–42.

Šarić, Ljiljana. "Balkan Identity: Changing Self-Images of the South Slavs." *Journal of Multilingual and Multicultural Development* 25, no. 5–6 (2004): 389–407.

Šašel Kos, Marjeta. "Celtic Divinities from Celeia and Its Territories: Who Were the Dedicators?" In *Dedicanti e Cultores nelle Religioni Celtiche*, edited by A. Sartori, 275–303. Milan: Cisalpino, 2008.

———. *Pre-Roman Divinities of the Eastern Alps and Adriatic*. Ljubljana: Narodni Muzej Slovenije, 1999.

Sassaman, Kenneth, and Wictoria Rudolphi. "Communities of Practice in the Early Pottery Traditions of the American Southeast." *Journal of Anthropological Research* 57 (2001): 407–25.

Šavli, Jožko, Matej Bor, and I. Tomažič. *Veneti: First Builders of European Community: Tracing the History and Language of Early Ancestors of Slovenes*. Vienna: Boswell, 1996.

Schacter, Daniel L. "The Seven Sins of Memory: Insights from Psychology and Cognitive Neuroscience." *American Psychologist* 54, no. 3 (1999): 182.

Schleier, Hans. "German Historiography under National Socialism: Dreams of a Powerful Nation-State and German Volkism Come True." In *Writing National Histories: Western Europe since 1800*, edited by Stefan Berger, Mark Donovan, and Kevin Passmore, 176–88. New York: Routledge, 1999.

Schlesinger, Walter. *Die Entstehung der Landesherrschaft. Untersuchungen vorwiegend nach Mitteldt. Quellen. Mit E. Vorbemerkung Z. Neudr*. Darmstadt: Wissenschaftliche Buchgesellschaft, 1941.

Schmid, Walter. "Südsteiermark im Altertum." In *Südsteiermark, ein Gedenkbuch*, edited by F. Hausmann, 1–27. Graz: U. Moser, 1925.

Schmitt, Jean-Claude. *The Holy Greyhound: Guinefort, Healer of Children since the Thirteenth Century*. Cambridge: Cambridge University Press, 1983.

Schnapp, Alain. *The Discovery of the Past*. New York: Harry N. Abrams, 1997.

Schönwälder, Karen. "Histories. The Fascination of Power: Historical Scholarship in Nazi Germany." *History Workshop Journal* 43 (1997): 133–54.

Schulze, Winfried. *Deutsche Geschichtswissenschaft nach 1945*. Munich: Oldenbourg, 1989.

Scott, Michael W. "The Matter of Makira: Colonialism, Competition, and the Production of Gendered Peoples in Contemporary Solomon Islands and Medieval Britain." *History and Anthropology* 23, no. 1 (2012): 115–48.

Serres, Michel, and Bruno Latour. *Conversations on Science, Culture, and Time.* Ann Arbor: University of Michigan Press, 1995.

Shanks, Michael, and Christopher Y. Tilley. *Re-constructing Archaeology: Theory and Practice.* 2nd ed. New York: Routledge, 1992.

Shaw, Rosalind, and Charles Stewart. *Syncretism/Anti-Syncretism: The Politics of Religious Synthesis.* London: Routledge, 1994.

Shennan, Stephen. *Archaeological Approaches to Cultural Identity.* Boston: Unwin Hyman, 1989.

Shore, Cris. "Imagining the New Europe: Identity and Heritage in European Community Discourse." In *Cultural Identity and Archaeology: The Construction of European Communities,* ed. P. Graves-Brown, S. Jones, and C. Gamble, 96–115. London; New York: Routledge, 1996.

Shuger, Debora. "Irishmen, Aristocrats, and Other White Barbarians." *Renaissance Quarterly* (1997): 494–525.

Shweder, R. A. "Enlightenment's Romantic Rebellion against the Enlightenment, or There's More to Thinking Than Reason and Evidence." In *Culture Theory: Essays on Mind, Self and Emotion,* edited by R. A. Schweder and R. A. Levine, 27–66. Cambridge: Cambridge University Press, 1984.

Siegmund, Frank. "Social Structure and Relations." In *Franks and Alamanni in the Merovingian Period: An Ethnographic Perspective,* edited by I. N. Wood, 177–99. Rochester, NY: The Boydell Press, 1998.

Sikes, E.E. *Anthropology of the Greeks.* London: D. Nutt, 1912.

Sillar, Bill. "Dung by Preference: The Choice of Fuel as an Example of How Andean Pottery Production Is Embedded within Wider Technical, Social, and Economic Practices." *Archaeometry* 42, no. 1 (2000): 43–60.

Sillar, Bill, and M.S. Tite. "The Challenge of 'Technological Choices' for Materials Science Approaches in Archaeology." *Archaeometry* 42, no. 1 (2000): 2–20.

Sindbæk, Søren M. "A Magyar Occurrence: Process, Practice and Ethnicity between Europe and the Steppes." *Acta Archaeologica* 70 (1999): 149–64.

Sinha, Chris, Vera Da Silva Sinha, Jörg Zinken, and Wany Sampaio. "When Time Is Not Space: The Social and Linguistic Construction of Time Intervals and Temporal Event Relations in an Amazonian Culture." *Language and Cognition* 3, no. 1 (2011): 137–69.

Skinner, Joseph. *The Invention of Greek Ethnography: From Homer to Herodotus.* New York: Oxford University Press, 2012.

Skrbiš, Zlatko. "The Emotional Historiography of Venetologists: Slovene Diaspora, Memory and Nationalism." *Focaal: European Journal of Anthropology* 39 (2002): 41–55.

———. "The First Europeans: The Case Study in Slovene National Imagining in Diaspora." *The Australian Sociological Association Annual Conference,* Sydney, 15 December, 2001. . Retrieved 6 Nov. 2013 from http://www.hasaarchives.com/uploads/pdf/The%20 First%20Europeans%20-%20The%20Case%20Study%20in%20Slovene%20National%20 Imagining%20in%20Diaspora%20-Skrbis.pdf

Slapšak, B., and Predrag Novakovič. "Is There National Archaeology without Nationalism? Archaeological Tradition in Slovenia." In *Nationalism and Archaeology in Europe,* edited by Margarita Diaz-Andreu and Timothy Champion, 256–93. London: UCL Press, 1996.

Slotkin, James Sydney. *Readings in Early Anthropology.* Chicago: Aldine Pub. Co., 1965.

Słupecki, Leszek. "Slavic Religion." In *The Handbook of Religions in Ancient Europe,* edited by Lisbeth Bredholt Christensen, Olav Hammer, and David Warburton, 338–58. New York: Routledge, 2014.

Smail, Daniel Lord. "Genealogy, Ontogeny, and the Narrative Arc of Origins." *French Historical Studies* 34, no. 1 (2011): 21–35.

Smith, Anthony D. *The Antiquity of Nations.* Cambridge; Malden, MA: Polity, 2004.

————. "Authenticity, Antiquity and Archaeology." *Nations and Nationalism* 7, no. 4 (2001): 441–49.

————. "The 'Golden Age' and National Renewal." In *Myths and Nationhood*, edited by G. Hosking and G. Schopflin, 36–59. New York: Routledge, 1997.

Smith, A. Livingstone. "Processing Clay for Pottery in Northern Cameroon: Social and Technical Requirements." *Archaeometry* 42, no. 1 (2000): 21–42.

Smith, Adam T. "The End of the Essential Archaeological Subject." *Archaeological Dialogues* 11, no. 1 (2004): 1–20.

Smith, Julia M.H. *Europe after Rome: A New Cultural History 500–1000.* New York: Oxford University Press, 2005.

Smith, Woodruff D. *Politics and the Sciences of Culture in Germany, 1840–1920.* New York: Oxford University Press, 1991.

Sørensen, Hans Christian. "The So-Called Varangian-Russian Problem." *Scando-Slavica* 14, no. 1 (1968): 141–48.

Squires, Susan, and Michael L. Van De Vanter. "Communities of Practice." In *A Companion to Organizational Anthropology*, edited by D. Douglas Caulkins and Ann T. Jordan, 289–310: New York: John Wiley & Sons, Ltd, 2012.

Šribar, V. „Der Karantanisch-Köttlacher Kulturkreis, Aquileja Und Salzburg." *Aquileia nostra* 54 (1983): 270–319.

Šribar, V., and V. Stare. "Das Verhältnis der Steiermark zu den übrigen Regionen der Karantanisch-Köttlacher Kultur." *Schild von Steier* 15/16 (1978/79): 209–25.

Stagl, Justin. *A History of Curiosity: The Theory of Travel, 1550–1800.* London: Routledge, 1995.

Stark, Miriam T., Ronald L. Bishop, and Elizabeth Miksa. "Ceramic Technology and Social Boundaries: Cultural Practices in Kalinga Clay Selection and Use." *Journal of Archaeological Method and Theory* 7, no. 4 (2000): 295–331.

Stark, Rodney. "Efforts to Christianize Europe, 400–2000." *Journal of Contemporary Religion* 16, no. 1 (2001): 105–23.

Starzacher, Karl. "Oberkrain, Deutscher Kulturboden." *Deutsche Volkskunde* 5, no. 2 (1943): 69–71.

Stewart, Charles. *Dreaming and Historical Consciousness in Island Greece.* Cambridge, MA: Department of the Classics, Harvard University, 2012.

————. "Historicity and Anthropology." *Annual Review of Anthropology* 45 (2016): 79–94.

Štih, Peter. "The Carolingian Period of the 9th Century." In *The Land Between: A History of Slovenia*, edited by O. Luthar, 93–109. New York: Peter Lang, 2008.

————. *The Middle Ages between the Eastern Alps and the Northern Adriatic: Select Papers on Slovene Historiography and Medieval History.* Leiden: Brill, 2010.

————. "The Slavic Settlement and Ethnogenesis." In *The Land Between: A History of Slovenia*, edited by O. Luthar, 81–92. New York: Peter Lang, 2008.

Stock, Brian. "The Middle Ages as Subject and Object: Romantic Attitudes and Academic Medievalism." *New Literary History* 5, no. 3 (1974): 527–47.

Stocking, George W. *Race, Culture, and Evolution; Essays in the History of Anthropology.* New York: Free Press, 1968.

Stoler, Ann Laura. *Along the Archival Grain: Epistemic Anxieties and Colonial Common Sense.* Princeton, NJ: Princeton University Press, 2009.

Strakosch-Grassmann, Gustav. *Geschichte der Deutschen in Österreich-Ungarn.* Vol. 1. Vienna: Carl Konegen, 1895.

Strathern, Marilyn. *The Gender of the Gift: Problems with Women and Problems with Society in Melanesia*. Berkeley: University of California Press, 1988.

Strickland, Debra Higgs. "The Exotic in the Later Middle Ages: Recent Critical Approaches." *Literature Compass* 5, no. 1 (2008): 58–72.

Štular, B., and I.M. Hrovatin. "Slovene Pagan Sacred Landscape Study Case: The Bistrica Plain." *Studia Mythologica Slavica* 5 (2002): 43–68.

Sugar, Peter. "The Nature of Non-Germanic Societies under Habsburg Rule." *Slavic Review* 22 (1963): 1–30.

Sutton, David E. *Memories Cast in Stone: The Relevance of the Past in Everyday Life*. New York: Berg Publishers, 1998.

Symes, Carol. "The Middle Ages between Nationalism and Colonialism." *French Historical Studies* 34, no. 1 (2011): 37–46.

———. "When We Talk about Modernity." *The American Historical Review* 116, no. 3 (2011): 715–26.

Symonds, Leigh. "Death as a Window to Life: Anthropological Approaches to Early Medieval Mortuary Ritual." *Reviews in Anthropology* 38, no. 1 (2009): 48–87.

Taylor, Charles. *The Malaise of Modernity*. Toronto, CA: The House of Anansi Press, 2003.

Teschke, Benno. "Geopolitics." *Historical Materialism* 14 (2006): 327–35.

Thaler, Peter. "The Discourse of Historical Legitimization: A Comparative Examination of Southern Jutland and the Slovenian Language Area." *Nationalities Papers* 40, no. 1 (2012): 1–22.

Thomas, Nicholas. *Out of Time: History and Evolution in Anthropological Discourse*. Cambridge; New York: Cambridge University Press, 1989.

Thompson, James Westfall. *Feudal Germany*. Chicago: University of Chicago Press, 1928.

Todorov, Tzvetan. *The Conquest of America: The Question of the Other*. 1st ed. New York: Harper & Row, 1984.

Todorova, Maria Nikolaeva. *Imagining the Balkans*. New York: Oxford University Press, 1997.

Trigger, Bruce G. *A History of Archaeological Thought*. Cambridge; New York: Cambridge University Press, 1989.

Trouillot, Michel-Rolph. "Anthropology and the Savage Slot: The Poetics and Politics of Otherness." In *Recapturing Anthropology: Working in the Present*, edited by Richard Gabriel Fox, 17–43. Sante Fe: SAR Press, 1991.

———. *Silencing the Past: Power and the Production of History*. Boston, MA: Beacon Press, 1995.

Turetzky, Philip. *Time*. New York: Routledge, 1998.

Turner, Sam. *Making a Christian Landscape: The Countryside in Early Medieval Cornwall, Devon and Wessex*. Exeter: University of Exeter Press, 2006.

Uebel, Michael. *Ecstatic Transformation: On the Uses of Alterity in the Middle Ages*. New York: Palgrave Macmillan, 2005.

———. "Opening Time: Psychoanalysis and Medieval Culture." In *Cultural Studies of the Modern Middle Ages*, edited by Eileen Joy, M. Seaman, K. Bell, and M. Ramsey, 269–300. New York: Palgrave, 2007.

van der Leeuw, Sander. "Giving the Potter a Choice: Conceptual Aspects of Pottery Techniques." In *Technological Choices: Transformation in Material Cultures since the Neolithic*, edited by P. Lemmonier, 238–87. London: Routledge, 1993.

Van Engen, John. "The Christian Middle Ages as an Historiographical Problem." *The American Historical Review* 91, no. 3 (1986): 519–52.

Vásquez, Manuel A. *More Than Belief: A Materialist Theory of Religion*. Oxford; New York: Oxford University Press, 2011.

Veit, Ullrich. "Ethnic Concepts in German Prehistory: A Case Study on the Relationship between Cultural Identity and Archaeological Objectivity." In *Archaeological Approaches to Cultural Identity*, edited by Stephen Shennan, 33–56. New York: Routledge, 1989.

Venn, Couze, and Mike Featherstone. "Modernity." *Theory, Culture & Society* 23, no. 2–3 (2006): 457–65.

Vermeulen, Han F., and Arturo Alvarez Roldán, eds. *Fieldwork and Footnotes: Studies in the History of European Anthropology.* London; New York: Routledge, 1995.

Vinski, Z. "Köttlacher Kultur." In *Enzyklopädisches Handbuch zur Ur- und Frühgeschichte Europas,* edited by J. Filip, 632–33. Stuttgart: W. Kohlhammer, 1966.

Voget, Fred W. *A History of Ethnology.* New York: Holt, Rinehart and Winston, 1975.

Vošnjak, Bogumil. *A Bulwark against Germany; the Fight of the Slovenes, the Western Branch of the Jugoslavs, for National Existence.* New York: Fleming H. Revell Company, 1919.

Wallerstein, Immanuel. "Eurocentrism and Its Avatars: The Dilemmas of Social Science." *New Left Review* 226 (1997): 93–108.

———. *Unthinking Social Science: The Limits of Nineteenth-Century Paradigms.* Philadelphia: Temple University Press, 2001.

Walter, Philippe. *Christianity: The Origins of a Pagan Religion.* 1st US ed. Rochester, VT: Inner Traditions, 2006.

Ward-Perkins, Bryan. "Reconfiguring Sacred Space: From Pagan Shrines to Christian Churches." In *Die spätantike Stadt und ihre Christianisierung,* edited by B. Gunnar and H.-G. Severin, 285–90. Wiesbaden: Reichert Verlag, 2003.

Warnier, Jean-Pierre. "A Praxeological Approach to Subjectivation in a Material World." *Journal of Material Culture* 6, no. 1 (2001): 5–24.

Wattenbach, Wilhelm. "Die Germanisierung der östlichen Grenzmarken des deutschen Reichs." *Historicsche Zeitschrift* 9 (1863): 386–417.

Weber, Max. *Economy and Society.* Berkeley: University of California Press, 1978.

Wenskus, Reinhard. *Stammesbildung und Verfassung; das Werden der frühmittelalterlichen Gentes.* Cologne: Böhlau, 1961.

Westrem, Scott D., ed. *Discovering New Worlds: Essays on Medieval Exploration and Imagination.* New York: Garland, 1991.

White, Hayden V. *Metahistory: The Historical Imagination in Nineteenth-Century Europe.* Baltimore, MD: Johns Hopkins University Press, 1973.

Wickham, Chris. "The Early Middle Ages and National Identity." *Storica* 27 (2006): 7–26.

Wiessner, Polly. "Style and Social Information in Kalahari San Projectile Points." *American Antiquity* 48 (1983): 253–76.

Williams, Howard. "Material Culture as Memory: Combs and Cremation in Early Medieval Britain." *Early Medieval Europe* 12 (2003): 89–128.

Wolf, Eric R. *Europe and the People without History.* Berkeley: University of California Press, 1982.

Wolfart, Johannes C. "The Rise of the Historical Consciousness." *Religion Compass* 3, no. 1 (2009): 86–98.

Wolff, Larry, and Marco Cipolloni, eds. *The Anthropology of the Enlightenment.* Stanford, CA: Stanford University Press, 2007.

Wolfram, Herwig. *Conversio Bagoariorum et Carantanorum: das Weissbuch der Salzburger Kirche über die erfolgreiche Mission in Karantanien und Pannonien.* Vienna: H. Böhlaus Nachf, 1979.

———. *History of the Goths.* New and completely rev. from the 2nd German ed. Berkeley: University of California Press, 1988.

Wood, Ian. "Barbarians, Historians, and the Construction of National Identities." *Journal of Late Antiquity* 1, no. 1 (2008): 61–81.

Wynne-Jones, Stephanie. "It's What You Do With It That Counts: Performed Identities in the East African Coastal Landscape." *Journal of Social Archaeology* 7, no. 3 (2007): 325–45.

Yelvington, Kevin A. "History, Memory and Identity: A Programmatic Prolegomenon." *Critique of Anthropology* 22, no. 3 (2002): 227–56.

Young, Bailey K. "The Myth of the Pagan Cemetery." In *Spaces of the Living and the Dead: An Archaeological Dialogue,* edited by C. Karkov, K. Wickham-Crowley, and B. Young, 61–85. Oxford: Oxbow, 1999.

Zammito, John H. *Kant, Herder, and the Birth of Anthropology.* Chicago: University of Chicago Press, 2002.

Index

MAKING SENSE OF HISTORY
Studies in Historical Cultures
General Editor: Stefan Berger
Founding Editor: Jörn Rüsen

Bridging the gap between historical theory and the study of historical memory, this series crosses the boundaries between both academic disciplines and cultural, social, political and historical contexts. In an age of rapid globalization, which tends to manifest itself on an economic and political level, locating the cultural practices involved in generating its underlying historical sense is an increasingly urgent task.